VOICING THE ESSAY

READING AND WRITING FOR DEPTH

VOICING THE ESSAY

READING AND WRITING FOR DEPTH

John Whatley

SIMON FRASER UNIVERSITY
PUBLICATIONS

Library and Archives Canada Cataloguing in Publication

Whatley, John, 1944-, author
     Voicing the essay : reading and writing for depth / author: John Whatley; editor: Katherine McManus.
Includes bibliographical references and index.
ISBN 978-0-86491-352-4 (pbk.)
     1. English language--Rhetoric. 2. Report writing. 3. Creative writing. I. McManus, Katherine, 1948-, editor II. Title.

PE1471.W43 2013   808'.0427   C2013-907995-5

Printed in Canada by Hignell Book Printing
Cover design by Greg Holoboff
Book Design and Typesetting by Robert D. MacNevin

Simon Fraser University Publications
1300 West Mall Centre
8888 University Drive
Burnaby, British Columbia V5A 1S6
Canada

 PUBLICATIONS

Contents

Preface

Why use the idea of "voice" to talk about the literary essay and student writing? First it comes out of experience with students; second it reaches deeply into both writing as a social practice and writing as a creative practice. Let me explain:

As a university instructor I have often wondered how a student best learns to write in an academic setting. It was clear almost from my beginnings as a lecturer in English that my students had a hard time with academic formality. After a few years of teaching, and marking a few thousand essays, and after studying more than a number of texts and manuals on academic writing it became clear to me that one reason for this difficulty was that the "formal voice" used in the university was *terra incognito*, especially for first-year students, and that I did not teach it very well, or did not teach it in a way that was having a great effect. My students simply had very little experience with the professional academic enterprise — unless they were lucky enough to be the child of a professor, or were a mature student, they could only guess at what was involved in the university rituals of research, publishing, teaching, conference presentation and the arcane hierarchies of academic advancement and titles — thus their lack of attention to formal discourse and its reflection in writing. This is likely something most English instructors know well. The problem is that most approaches to teaching this formal academic voice either as writing or as discourse, do so in isolation. Most approaches simply describe, define, exercise and train students in academic forms of writing and speaking with no real tie to the underlying practices of academia, and very little attention paid to why these changes in address, idiom, lexis, attitude, tone, are important.

It occurred to me that this approach has a definite drawback — first it trains students that the academic essay is the singular form of essay writing, and second, it neglects the technical problem of learning to distinguish accurately between formality and familiarity. Academic formality is often well discussed, excellently defined, well theorized, fully exemplified. Familiarity, however, is pretty well dismissed as entirely secondary, and as a distinct error when it appears in the academic style. Students are told, sometimes with absolute and magisterial certainty, that they should never use the "I" pronoun and its relatives. "Your opinion, your anecdotes, your feelings do not matter," we say. "What matters is breadth of research, proof, correct citation, layout of ideas, the fronting of your claim and what you are writing about." But the reasons for this injunction are really left unstudied, are never fully discussed, and thus the advantages and disadvantages of leaving familiarity to write and think formally are not really understood. Students are asked to take these injunctions and boundaries on faith. I think this is one of the significant reasons that students are often not steady in the formal voice for a longer time than necessary — they must fill in the gaps themselves, sometimes having to wait for graduation to see what the whole of the experience of their introduction to scholarship was about.

Once the problem was seen, another way became evident, and I began to write this text. The goal was to take more time to explain the familiar voice and set it in adequate relation to the formal voice. In practice over a number of years this approach has shown its value. Academic formality itself became more clear, formal procedures become more available, the academic project becomes understandable and even, perhaps, something positive. After a more careful grounding in and comparison with familiarity, the student improves his or her own formal voice and for good reasons, not from faith alone.

This book has grown out of that original insight. It has grown now to an attempt to bring in as many relevant voices as possible and put the formal, scholarly voice in relation to them. It became evident as this work progressed that more than two voices were at stake. The narratives that students of literature are asked to analyze also had to be taken into account, and it was again more accessible when considered as a "voice" rather than only as text. My struggles with teaching the literary essay, and to introducing this formal register, led to further critical knowledge on my part. I realized that the storyteller and narrator modulate their approaches in relation to familiarity and formality. Once having seen the potential of these, now three, voices to explicate the literary essay, it became equally clear that the essay and indeed much of literature is made up of hybrids of these voices.

At about the third year of university, I suspect students have, if they survive, become expert at writing essays and have had more than enough of writing essays. But it may help to remember that the essay is not only an exercise done in universities but also a creative form that has been with us at least since Montaigne. The essay is a literary form. This may not be news but it is an interesting fact. Some brilliant essayists have come before us, and their work is worth the application of a category or two and worth study as a literary form. Essayists have provided us with both a stable and a volatile shape. If quality is measured in amount and endurance, surely the essay is one of the most tenacious and prolific of literary forms. If quality is measured in changeability, ability to shift, to reassign significance and the elements of literary convention, to revise form, then the essay is one of the most volatile and radical of forms. But I also cannot imagine anything more stable than the academic essay. My hope is that this text will help students realize the beauty and value in the essay, as one of the more neglected of literary forms. With luck this book will help students to both recognize this value, and develop their own abilities in writing analysis and commentary. I also have a hope that, outside the rigours of writing university essays, students who read this text will also be enough inspired that they will be tempted to try their own hand and experiment with the creative possibilities of the literary essay themselves.

Acknowledgements

With much appreciation to my wife, Laurel, for her gifts of grace, time and the encouragement to write this text. — *John Whatley*

Permissions

The articles in this text that are not in public domain have been reprinted with permission. We acknowledge:

Erika Anderson and *Creative Nonfiction* for "Man on the Tracks," *Creative Nonfiction* Issue #49, Summer 2013.

Shawn Syms and *Quill & Quire*, for "Brian Fawcett, Human Happiness," *Quill & Quire*, February 2012.

The cover photo of Maya Angelou is used under the Creative Commons License, Attribution-Share Alike 2.0 Generic. Author, Adria Richards, photo Date 26 Feb. 2009.

VOICING THE ESSAY

READING AND WRITING FOR DEPTH

Introduction

What happens when you hear the word "voice"? You likely think about an Opera or pop star, or what we do in conversation with our vocal chords, and many other instances drawn from singing or speech. You likely do not think of the more technical sense used by linguists and literary scholars, of say, "the forms of talk" to use Irving Goffman's phrase, or "modes of discourse" or "mind style" to use Roger Fowler's concepts. Such scholars have made much of this distinction. Drawing on such ideas, I will be using the term "voice" in a very broad sense, to map a very human activity that is a recognizable part of our lives. We are, after all "the discoursing animal" and shape our voices to the job at hand. It is a complex process.

Your speaking voice involves tone, vocabulary, stress, volume, context, feeling, point of view, gesture, expression, syntax, and many other aspects and skills. Think of the different voices you would use when presenting in class, writing a letter of complaint to an airline when they changed seating without notifying you, or composing an application for a job. You would not confuse these situations. The voice you use when asking for a refund, or the tone with which you shape the glowing narrative of your work history, are different. We recognize the difference. These voices occur in social space and we shape our address to this space; yet, in all these situations, there is a constant. To speak effectively, we must fashion our voice to a situation. The same occurs in texts. Texts are also "social discourse." We talk and listen, read and write, sign and countersign — and text message — in a social context. Literature, where voice has become text, deals with these subtleties of voice and the tension between private and social voices in great depth and with considerable freedom of scope. This book applies this idea of text as voice, to the literary essay. In it we will be following three voices, the familiar voice, expression close to (but not the same) as our everyday voice, the formal voice we use in academic essays and presentations, and the narrative voice used when we tell and write stories. The essay and much other prose is a mixture of these voices. My hope is that by disentangling them and finding out how authors use them together and separately, we gain insight into how literary texts are constructed, and how to write about them effectively.

1 Essays from the Past: Familiar, Formal, and Narrative Voices

He [Pirandello] is contesting the very logic of mimesis; the obligation of art to imitate an imperceptible order, the paradox that make-believe must be credible while history is not, that fictions are called upon to embody a "universal human significance and value" not present in fact. (Thomas Harrison, *Essayism*, 89)

Sources

Mary Astell, *A Serious Proposal to the Ladies for the Advancement of Their True and Greatest Interest* (1694)

Erika Anderson, "Man On The Tracks" *Creative Nonfiction* Issue #49 (2013)

Francis Bacon, "Of Revenge" *Essays* (1612)

Charles Dickens, "Night Walks" from *The Uncommercial Traveller* (1859)

Michel de Montaigne, "Of Vanity" *Essays* (1588)

Dorothy Wordsworth, *The Alfoxden Journal* (1798)

Objectives

In this chapter, we begin a close examination of three prose voices: (1) the familiar voice, (2) the formal or academic voice, and (3) the voice of the story teller or narrator. Our tools will be grammatical elements like pronouns, demonstrative adjectives, and tense; narrative elements like point of view, character, and figures of speech; and formal elements like the amount of evidence, and the uses of terminology and logical relation. In addition I will be using terms drawn from communicative linguistics like "deictic markers," "usage," and "register." With these tools we can begin to see the differences between the three prose voices. At the end of the chapter, you should be able to recognize them in a number of prose settings, though the literary essay will be our main focus. And as we proceed, we will pose some questions about your own approach to writing essays.

The essay is one of the most flexible forms of prose and provides us with a good lens through which to analyze the shapes prose can take. It has a long and interesting history. It began in Renaissance France with Montaigne in the last third of the 15th century; it flourished in Europe, especially during the English Enlightenment of the 18th century, and today is going strong and world-wide in university publications, student assignments, magazines, scholarly journals and vigorously on the Internet. Most of us are well aware of essays as we have likely written many of them; and we have learnt to expect certain structures from them, though we may not be aware of their literary qualities, or their past.

Another goal of this chapter, then, is to raise your awareness of the literary aspects of the essay. Prose in the literary essay can convey subtle and complex meaning like irony and figurative implication, or a satirical characterization that turns on the use, or abuse, of a single word, and because the form is over four hundred years old, essays can tell us much about the past's sense of truth, beauty, justice, culture, or gender. In any given essay you will find that one voice may be predominant; but literary essayists often include all three. Through such intersections of voice, additional meaning is communicated; and in many instances thought is implied rather than directly stated. When we encounter this additional or highlighted meaning, our text becomes problematic and we must engage in a close reading. Another goal of this chapter, then, is to introduce you to this disciplined, sustained type of study of a literary text. A close reading is required when you wish to write cogently about literature, the most difficult and richest kind of text we can produce.

We begin our exploration with some classic essays of the past. The historical approach has the advantage of showing the forms we are going to study when they were new and their shapes were in the foreground and clear. The originating writers I have chosen are Michel de Montaigne, Lord Bacon, Mary Astell, and the nineteenth century's Charles Dickens. Using these sources we will explore the basics of the literary essay. In upcoming chapters, we change focus to the way essayistic prose now appears in current magazines, journals, or online and in the popular press. But we need to get our historical bearings first. Texts from the past can be challenging. Our reading will focus on the types of address we find in them and we will ask whether they are expressing *familiarity, a narrative,* or a *formal argument.* But first, a number of preliminary questions: How can you tell the voices apart? Which voice is at work in any given essay? How can we evaluate them? How are they related to the way you write in a university? As a start toward answers, and using the method of close reading, our operative question will be whether we have analyzed these essays for the range of voices they use, and the depth of meaning they express.

The Familiar Voice of Michel de Montaigne

Though an "essay-like" kind of writing existed long before his time, Michel de Montaigne is usually regarded as the inventor of the essay form. The events of Montaigne's life and the beginnings of the literary essay are closely interwoven, so we will first review his background in order to understand the structures of the prose style he created.

Background

Michel de Montaigne was born in 1533 into a minor branch of the French nobility. He was aware of formality early. Legend has it that Montaigne's father trained him in Latin as soon as he could speak. Whatever the truth of the story, the elder Montaigne believed in the virtues of formal knowledge and provided his son with a university education. In keeping with his social position and training, Michel was expected to take on a public position, and he eventually became a lawyer in the *Parlement* for Bordeaux. He there met Étienne de la Boétie, a fellow counselor, who was to become his best friend and with whom he formed what was probably the closest relationship of his life. Montaigne was married in 1565 and had five children, only one of whom, Léonore, survived him. Later, as his tact and verbal skill became widely known, he was called on to perform many diplomatic missions and to lead troops in the religious wars that erupted in France toward the end of the century.

Both his father and his friend La Boétie died in 1568, and this severe double blow is often seen as a motive for Montaigne's taking up a literary and philosophical life. In 1571, Montaigne retired from the politics of the court to his 3,000-volume library, and in 1572, in the quiet seclusion of his chateau tower, began to develop a form of writing he called the "essai." In 1581, the king (Henry III) asked him to take office as the mayor of Bordeaux. He did as he was bid, but success in the fractious public sphere of his day was never Montaigne's aim. He considered his public life secondary to the life of the mind and wished no more than to return to his chateau to study and meditate on ancient writers and to write essays about his meditations.

The French word *essai* has a number of connotations in English, and among them is the equivalent of the well-known form of composition called "the essay." The word's root meaning, however, is "to assay," to test, experiment with, or attempt something. The allusion to the first siftings and weightings in evaluating a potential mining site for gold or precious stones is apt and gives us a glimpse of the attitude writers after Montaigne brought to the new genre. In order to see what was at stake in this new form, why it is significant for us, we need to change focus slightly and place Montaigne's *essais* in a broader context.

Montaigne wrote during a period of intense social struggle in which two powerful intellectual trends arose and came into conflict. According to historian Donald Frame, the first of these was the Humanism of the European Renaissance (14th to 16th centuries) with its concentration on human skills and abilities, its love of both the past and experiment, and its thirst for new knowledge. In this far-reaching change in worldview, thinkers found a new method of reasoning, new values, and an artistic rebirth as the ideals of the Greek and Roman past were rediscovered by the West (often through the Middle East). With his love of classical knowledge, his curiosity, and his tolerance, Montaigne is a symbol of the late Renaissance, and there are many allusions to the Greek and Roman thinkers in his writing. The other important social change that affected Montaigne was the Reformation (16th Century) — the European-wide reaction against the authority of the Roman Catholic Church. The Protestant-Catholic conflict was not a matter of calm discussion, nor was it a disinterested debate about differing values: "the great conflict ... culminated in the bloody religious civil wars of the later years of the century" (Frame xiv).

Montaigne wrote, then, during a period that was intellectually stimulating but also dangerously conflict-ridden. The year in which he began to write his essays, 1572, was also the year of the St. Bartholomew's Day Massacre. Suspicious of Protestant leaders for their supposed part in a plot to overthrow the Crown, Catherine de Medici, the Catholic Queen Mother, and her son, Henry III, ordered the assassination of a key Protestant adviser, Admiral Coligny. The order sparked acts of violence against Protestants across France, and before the conflagration had burned itself out, 10,000 or more Huguenots (Protestants) had been killed (Elliot 215–227, Wilson, 212–213).

On the surface, Montaigne's period does not look auspicious for the creation of a new literary form. But the social turmoil was, in fact, a likely reason for its appearance, at least for Montaigne. While Montaigne was a devoted monarchist and on the Catholic side, he struggled to keep alliances in both camps and garnered a reputation for maintaining a level-headed approach to the overheated emotions of the day. In the doubt and divided loyalties of the civil war (his own family was split by it; his mother was Jewish, though Protestant by choice, and his father Catholic), he created a kind of writing he hoped would give his reader a perspective on the social chaos and tensions that threatened to reduce France to anarchy. At its outset, Montaigne's new "essai" questioned system and dogma. In it, he records his personal experience in a way that loosens entrenched positions and replaces them with the observations and questions of an open and independent mind.

Montaigne's Difference: The Familiar Voice

Thus, although Montaigne is surrounded by intense debates in the highly formal discourses of philosophy, religion, science, and law, his essays contain a refreshing difference in style — they are informal, digressive, and often intensely personal. Our first excerpts[1] from the essay, "Of Vanity," are taken from Book III of "The Essays" and show Montaigne at his skeptical and mellow best. While his theme is serious and he often refers to the "dissensions" of his time, he writes in an easy, conversational way and with typical self-depreciation:

From "Of Vanity"

But there should be some restraint of law against foolish and impertinent scribblers, as well as against vagabonds and idle persons; which if there were, both I and a hundred others would be banished from the reach of our people. I do not speak this in jest: scribbling seems to be a symptom of a disordered and licentious age. When did we write so much as since our troubles? when the Romans so much, as upon the point of ruin? Besides that, the refining of wits does not make people wiser in a government: this idle employment springs from this, that every one applies himself negligently to the duty of his vocation, and is easily debauched from it. The corruption of the age is made up by the particular contribution of every individual man; some contribute treachery, others injustice, irreligion, tyranny, avarice, cruelty, according to their power; the weaker sort contribute folly, vanity, and idleness; of these I am one. It seems as if it were the season for vain things, when the hurtful oppress us; in a time when doing ill is common, to do but what signifies nothing is a kind of commendation. 'Tis my comfort, that I shall be one of the last who shall be called in question; and whilst the greater offenders are be-

---

1   These excerpts are taken from online sites. See the online versions of Montaignes' *Essays*: (1) the Gutenberg edition online: www.gutenberg.org/files/3600/3600-h/3600-h.htm (2) another edition can be found on *The Philosophy Pages*, http://www.davemckay.co.uk/philosophy/ and the specific references to the essay Of Vanity are taken from http://www.davemckay.co.uk/philosophy/montaigne/montaigne.php?name=essays.book3.102]

ing brought to account, I shall have leisure to amend: for it would, methinks, be against reason to punish little inconveniences, whilst we are infested with the greater. As the physician Philotimus said to one who presented him his finger to dress, and who he perceived, both by his complexion and his breath, had an ulcer in his lungs: "Friend, it is not now time to play with your nails." — (Plutarch, "How we may distinguish a Flatterer from a Friend.")

[Montaigne, Michel de, *Essays*, Book III, Chapter IX "Of Vanity" Tr. Charles Cotton, Ed. William Carew Hazlitt, [1877 edition] www.gutenberg.org/files/3600/3600-h/3600-h.htm#2HCH0102, (Accessed May 19, 2011)]

At another point in "Of Vanity" Montaigne lets us in on a personal trait we might also recognize.

For my part, I have that worse custom, that if my slipper go awry, I let my shirt and my cloak do so too; I scorn to mend myself by halves. When I am in a bad plight, I fasten upon the mischief; I abandon myself through despair; I let myself go towards the precipice, and, as they say, "throw the helve [handle] after the hatchet"; I am obstinate in growing worse, and think myself no longer worth my own care; I am either well or ill throughout. 'Tis a favour to me, that the desolation of this kingdom falls out in the desolation of my age: I better suffer that my ill be multiplied, than if my well had been disturbed. — [That, being ill, I should grow worse, than that, being well, I should grow ill.] — The words I utter in mishap are words of anger: my courage sets up its bristles, instead of letting them down; and, contrary to others, I am more devout in good than in evil fortune, according to the precept of Xenophon, if not according to his reason; and am more ready to turn up my eyes to heaven to return thanks, than to crave. I am more solicitous to improve my health, when I am well, than to restore it when I am sick; prosperities are the same discipline and instruction to me that adversities and rods are to others. As if good fortune were a thing inconsistent with good conscience, men never grow good but in evil fortune. Good fortune is to me a singular spur to modesty and moderation: an entreaty wins, a threat checks me; favour makes me bend, fear stiffens me.

[www.gutenberg.org/files/3600/3600-h/3600-h.htm#2 HCH0102]

This is something like the German term *Schadenfreude*, the joy in other's tragedy, though it is turned inward on Montaigne's own tragedies. And here is another example of this familiar style from a little further along:

> This greedy humour of new and unknown things helps to nourish in me the desire of travel; but a great many more circumstances contribute to it; I am very willing to quit the government of my house. There is, I confess, a kind of convenience in commanding, though it were but in a barn, and in being obeyed by one's people; but 'tis too uniform and languid a pleasure, and is, moreover, of necessity mixed with a thousand vexatious thoughts: one while the poverty and the oppression of your tenants: another, quarrels amongst neighbours: another, the trespasses they make upon you afflict you....

[www.gutenberg.org/files/3600/3600-h/3600-h.htm#2 HCH 0102]

Can you hear the voice in these excerpts? Montaigne's writing shows his social level and education, but his diction is informal, even casual; it is close to the kind of speech we can imagine him using in everyday life. Though his work is directed to a wide audience, Montaigne strikes an intimate, familiar tone. For Frame, "nearly every reader finds in Montaigne a friend. Like a painted portrait whose eyes seem to follow the spectator wherever he goes, Montaigne's written portrait seems to each reader to be addressed especially to him" (xxviii). Montaigne is talking as a private individual to an audience he expects will be friendly and receptive: that is, to an audience of private individuals like himself. He is more than a little skeptical of the systematic religious positions and formal debates that had produced the divisions and inhumanities of the French civil wars. At a time of great social upheaval, Montaigne writes frankly about himself, revealing his private thoughts, feelings, and problems.

This openness about the intimate side of life was to become one of the features of the *familiar* or *autobiographical* essay with its use of the first person singular pronoun and its closeness to the writer and the immediate context in which it was written. The point of view is personal in thought and expression, in distinction, say, to the cerebral, abstract, or legalistic use of pronouns like "one" or the authoritative use of "we."

Montaigne and the Formal Voice

But, despite its personal cast, Montaigne's essay does have a more formal dimension. Its pages are, for instance, studded with quotations from the works of classical Roman thinkers like Lucretius, Ovid, and Horace. A statement is general if it refers to wide-reaching events or experience beyond the direct experience of an individual speaker. The statement "Plants have an inner vascular structure composed of phloem and xylem cells" is general because it sums up characteristics that all plants have in common and does not have much relevance to, say, weed pulling. Use of such generalities is one of the important features of a more formal voice, and we can find examples of it in Montaigne's text. In talking about his own quixotic nature, he notes later in the essay that once he feels chagrin or frustration, he will goad himself into enlarging the feeling: "for the most trivial cause imaginable, I irritate that humour, which afterwards nourishes and exasperates itself of its own motion; attracting and heaping up matter upon matter on which to feed." Then he sums up his experience, the overall effects of this neurotic picking at his own irritation, with a general saying from Lucretius (in the original Latin of his text, *Stillicidi casus lapidem cavat*):

> The ever falling drop hollows out a stone. — Lucretius, i. 314.

Such nuggets of general wisdom are called *aphorisms*. This one could be applied to many situations. Montaigne uses it to show us how he makes small irritations into big ones, but you could, for instance, use it to mean that many small efforts gradually add up to big successes or that persistence pays off. Like the xylem and phloem example, the saying is highly general and captures essential features that belong to a number of differing situations, something like "small actions can add up to make big differences." Try to invent an aphorism that has the same meaning but uses a different image, and you will see the process and also the difficulty of coming up with an effective and stylish example.

But while Montaigne draws from a wide range of classical sources to cast light on his own experience, he does not give much proof for these aphorisms, nor does he develop their general perspectives much further or try to organize them into a life-view of some kind. The formal dimension, then, is not highly developed or is at least well balanced with familiarity.

In "Of Vanity" we are led through a fascinating analysis of Montaigne's inner world that exposes something familiar to us all: the *unsystematic* nature of our everyday lives. He finds, for instance, that he does not want to live up to the public's expectation that he act like a respectable nobleman who sets an example and tends his estate carefully and consistently even though he evidently *is* a respected nobleman who runs his estates well. He confesses to a certain level of creative ignorance about his own financial situation and his public responsibilities and concludes that he does not care much about the view others of his station have of him in this regard. He is sensitive even to the expectation that he be methodical and consistent, noting that any attempt on his part to be so inevitably breaks down. His self-analysis extends to showing how he dislikes any order imposed on experience through a rational system of values or the wide conceptual orientation and comprehensive terminology given by a philosophy. Such an order would require a machine-like consistency. He states his doubts openly:

> We occupy our thoughts about the general, and about universal caus-es and conducts, which will very well carry on themselves without our care; and leave our own business at random, and Michael much more our concern than man. Now I am, indeed, for the most part at home; but I would be there better pleased than anywhere else.... ("Of Vanity")

Thus, where you might expect him to develop a more systematic view, per-haps leading from his own experience to ideas about humanity in general, Montaigne becomes ironic, gently poking fun at the tendency and himself. Commenting on his own digressive style, he tells us that "I, moreover, fear, in these fantasies of mine, the treachery of my memory, lest, by inadvertence, it should make me write the same thing twice. I hate to examine myself, and never review, but very unwillingly, what has once escaped my pen." He studies and writes as he pleases, following an individualistic, digressive line of development, and will resist any method that requires that he revise his thoughts to gain a more logical precision and order.

The two voices, the familiar and the formal, are intricately entwined in Montaigne's essay, but in the end, we call his approach *skeptical* of formality. Montaigne distrusts the application of a system of general ideas made up by a philosopher to explain real, ongoing, everyday problems or to guide us through our familiar and social lives. As Montaigne shows us, he is a limited, individual human being who knows his own failings in applying extended reasoning and logical disciplined thought to his life. Although we cannot conclude that he is anti-rational or amoral, throughout "Of Vanity" Montaigne calls our attention to the dangers posed by systems of explanation, and he uses a less strict form of expression and thought, a more tolerant and less practiced kind of thinking and writing about the world—the "Essai." His "digressions" are strategic. By showing us his own vanities and failings, he points up the limits and problems of finished general positions like "Protestantism" or "Humanism." Views that can be applied to all of humanity tend to become rigid and can lead to dogma-tism, violent disagreement, and, finally, to the dangerous social disruption with which he was surrounded. Humanity, according to Montaigne, may not be ready for the complete awareness, constant vigilance, and self-control required by such systematic world views.

We will leave Montaigne with a few further quotations from "Of Vanity." All explore the failings of systematic thought and strongly imply that human knowledge is flawed and limited and that it is absurd to try applying grandiose systems to explain and manage our lives. For the Montaigne of "Of Vanity," human life always proceeds on an individual plane, not through a system of general ideas:

> All these fine precepts are vanity, and all wisdom is vanity:
>
> > "Dominus novit cogitationes sapientum, quoniam vanae sunt."
> > ["The Lord knoweth the thoughts of the wise, that they are vain." —Ps. xciii. II; or I Cor. iii. 20.]
>
> These exquisite subtleties are only fit for sermons; they are discourses that will send us all saddled into the other world. Life is a material and corporal motion, an action imperfect and irregular of its own proper essence; I make it my business to serve it according to itself....
>
> To what end are these elevated points of philosophy, upon which no human being can rely? and those rules that exceed both our use and force?
>
> [www.gutenberg.org/files/3600/3600-h/3600-h.htm#2 HCH0102]

There is a dialogue in Montaigne's essay between a familiar voice and a more formal generalizing or philosophical voice. The familiar voice has the upper hand and usually undercuts the formal voice. Montaigne wants us to keep our feet solidly on the ground and to distrust the authority of human systems of explanation — they are to him usually egotistical, grandiose, and vain.

Summary: Construction of the Voices in "Of Vanity"

Whether or not you agree with this position (or is it a non-position?), Montaigne has introduced us to the difference between the *familiar* and the *formal voices*. The familiar voice is marked in Montaigne's text by the consistent use of a particular set of pronouns, (*I, me, mine*), direct, usually casual, addresses to his reader (*we, you, us, our*), and many references to a shared context. Remember, in our first quotation, Montaigne asked his readers a pointed question. "When did *we* ever write so much as since *our* civil wars?" [italics added]. The linguistic term for this kind of reference to a mutual context shared between writer and audience is *deixis* — the Greek word for pointing. *Deictic markers* like "we" and "our" are the words in a sentence that refer to the participants and to aspects of the place and time of an utterance.

In Montaigne's use of the familiar voice, we find descriptions of his immediate experience: his home life, the personal knowledge he has gained from running his estate and the tensions between himself, his workers, family, and friends. We are with him during time off, travel, and his casual, at-home experience, or we read along with him and share his meditations on what he has read. Through this disarming "anti-method," he shows us some of the rich diversity of his everyday life and sometimes stresses the most up-close part of this world — his own personal, material existence, sometimes the most basic level of this existence, his own body — its needs, pains, foibles, and limits. He, of course, uses general terms and sometimes proposes wide claims, but in "Of Vanity," they come to us as self-contained *aphorisms* and are held provisionally, only for the moment needed. Each communicates one very local general insight, and as they are drawn from many authors, they could not together really make up a coherent system. Montaigne has discovered a rich source from which to write — the inexhaustibly interesting world of his private idiosyncrasies.

One modern literary critic of the essay, Thomas Harrison, thinks that the essay is "antigeneric" and this most certainly fits Montaigne's essay "Of Vanity." At the very beginning of the modern form, we have a writer who shows with brilliant effect some of the limits of general and formal thought when it is applied to familiar life.

The Formal Voice of Francis Bacon

Montaigne had some brilliant followers in the art of the essay; they include Francis Bacon, Isaac Newton, John Locke, and other proponents of the *New Philosophy* of science. As we have already noted, Harrison's idea that there is an "antigeneric" strain in the early form of the essay seems to hold true in our short study of Montaigne. Especially in the middle and late phases of his life, Montaigne developed an engaging skepticism about the new systems of thought like the *empiricism* of the New Science, or the more worldly *humanist* position in philosophy that were creating controversy in the intellectual life of his day. But not all essayists who came after him used the familiar voice or shared his doubts about formal thought. The developing form soon incorporated a wide variety of styles, approaches, and content. Writers of the following centuries often forwarded rigorous, hard-headed thinking in their "essays," but again, in contrast to longer reports on scientific experiments or the development of a philosophical position, their work was also brief, topical, and trial-like.

Formal essayists think and analyze in ways that are more methodical than the familiar approach we have so far seen. Their use of language is more abstract, their overall tone is impersonal, and they usually attempt to make, and sometimes prove, a general claim.

Background

Francis Bacon (1561–1626), the first English essayist, wrote in this more impersonal style and was well aware of the essay's role as an advance guard of science. Like Shakespeare, he lived during the reigns of Elizabeth I and James I. Bacon's family held influential positions at court and in Parliament, and throughout his life he was close to power. He became a skilled politician as well as a philosopher of the new science. After a stint as solicitor general of England and through astute political infighting, he reached the important position of Lord Chancellor in 1618. As in Montaigne's period, religious and civil strife were in the air. England's own Civil War was in the wings. Again, like Montaigne, Bacon was writing within a context affected by the European Renaissance and the Reformation.

Bacon had the same kind of hope for the essay form we found in Montaigne. He hoped it would open things up for more calm discussion and exploration and help advance humanity. But Bacon also thought the form should be used as a vehicle for logical thought and science. He contemplated the social advances that would come about through liberation of scientific method from the older scholasticism, and he had a practical bent. He predicted the inventions of steel, unbreakable glass, and a method of speeding up the ripening process of fruit, and he died trying to find out how to preserve a chicken through cold storage — packing it in ice and snow. In a letter attached to a copy of his *Advancement of Learning* (1605) sent to the Earl of Salisbury he compares himself to "a bell-ringer which is first up to call others to church" [online]. Bacon heralded the vigorous new science both in his essays and in longer works. Since Bacon was a philosopher of science, his essays are full of pith and hard-edged thought. In contrast to Montaigne, he uses a terse, pared-down style that gets to the core of his subject.

Formality in "Of Revenge"

In Bacon's essay, "Of Revenge," we see the differences clearly. Where Montaigne is familiar, digressive, and "antigeneric," Bacon is impersonal, brief, and general. His prose has very few personal pronouns and other *deictic* markers for personal relations with others and a familiar context; the reader awareness and immediate context we found in Montaigne are not strongly present. In addition, Bacon keeps us strictly focused on one topic; everything extraneous to it is stripped away. The brevity and concentration of Bacon's style contrasts strongly with Montaigne's digressions. Most of Bacon's essays are about one specific topic, "Revenge" or "Youth and Age" or "Atheism." But where Montaigne's essay Of Vanity was sixty or so pages long, the following excerpt (about one-third of the total) is from an essay that is exactly one paragraph long:

Of Revenge

REVENGE is a kind of wild justice; which the more man's nature runs to, the more ought law to weed it out. For as for the first wrong, it doth but offend the law; but the revenge of that wrong, putteth the law out of office. Certainly, in taking revenge, a man is but even with his enemy; but in passing it over, he is superior; for it is a prince's part to pardon. And Solomon, I am sure, saith, It is the glory of a man, to pass by an offence. That which is past is gone, and irrevocable; and wise men have enough to do, with things present and to come; therefore they do but trifle with themselves, that labour in past matters. There is no man doth a wrong, for the wrong's sake; but thereby to purchase himself profit, or pleasure, or honour, or the like. Therefore why should I be angry with a man, for loving himself better than me? And if any man should do wrong, merely out of ill-nature, why, yet it is but like the thorn or briar, which prick and scratch, because they can do no other. The most tolerable sort of revenge, is for those wrongs which there is no law to remedy; but then let a man take heed, the revenge be such as there is no law to punish; else a man's enemy is still before hand, and it is two for one. Some, when they take revenge, are desirous, the party should know, whence it cometh. This is the more generous. For the delight seemeth to be, not so much in doing the hurt, as in making the party repent. But base and crafty cowards, are like the arrow that flieth in the dark. Cosmus, duke of Florence, had a desperate saying against perfidious or neglecting friends, as if those wrongs were unpardonable; You shall read (saith he) that we are commanded to forgive our enemies; but you never read, that we are commanded to forgive our friends. But yet the spirit of Job was in a better tune: Shall we (saith he) take good at God's hands, and not be content to take evil also? And so of friends in a proportion. This is certain, that a man that studieth revenge, keeps his own wounds green, which otherwise would heal, and do well. Public revenges are for the most part fortunate; as that for the death of Caesar; for the death of Pertinax; for the death of Henry the Third of France; and many more. But in private revenges, it is not so. Nay rather, vindictive persons live the life of witches; who, as they are mischievous, so end they infortunate.

[www.gutenberg.org/cache/epub/575/pg575.txt. Accessed May 31, 2011]

Though this passage is taken from one of the briefest of essays, you probably had to slow down when you read it. Not one word is wasted, and a carefully controlled, disciplined level of thought pushes the familiar level into the background.

Bacon's approach is general and objective rather than personal and subjective because his analysis holds for all instances of vengeful action — he uses phrases like "man's nature," "a man," "wise men," and "any man" [women seem to be left out of his equations] rather than showing us instances of revenge he might have experienced himself. When he does use examples, they are drawn from history, not from his own experience. Even in his most familiar sentence, "Therefore why should I be angry with a man for loving himself better than me?" the focus is on a general instance. It is "a man" who has acted vengefully; we are not given a specific act of revenge that Bacon suffered through or committed. This more impersonal voice also carries a note of authority. Bacon speaks about revenge in a knowledgeable way that appears to be the result of well-digested experience. You get the feeling that each of Bacon's general claims about revenge could be backed up; they have the added credibility of a method. In a prose style that has been much cut and reduced, he tells us about revenge from an expert's point of view. This generality, objectivity, precision, and authoritative tone make this essay a good first example of a more *formal voice*.

Familiarity in "Of Revenge"

However, even in this impersonal style Bacon uses the occasional "I" pronoun, "why should I be angry," and a marker usually found in conversation, "I am sure," though these are only brief notes of familiarity. The many short, compressed sentences also have an idiosyncratic feel — together they sound like an individual expression — this is *Bacon's* formal voice. In addition, he directly addresses the reader, though through the formal, debating device of a *rhetorical question* — a question posed with the answer already known. The subjective, familiar note is present enough that I sometimes wonder if there might not be a hidden personal reference in this essay, perhaps to an experience Bacon might have gone through — we know that his career was a series of life and death struggles with his opponents; and in those times, brutal acts of revenge were part of political life.

There is another familiar element in this essay. Each of Bacon's short, crisp sentences can almost stand alone. In contrast to those in "Of Vanity," *most* of his sentences are aphoristic; they are like short, pithy, and very quotable sayings — "revenge is a kind of wild justice," and "they do but trifle with themselves that labour in past matters." Bacon is trying for maximum effect with minimum material. This choppy aphoristic style comes about because there are not many *cohesion markers* in his text like "in addition," "first, second, third," or "in contrast." This downplaying of connections between sentences does not allow for much overall formal development. There is also not much sampling of the variety of acts of revenge or analysis of the elements that go up to making a vengeful act, no wider explanation of the legal system and the laws against revenge, and no reference to a counter-argument or to other authorities on the topic — with the exception of Solomon. To include extensive sampling, wider analysis, the answering of contrasting positions, or other supportive proof would require a longer account. This essay is then not a *systematic* exploration of its subject. Disciplined and general as it is, Bacon's "Of Revenge" has familiar elements; it is an appetizer, a foretaste of a more thorough, methodical study of the problem of defining human revenge that might come later.

Summary: The Essay's Formal Voice

In sum, with Bacon's more formal voice, we see features that are quite different from those of the familiar voice we found in Montaigne. Rather than treating a number of topics, a single general claim is presented and illustrated, and there is an *analysis* that uncovers some of the motives or reasons for vengeful acts. Bacon's tone is also not as reader-oriented as Montaigne's; it is more impersonal and authoritative, with almost no references to an immediate, familiar context. We see a methodical approach at work. Unlike the references to family, friends and immediate context used in the familiar voice, the main kinds of references Bacon uses are to ideas or the new discourse of science. His sentences tend to communicate facts or propositions rather than opinion or feeling, and his general claim has been thought-through; it is logically organized, and has been revised, through cutting everything extraneous, for effect.

The advantages of a brief prose form that allowed both formal and familiar modes was soon recognized, and the essay quickly became a popular genre. During the eighteenth century, the great period of the rise of middle-class literacy in England, many other shapes of the essay appear. Alongside the impersonal, more authoritative style of Bacon and the digressive, familiar style of Montaigne, we see in writers like Mary Astell and Joseph Addison, a middle style developing that mixes lightness and seriousness, the pleasures of self-expression and digression with disciplined ideas.

Mary Astell's Middle Style

Background

Mary Astell (1666–1731) was the daughter of a Newcastle merchant and was educated by an uncle (a clergyman) in Latin, French, mathematics, logic, and natural philosophy. One of her first poems (called "Ambition") was published anonymously in 1684 when she was eighteen: "I scorn to weep for worlds, may I but reign/And empire over myself obtain" (Gilbert and Gubar 189). She followed through in her quest for a serious life not hemmed in by the typical life offered women by going to London in 1688 where she continued studying. She published "A Serious Proposal to the Ladies" in 1694 and then, at about the same time, proposed a scheme for a ladies' college. It reached the highest circles of government and was looked on favourably by Queen Anne, though it was not carried out. She was included in *The Ladies Library* of 1714, edited by Richard Steele (companion editor of *The Spectator*), and was satirized in *The Tatler* by Jonathan Swift. Another work by Mary Astell is *The Christian Religion, as professed by a Daughter of the Church of England*, written in 1705.

Astell's Proposal

In the following excerpt, Astell proposes that a group of women retire temporarily from the temptations and digressions of their everyday lives and form a "monastery" of learning. In this early form of a university for women, they would read, meditate on, and discuss serious philosophy and ideas. Her reasoning was that in so doing they could become better wives and companions, but there was an ethical point about gender involved. Because women had been left out of the methods of teaching and learning allowed to men, they often lived in "a cloud of ignorance," and such a retirement would help right this imbalance. The ironic note you might sometimes detect arises because Astell's language is already philosophically informed and she is well equipped to generalize and to maintain her argument despite the lack of a university education.

> From *A Serious Proposal to the Ladies for the Advancement of Their True and Greatest Interest.* London, 1694.
>
> Therefore, one great end of this institution shall be, to expel that cloud of ignorance which custom has involved us in, to furnish our minds with a stock of solid and useful knowledge, that the souls of women may no longer be the only unadorned and neglected things. It is not intended that our religious should waste their time, and trouble their heads about such unconcerning matters, as the vogue of the world

has turned up for learning, the impertinency of which has been excellently exposed by an ingenious pen, but busy themselves in a serious inquiry after necessary and perfective truths, something which it concerns them to know, and which tends to their real interest and perfection, and what that is the excellent author just now mentioned will sufficiently inform them. Such a course of study will neither be too troublesome nor out of the reach of a female virtuoso; for it is not intended she should spend her hours in learning words but things, and therefore no more languages than are necessary to acquaint her with useful authors. Nor need she trouble her self in turning over a great number of books, but take care to understand and digest a few well-chosen and good ones. Let her obtain right ideas, and be truly acquainted with the nature of those objects that present themselves to her mind, and then no matter whether or no she be able to tell what fanciful people have said about them: And thoroughly to understand Christianity as professed by the Church of England, will be sufficient to confirm her in the truth, though she have not a catalogue of those particular errors which oppose it. Indeed a learned education of the women will appear so unfashionable, that I began to startle at the singularity of the proposition, but was extremely pleased when I found a late ingenious author (whose book I met with since the writing of this) agree with me in my opinion. For speaking of the repute that learning was in about 150 years ago, "It was so very modish," says he "that the fair sex seemed to believe that Greek and Latin added to their charms: and Plato and Aristotle untranslated, were frequent ornaments of their closets. One would think by the effects, that it was a proper way of educating them, since there are no accounts in history of so many great women in any one age, as are to be found between the years 15 and 1600.

[http://www.luminarium.org/eightlit/astell/]

Note how Astell's voice interweaves familiar and formal voices and some elements of narrative. A good example of the formal voice can be found in the first sentence of the excerpt where a high level of generality is present. We are dealing with an idea concerning all women. Astell asks for an adequate education such that "the souls of women may no longer be the only unadorned and neglected things." This more general level is found throughout the excerpt. Astell also claims that formal thought can have political implications. She asks who is excluded and who included in the distribution of the formal voice and the training required of it. She implies that there are social forces at work in deciding who can use each register, and that traditionally women have been excluded from advanced learning as well as the reading and formal reasoning it requires. Astell recognizes that formal language is a learned skill, and she is asking why more women are not trained in it.

In terms of the familiar voice, the "I" pronoun is at moments strongly present, even though a general claim is also presented and is well argued for. The two voices can be clearly seen in the following excerpt:

> Indeed a learned education of the women will appear so unfashion-able, that I began to startle at the singularity of the proposition, but was extremely pleased when I found a late ingenious author (whose book I met with since the writing of this) agree with me in my opinion.

Note the "I" pronoun, the stress on emotions ("startle," "was extremely pleased") and the reference to a good portion of the audience, "will appear so unfashionable." To whom would it appear so? Likely to most readers of the day. We also see something of a technical vocabulary in the term "female virtuoso." This phrase is a good example of the way in which vocabulary and context can be related. Today, the term would be a way of referring to a practiced professional singer or musician, but, according to the note to the essay, in Astell's day "virtuoso" meant simply someone interested in the pursuit of knowledge. An additional deictic marker can be seen in the reference to "a late ingenious author, (whose book I met with since the writing of this) [who] agree[s] with me in my opinion)...." which the editor also states is a reference to William Wotton's 1691 *Reflections upon Ancient and Modern Learning.* Such a mixture shows this text to be a good example of the *middle style,* in which a formal claim is mixed with a more relaxed connection to local events and to personality.

We can also detect a faint trace of characterization, one aspect of a narrative. We find it in the use of the "she" pronoun in the first part of the essay. There is a sketch of a female scholar in "Nor need she trouble her self in turning over a great number of books, but take care to understand and digest a few well-chosen and good ones." Astell is creating a new model of a well-educated woman. The image is detailed enough that the reader can just see the outline of such a character, created perhaps to show that she may not be all that threatening, but is, in the terms of the time, truly a more useful, pious and worthy individual for her education.

Narrative in the Essay and Creative Non-Fiction

Here is a brief excerpt from one of the journals of Dorothy Wordsworth, sister to the English Romantic poet William Wordsworth. She is sometimes credited with providing some of the basic ideas for his poetry, and we can see something of her gift in prose from the following entry from one of her most well-known prose works, the *Alfoxden Journal* written in 1798. It is really a precursor to what is today called, "creative non-fiction":

> *26th.* — Coleridge came in the morning, and Mr. and Mrs. Cruikshank; walked with Coleridge nearly to Stowey after dinner. A very clear afternoon. We lay sidelong upon the turf, and gazed on the landscape till it melted into more than natural loveliness. The sea very uniform, of a pale greyish blue, only one distant bay, bright and blue as a sky; had there been a vessel sailing up it, a perfect image of delight. Walked to the top of a high hill to see a fortification. Again sat down to feed upon the prospect; a magnificent scene, *curiously* spread out for even minute inspection, though so extensive that the mind is afraid to calculate its bounds. A winter prospect shows every cottage, every farm, and the forms of distant trees, such as in summer have no distinguishing mark. On our return, Jupiter and Venus before us. While the twilight still overpowered the light of the moon, we were reminded that she was shining bright above our heads, by our faint shadows going before us. We had seen her on the tops of the hills, melting into the blue sky. Poole called while we were absent.

> *Dorothy Wordsworth's Journal, Written at Alfoxden from 20th January to 22nd May 1798.* [www.gutenberg.org/files/42856/42856-h/42856-h.htm]

The description of the setting of her walk with Coleridge and the landscape and the walk back from Stowey is given figurative, poetic resonance by the personification of the moon. It contains additional meaning, though accurately determining it would take some analytical work "… our faint shadows going before us" speaks perhaps of some magical dimension of her relation with Coleridge, or a transcendent moment with William's friend and author of the "The Rhyme of the Ancient Mariner."

Such creative use of prose distinguishes the literary essay from the more formal types we have seen with Bacon and Astell, and the familiar autobiographical prose of Montaigne. In the history of the genre, authors quickly found that complex narrative techniques could be blended with discursive (formal) structures to form an interesting interplay between factual, non-fictional references and the techniques of short story and the novel.

In another example from Charles Dickens's essay "Night Walks" about a late night-early morning ramble through 19th century London, (1859) the narrative element is clear. Early in his evocation of setting, Dickens plays novelistically with *point of view*. He does so by momentarily forming himself as a character in his own essay. The point of view moves from the standard "I" narrator to the "he" of the third person narrator.

> Some years ago, a temporary inability to sleep, referable to a distressing impression, caused me to walk about the streets all night, for a series of several nights....
>
> ****
>
> At length these flickering sparks would die away, worn out — the last veritable sparks of waking life trailed from some late pieman or hot-potato man — and London would sink to rest. And then the yearning of the houseless mind would be for any sign of company, any lighted place, any movement, anything suggestive of any one being up — nay, even so much as awake, for the houseless eye looked out for lights in windows.
>
> ****
>
> Walking the streets under the pattering rain, Houselessness would walk and walk and walk, seeing nothing but the interminable tangle of streets, save at a corner, here and there, two policemen in conversation, or the sergeant or inspector looking after his men. [xiii paras 1, 5, 6]

You can trace this transformation through the subtle *deixis* Dickens uses, for example, when he changes the adjective "houseless" to a noun phrase "the houseless eye" [meaning himself] to an adjective used as a proper noun, "Houselessness" also referring to himself. And when he comes upon a man lurking in a doorway, he says, "Houselessness and this gentleman would eye one another from head to foot" (2). The narrator is then leaving his own familiar "I" narrator and the secure essayist position and has momentarily become a fictional character himself, "Houselessness." Why? Again, something that was settled and taken for granted, this time the narrative point of view, becomes a problem for the reader and requires more thought. Can you find the significance of this typically Dickensian play of language? Such a problem would make a good theme for the explication of an essay.

Leaving this overview of essays from the past, let's look briefly at what can be done with this blend of fact and fiction today. Modern and postmodern essayists have taken these possibilities to another level. In quite a different vein, and showing how far this hybrid approach of mixing fiction and fact can be taken, here is an excerpt from Erika Anderson's "Man on the Tracks" from the online journal *Creative Nonfiction (2013)*:

When you watch a man on the tracks before an oncoming train,
that's exactly what you do: watch.

You can shout at him.
You can yell, "Train!"
You can grip your *New Yorker* and suck in your breath.
You can exhale when the Brooklyn-bound A stops twenty feet short.
You can widen your eyes when the man stumbles in your direction,
toward the platform where you await the Manhattan-bound A.
You can gasp when the man steps over the electrified third rail.
You can listen to the Manhattan-bound A train barrel down.
You can see its blue circle of light.
You can stare at the man, who now stands before you, on the tracks.

Erika Anderson, *Creative Nonfiction*, Issue #49, Summer 2013, [www.creativenonfiction.org/online-reading/man-tracks. Accessed Oct. 8, 2013].

Note the grip this first paragraph has on you. The text is based on a real event, perhaps one you have experienced, but its technique, like Dickens's, is narrational. We begin with a highly dramatic moment, unusual, it stops us, we are ready to have it unfold in tragedy or in safety, we are not sure which. It seems to be quickly resolved, only to be tightened to the breaking point once again with the "A train" oncoming from the opposite direction. The gripping presentation of the facts is done through sequencing, that is through effective manipulation of temporal setting, speeding up and slowing down the reading rate, and through repetition of the pronoun "you," which are techniques found in poetry, or in a short story or novel.

Anderson also "shows rather than tells" in this creatively fictional essay. We do not know whether the event is real or fictional. Perhaps that is her stylistic point. When something like this happens we often say, "if felt as if I were in a movie." She poses the question about reality very well through the ambiguities of this new genre: am is seeing this? Is it real? Am I in a dream? I do not believe what I am seeing. Creative nonfiction captures those experiential moments when the difference between reality and fiction are obscured and nothing is clearly real or fictional.

The best essays lead us into the unexpected. Note that in the more formal voice of Bacon's essay, the theme is developed directly, and it is highlighted by repetition and illustration — there are few surprises. In Wordsworth's Dickens's and Anderson's more literary voices, the theme is not stated directly; it comes to us through the details and insights the narrator mentions as they show us a night walk in a great city, one of the dangers of the subway, or a walk over the English countryside in moonlight.

Conclusion, Voices and Prose

We have been studying some well-known aspects of prose in these essays of the past — how writers use the formal and familiar registers, support general claims, and use narrative techniques like point of view, temporal setting, and characterization. But, I think you can see that the literary essayist's voice is unusual, quite unlike the approach taken by those writers who work wholly with either systematic thought or with novels and short stories. This is one of the intriguing features of essayistic prose; in one essay we can have both a familiar voice that speaks directly to us about personal matters and a narrator who uses extended irony or the kinds of characterization or setting we find in a short story. In addition, we could also find an authoritative formal voice that presents us with the analysis, illustration, and proof of a general claim. To complicate matters further, essayists delight in bringing these types of discourse together so they can check and augment one another in a profusion of ways. You may have begun to see the complexity of the essay as a form and to understand that a number of specific problems about voice and context must be solved before you can read essays well.

*In the **literary essay**, no level or type of discourse is absolute.*

In certain contexts, the familiar voice may not be so reliable as a touchstone, and its first protagonist, Montaigne, is also aware of its limits. On the other hand, Lord Bacon was an exacting scientist and social critic, and his style is impersonal; he did not work in the familiar mode begun by Montaigne. And as Astell shows us, for women of the 18th century, the formal voice of philosophy offered an alternative to a limited training for women in empty verbal etiquette and elegance. We have to take into account a multiplicity of registers in the literary essay; we are usually dealing with *voices,* decidedly in the plural, and with their interaction.

This difficult pluralist aspect of the essay demands a kind of tolerance in your reading — a willingness to suspend the need to define the whole of an essay in terms of any one kind of voice until we see and understand its possible literary value in relation to the other voices.

In our upcoming chapters we will study the essay as an experimental, open kind of writing, sometimes close to the life of the author, which often uses a number of voices (polyphony) and a pluralism of viewpoint. In many essays, there is a lively interaction between formal, literary, and familiar discourses with the result that authority is often questioned through techniques like irony, counterpoint, juxtaposition, or narrative.

At the end of this brief overview of the essays of the past and the styles they experimented with, I can only point to the many other period essayists and uses of voice we have not covered, but if you are interested, you might wish to read them. The Enlightenment period produced a variety of essays and well know names: Jonathan Swift, Samuel Johnson, and Frances Burney. The Romantic period: William and Dorothy Wordsworth, Liegh Hunt, Percy Bysshe Shelley, Lamb, Hazlitt, Thomas de Quincey, and Joanna Baillie. The Victorians, for instance, produced many brilliant essayists: Thomas Carlyle, John Stuart Mill, Charlotte Brontë, George Eliot, John Ruskin, Matthew Arnold, Thomas Huxley, Oscar Wilde, and George Bernard Shaw (as well as Dickens) — and brilliant essays were appearing in Canada and the United States in this period as well. Sarah Jeannette Duncan, Emerson, and Thoreau wrote a number of them. I hope to have shown you how many levels of information and voice can be found in essays, and I have stressed the notion that essay content involves much more than formal ideas alone. Carlyle's mythical Teufelsdroeck in *Sartor Resartus* who can find a new religious insight only through struggling in the desert of his familiar life and Oscar Wilde's life and death struggle with homophobia in "De Profundis" show us again that finding the interplay of voices is a useful key to reading essays well.

Study Questions

1. Which voice (or voices) do you use in your own essay writing?
2. What voice or voices are you required to use in writing an academic essay? Do you agree with the "regulations" of the formal voice you have learned?
3. How would you begin an evaluation of Montaigne's "Of Vanity"? What criteria would you use to judge its worth?
4. Try your hand at an evaluation of Bacon's essay. Are there elements missing in his coverage that you would need in order to agree to Bacon's claim? He advises we forgive rather than act out a revenge. Do you agree with him about his theory of the "green wound"?
5. The passages extracted from Astell's essay are often quite formal and abstract. Describe the elements of this formality. Give examples.
6. Do you agree that Astell is using a "middle style?" How would *you* describe the level of her vocabulary? For you, is it high, (formal) low, (familiar) or middle?
7. If you were to make your living writing essays, what kind of essay would you write? Would you use a familiar, formal, or narrative voice?

8. What would be gained and what lost if you included familiarity in one of your own academic essays? Would you have to seek permission?

Check List

- What kind of voice am I hearing when I read? *Familiar, formal, or story-telling (or narrative)*
- Can I detect a mixture of voices?
- How can I tell which voice is being used?
- What kind or type of text is this? Essay, journal, diary, true story, creative nonfiction, anecdote, memoir, autobiography?
- What deictic markers can I find? *Me, mine, you, your, I, they, he, she, it etc.* (deictic markers refer to the members of a discussion and can point to events outside the text).
- What general ideas can I find?

Key Terms

Formal voice

The level of voice used in serious argument and academic prose; it rarely uses the "I" pronoun and its complementary set of pronouns, me, us, we, you; author takes an objective stance, concerned with logical argument, inclusion of other positions, coverage, support, proof, or expertise to convince an audience that a general proposition is credible or accurate.

Familiar voice

The tone in prose that is close to the casual voice used in everyday discourse; it is found in the familiar essay. The voice is not entirely the same as the way we speak, as it is yet a text, and terms that are so individual they could not communicate are removed. This voice uses many *deictic markers* that tie the discourse to a context of utterance.

Narrative

The story-telling voice. One of the most complex of the prose voices. It can involve the other two voices and all of the shapings and literary structures we can find in ancient Greek myth, a West Coast Salish folk tale, a stand up comedian's "bit," a novel by George Eliot, or a short story by Toni Morrison or Edgar Allen Poe.

Characterization

The art of creating fictional beings who exist in literature (and sometimes elsewhere). Shakespeare's Hamlet, Milton's Satan, Dickens's Wackford Squeers, and many thousands of others are projections of an author's understanding of how another human being (and sometimes an animal or alien) may work psychologically, biologically, and socially. How the great, believable, "living" characters of literature are created has puzzled literary critics for centuries.

Literary (or creative) non-fiction

The use of literary techniques to report on or recreate actual events and people. Joan Didion's "On Going Home," Michael Ondaatje's *Running in the Family* are good examples.

Chronology

A list of dates and explanations showing the temporal sequence of an event. Can be used to organize a brief anecdote or a long involved history. It is essentially a list of dates and the events that happened on them.

Time line

A description of the simple unfolding in time of the events in a work of fiction. The phrase can also describe time in a film as well. It is related to plot, but is simpler than plot. If you were to sketch the time line in a text, you would say "The events in this text began on Dec. 8ᵗʰ 1944 just after WWII with the birth of Familiar Jones. In year one Jones dies; in year two Squires is married…," and so on. Briefly said, a time line is the temporal organization of a plot. Time lines can go backward or forward.

Deictic marker

The pointers to context in a text. They can include all the pronouns that refer to the speaker and to his or her listener/readers; but also references to events that are occurring or have occurred in the context of a text, or physical or temporal elements in the context. *You, I, she, he, Homelessness, Bedlam,* and Astell's "a late ingenious author (whose book I met with since the writing of this)," or Wordsworth's "Coleridge" are such markers.

Cohesion markers

The language of a text that links parts of it together. These include, the adverbs, "thus," "therefore" "in conclusion," or listing devices as when you make a list of elements you are going to cover, and then do so.

Close reading

Generally, the in-depth reading of a literary text. An approach to reading that does not allow much of the significant meaning in a passage to escape. The skill lies in keeping in contact with the text through analysis of specific passages, these can be on the paragraph level, individual phrases or significant words. A close reading is usually done in stages like the following: First, read the text and make notes, and keep a record of your observations and insights. Next, see if you can find further examples of your insights in the text. Write these out as the first stage of a paper. Remember to keep records of your analysis and especially the page numbers where your insights or responses occur.

Point of view

There are a number of these and they are often quite complicated in the way they function in any text. They include, the third person; the third person omniscient; the second person narrator, — "you"; the "I" narrator or first person; and the limited first person.

Rhetorical question

A question posed to which you already know the answer. Your audience is not really supposed to answer the question, but simply to hear its persuasive value. "How many of people in Canada, truly believe we are a completely separate nation from the US?" The answer would be hard to find, but the persuasive meaning is clear — we are not so separate.

Register

The level of language of a text or speech. A register can be seen as a range from formal or familiar, but the meaning is social. Formality is the way in which you would talk in formal social situations; you would address people at a university convocation in a different manner than at a wedding or a funeral. A more familiar register would involve idiomatic expressions as well as the "I" pronoun.

Works Cited

Anderson, Chris. "Teaching Students What Not to Say: Iser, Didion, and the Rhetoric of Gaps" *JAC: A Journal of Rhetoric, Writing, Culture, and Politics,* Volume 7, Issue 1/2 Double Issue, 1987, 2006.

Anderson, Erika."Man on the Tracks" *Creative Nonfiction,* Issue #49, Summer 2013. https://www.creativenonfiction.org/online-reading/man-tracks [Accessed Oct. 8, 2013].

Astell, Mary. Excerpt from *A Serious Proposal to the Ladies for the Advancement of Their True and Greatest Interest*. London, 1694. See the *Luminarium* website: http://www.luminarium.org/eightlit/astell/ [Accessed Aug. 8, 2011].

Bacon, Francis. "Of Revenge." *Essays* (various editions, 1597–1625). www.gutenberg.org/cache/epub/575/pg575.txt [Accessed Aug. 13, 2007].

Bacon, Francis. *The Advancement of Learning*. www.gutenberg.org/cache/epub/5500/pg5500.txt [Accessed Oct. 11, 2013].

Dickens, Charles. "Night Walks" from *The Uncommercial Traveller*. The Project Gutenberg e-Book of *The Uncommercial Traveller*, by Charles Dickens (#23 in series by Charles Dickens) www.gutenberg.org/cache/epub/914/pg914.txt [Accessed Oct. 11, 2013].

Frame, Donald M. *Montaigne: A Biography*. London: H. Hamilton, 1965.

Fowler, Roger. *Linguistic Criticism*. Oxford: Oxford University Press, 1986.

Gilbert, Sandra and Susan Gubar eds. *The Norton Anthology of Literature by Women: The Traditions in English*, 2nd ed. New York: W.W. Norton, 1996.

Good, Graham. *The Observing Self: Rediscovering the Essay*. London: Routledge, 1988.

Harrison, Thomas. *Essayism: Conrad, Musil & Pirandello*. Baltimore: Johns Hopkins University Press, 1992.

Hitchins, Christopher. "The Dark Side of Dickens: Why Charles Dickens was among the best of writers and the worst of men" *The Atlantic* (May 2010 para 6). Web, November 14, 2011. http://www.theatlantic.com/magazine/archive/2010/05/the-dark-side-of-dickens/8031/ [Accessed Sept. 20, 2011].

Montaigne, Michel de. "Of Vanity." [See the online version of Montaigne's *Essays*, from the Gutenberg edition online: www.gutenberg.orgfiles/3600/3600-h/3600-h.htm.

Wilson, David. *A History of England*. Holt, Rhinehart and Winston, Inc., 1967.

Wordsworth, Mary. *Dorothy Wordsworth's Journal, Written at Alfoxden from 20th January to 22nd May 1798*. Web access Oct., 2013.

2   The Familiar Voice

It is not easy to write a familiar style. Many people mistake a familiar for a vulgar style, and suppose that to write without affectation is to write at random. On the contrary, there is nothing that requires more precision, and, if I may so say, purity of expression, than the style I am speaking of. It utterly rejects not only all unmeaning pomp, but all low, cant phrases, and loose, unconnected, slipshod allusions. It is not to take the first word that offers, but the best word in common use; it is not to throw words together in any combinations we please, but to follow and avail ourselves of the true idiom of the language. (William Hazlitt, "On Familiar Style," Essay xxiv, 217)

Sources
Joan Didion, "On Going Home" (1961)
Shawn Syms, *Quill & Quire* review (2012)
Elizabeth Hardwick, book review (1996)
Lisa Grekul, "Inspiring and Uninspired" (2007)

Objectives
When you finish this chapter you should be able to recognize the following aspects of the familiar essay:

- *The pluralism of the familiar essay.* How the three essayistic voices can interact in a modern personal essay with an "I" narrator;

- *Commentary and evaluation.* Excerpts from reviews show how experts evaluate and comment on the familiar essay and memoir;
- Two patterns of narrative in the familiar anecdote: *time line* and *plot*;
- General ideas in the familiar. Using the technique of *close reading*, finding and supporting a theme in the familiar essay;
- *Authorial commentary.* How familiar essayists signal themes and issues through adjectival expressions, modality, and a mixture of general and specific;
- The differences between *general* and *specific words* and their relation to proof, support, and analysis; and
- Uses of *modality* to nuance relations to an action or event.

Introduction

The modern familiar essay is grounded in personal experience; you will not then find a consistently formal or impersonal tone in the essays we will study in this chapter. You can, however, come across occasional elements of argument, evaluation, preliminary analyses, or general ideas. Essays like Joan Didion's "On Going Home" or Dickens's "Night Walks" often show a level of wider concern and generality, sometimes a recognizable formal voice is mixed in with the predominant familiarity and anecdote. The challenge in reading these delightful texts is first to recognize and then unpack their subtle changes in voice and perspective. The approach to this kind of analysis is called *close reading.* Such in-depth reading can form the basis for decisions about your own writing, and can show you clearly the difference between a familiar style and a formal style.

Through study of this occasional formality, this chapter will introduce you to university writing about literature. Writing about the familiar essay is a good place to begin development of this skill. The multiple voices in the familiar essay, (its polyphony) and the difficulties you sometimes find with its shifts in levels of voice and generality can make good subjects for your own writing. This chapter will show you how to read for a theme in order to begin an analysis, and to work up an argument.

Formal discourse about literature including the familiar essay is called *literary criticism* or *literary theory.* Your challenge is in this chapter is to begin use of this formal language accurately but with full care for the living quality of familiar essays.

Commentary and Reviews

In order to build up your vocabulary of literary terms and approaches, we begin with a study of examples of commentary found in professional reviews of familiar essays and memoirs. This step will show you the differences between specific and general language and how reviewers use it to summarize the texts they are reviewing, clarify their themes and sometimes evaluate them. After this we can more easily find these levels, and how familiar essayists also use commentary.

In the Canadian review, *Quill & Quire* of February, 2012 Shawn Syms gives a quick synopsis of Brian Fawcett's memoir *Human Happiness*, also of the same year.

> In his new memoir, essayist and fiction writer Brian Fawcett offers a thoughtful and beautifully written dissection of the long-standing relationship between two people who could rarely stand one another: his parents. While that duelling duo never truly reconciled, Fawcett has ultimately written a love story, albeit one that takes place between another embattled pair: the author and his alpha-male father.
>
> Fawcett's previous books have blurred boundaries between fiction, journalism, politics, and memoir, and have often been very personal in nature. In his latest, he questions the concept of happiness espoused by his parents' generation — in particular, its emphases on privilege, material comfort, and a lack of guilt. Key to his inquiry is the increasingly fractured nature of the contemporary family.
>
> The author's father, Hartley, was aggressive, unforgiving, and competitive, both at work and at home. His mother, Rita, believed in family unity at all costs, though she openly confessed to her son that she hated her husband, who refused to comfort her at the best of times, and especially while she fought breast cancer. The marriage lasted more than a half-century until Rita's cruel death following a stroke, but there was a cost paid by the next generation. The author, his brother, and his two sisters have gone through a total of 14 divorces trying to avoid their parents' mistakes.
>
> In skilful prose, Fawcett sets his parents' combat in social and historical context, and explores how his own coming of age allowed him to view their struggles more clearly. In a pair of particularly revealing chapters, he interviews each of his parents, asking them the same set of questions about love, sex, society, and religion, eliciting responses light years apart.
>
> Rita's death releases Hartley from the unhappy relationship, transforming his personality in the process. He lives to be over 100 and exposes a romantic and sensitive side his son had never before noticed. As Fawcett comes to see how much he shares his father's difficult traits, they reach a new understanding. The book's structural build-up to this reconciliation makes for a profoundly moving reading experience.

Syms begins at a high level of generality: He notes that Fawcett's writing "breaks the usual boundaries between genres," or, in our terms, he mixes familiarity and formality; Fawcett's books have "blurred boundaries between fiction, journalism, politics, and memoir, and have often been very personal in nature." While Fawcett's familiar milieu is a focus, Syms reduces his memoir to an economical overview. His review is five paragraphs long, (about one-and-a-half essay pages, or 350 words) and this requires a high level of generality; he was likely given a word count to work within by his editor. The level of generality is shown in other ways: we are, for instance, told about the general makeup of "Fawcett's previous books" but not given a list of specific works. And, again because of the limited space, there is no quotation or paraphrase from the memoir itself. However, Fawcett's parents are named, some details are given, and there are a few evaluations of the quality of Fawcett's portrayal of his family. The purpose is to give a brief sketch, a summary, and not to judge the text overmuch. Syms has also found a clear theme in the memoir: he says Fawcett "questions the concept of happiness espoused by his parents' generation." And there is enough detail to support this general idea and thus engage us: his father for example was competitive and aggressive and his mother disliked him. We are given one telling example of this "battling duo": his father's reported indifference to his mother's breast cancer. In addition, "... there was a cost paid by the next generation. The author, his brother, and his two sisters have gone through a total of 14 divorces trying to avoid their parents' mistakes." These details were carefully chosen to support the idea of a dysfunctional relation based on a faulty "concept of family happiness" and may interest us enough to want to follow through and read Fawcett's memoir. Syms has found what he takes to be the essential point of the memoir — that is, its theme. We are shown an interaction between examples and a general level; that is, between family events and a wider level of ideas about them. Book reviews balance a wide general view of a work with enough specifics drawn from the text such that this view is supported and the reader engaged in the theme.

Here is another excerpt from an October, 1996 book review of Joan Didion's *The Last Thing He Wanted* in the *New York Times Review of Books*. The reviewer, Elizabeth Hardwick, has summed up what she sees as the most important feature of Didion's novels, the "broken" or fractured quality of the characters' awareness. To Hardwick, Didion presents this quality through her ability to recognize *register* — a term for the social level or usage of language — in this case everyday speech and jargon.

> Joan Didion's novels are a carefully designed frieze of the fracture and
> splinter in her characters' comprehension of the world. To design a

structure for the fadings and erasures of experience is an aesthetic challenge she tries to meet in a quite striking manner; the placement of sentences on the page, abrupt closures rather like hanging up the phone without notice, and an ear for the rhythms and tags of current speech that is altogether remarkable. Perhaps it is prudent that the central characters, women, are not seeking clarity since the world described herein, the America of the last thirty years or so, is blurred by a creeping inexactitude about many things, among them bureaucratic and official language, the jargon of the press, the incoherence of politics, the disastrous surprises in the mother, father, child tableau.

The method of narration, always conscious and sometimes discussed in an aside, will express a peculiar restlessness and unease in order to accommodate the extreme fluidity of the fictional landscape. You will read that something did or did not happen; something was or was not thought; this indicates the ambiguity of the flow, but there is also in "did or did not" the author's strong sense of a willful obfuscation in contemporary life, a purposeful blackout of what was promised or not promised — a blackout in the interest of personal comfort, and also in the interest of greed, deals, political disguises of intention. (1)

The kind of commentary we find in a book review often proceeds this way. We have a wide general statement about Didion's work. Her novels are "a carefully designed frieze of the fracture and splinter in her characters' comprehension of the world." This concerns the family, as did Fawcett's memoir, but also bureaucracy and politics. The view is also wider than one work. A reviewer will sometimes summarize a number of works by finding the common or habitual theme to which a writer consistently returns.[1] Note also that literary reviews often begin with analysis of an aspect of language. In this case the focus is on Didion's distrust of verbal inexactitude as she finds it in both everyday speech and in bureaucratic and official language, journalistic jargon and the willful incoherence of political speeches. The wider view is balanced, once again, with just enough lower level detail that we can see the point of the commentary. Verbal imprecision is found for instance in "abrupt closures rather like hanging up the phone without notice, and an ear for the rhythms and tags of current speech...." In an incisive comment, Hardwick finds that these sudden closures and inexactitudes mask "A purposeful blackout of what was promised or not promised — a blackout in the interest of personal comfort, and also in the inter-

---

[1]   Often called an author's *leitmotif.*

est of greed, deals, political disguises of intention." Hardwick's commentary thus includes a theme, a level of generality (the critique of truncated expression as a disguise of motive, across Didion's novels) supported with enough examples drawn from the text to allow us to see it clearly. We sense a positive evaluation of Didion's way of showing this theme; clearly the reviewer is onside. Note again, the mix of general and specific, a higher level of ideas used to describe the theme, and a lower level of detail used to support it.

Here is a review that compares and contrasts *All of Baba's Children*, (1977) a ground breaking memoir by Canadian-Ukranian writer Myrna Kostash with another work, Marsha Forchuk Skrypuch's *Kobzar's Children: A Century of Untold Ukrainian Stories* (2006). In this review we find more direct, *verbatim*, or word-for-word quotation from the two source texts in the review. The reviewer is Lisa Grekul, her somewhat negative title is "Inspiring and Uninspired"; the review was published in 2007 in the literary journal *Canadian Literature*. For Grekul, Kostash's 1977 memoir set the standard for the kinds of personal and revealing narratives about the Canadian-Ukranian community not found in the later text by Skrypuch.

> Written in the probing journalistic style that she would hone in her later work, the book explores the history of Two Hills, a predominantly Ukrainian Canadian community in Alberta. Kostash divides the text into sixteen chapters, each focused on a different aspect of Two Hills' past ("Emigration," "The Homestead," "Politics," "Mythologies"), combining information from archives and academic sources with first-hand insights and observations (she lived in Two Hills for four months in 1975, during which she interviewed many long-time residents). Not unlike some of her later work — *Bloodlines*, most notably — *All of Baba's Children* opens with Kostash's confession that her decision to write it was a "surprise": "[o]f all the things to write about," she asks, "why would I choose the Ukrainian-Canadians? I did not feel particularly attached to their community; I did not speak Ukrainian; lessons in Ukrainian history and literature had made no impression." Yet it is precisely Kostash's insider/outsider-ness vis-à-vis the Ukrainian community — her status as a second-generation "ethnic," relatively disconnected from her roots — that enables her to provide compelling and controversial commentary not only on the Ukrainian community in and around Two Hills but also on ethnic identity in Canada more generally.
>
> Indeed, while residents of Two Hills were overwhelmingly delighted that a writer (one of "their own," no less) had written a book

about their community (other readers, too, from across the country, thanked Kostash for retrieving "*their* history" from the "margins of official ethnic history"), *All of Baba's Children* caused a stir when it was first published because of its radical perspective on both national identity (questioning the celebratory rhetoric of multiculturalism, exposing the lingering aftermath of assimilation) and Ukrainian Canadians' experiences in Canada. As George Melnyk explains in his foreword to the 1992 edition, the book garnered "immediate national attention"; not all reviews, however, were positive. Some Ukrainian Canadians, angered by Kostash's discussions of sexism, anti-Semitism, and communism in the Ukrainian Canadian community, "attacked [her] for having aired the community's dirty laundry in public." But regardless of the varied responses it received, Melnyk is right when he draws attention to how the book "engages its audience," making it "difficult to be detached when reading *All of Baba's Children*." He is right, too, when he refers to the text as a "manifesto yet to be surpassed." (145–147)

As this review shows, evaluation and commentary can clarify or *explicate* a text. In literary use, an *explication* provides a detailed explanation; it usually grapples with an obscure text or attempts to solve a problem in our ability to read a text accurately; usually, however, explication is the ground for an evaluation. Grekul presents a quotation from the author, showing why she chose the Ukranian-Canadian community, and the difficulty it presented to her. Note that the quotation is adequately prepared for and is from the opening of the work,

> [Kostash's] decision to write it was a "surprise": "[o]f all the things to write about," she asks, "why would I choose the Ukrainian-Canadians? I did not feel particularly attached to their community; I did not speak Ukrainian; lessons in Ukrainian history and literature had made no impression." Yet it is precisely....

This type of quotation is called "run in" because it is part of the flow of the text and not set apart through indentation, as is a "block quotation". In terms of the theme, the quotation is used to show the advantage given Kostash by the distance from her Ukranian roots — it allows her to reveal parts of the community she may not have been able to show if she were a more active member. The quotation has relevance then to the reviewer's purpose of helping the reader understand the upcoming evaluation of the more recent text. Grekul then takes us through the publishing history of *All of Baba's Children*, its effect in the community, and examples of early reviews. Again, her overview is supported through direct quotation and paraphrase. She now engages the issue presented by this work, the controversy surrounding Kostash's questioning of what she calls "the celebratory rhetoric of multiculturalism," pointing to the difference between celebration and continuing marginalization. She uses other critics who have also commented as an entry into her own position. One critic is selected, George Melnyk, who explains that the work led to "immediate national attention"; though not all reviews were positive. Some Ukrainian Canadians, "attacked [her] for having aired the community's dirty laundry in public." Note how Melnyk's opinion is used to both open the issue and to begin Grekul's evaluation. This is a short review, (six paragraphs, 1,148 words) but it manages to pack in much detail and illustration in order to show the reader some of the significant dimensions of an important issue about multiculturalism and how one text achieves a high standard of discussion and another did not.

Literary commentary based on explication and evaluation is found in many forms. In critical approaches to other genres, like poetry for instance, the method is similar. The following is taken from the Victorian critic Matthew Arnold's well-known 1879 essay on the English romantic poet, William Wordsworth. Wordsworth is known for his introduction of a familiar voice in poetry:

> The *Excursion* and the *Prelude*, his poems of greatest bulk, are by no means Wordsworth's best work. His best work is in his shorter pieces, and many indeed are there of these which are of first-rate excellence. But in his seven volumes the pieces of high merit are mingled with a mass of pieces very inferior to them.

Arnold's comments, like Hardwick's and Syms's summarize a large amount of study and reading; in this case, all of Wordsworth's writing. The adjectives do a lot of work here. Arnold, unlike Hardwick, is sorting Wordsworth's poetry into categories like good and bad, worst and best, of high and low merit, first and second rate, superior and inferior. His comments are not only descriptive or summative like Sym's and Hardwick's, but directly evaluate; though, as we noted, Hardwick's summation carries some evaluation; note again how she uses "prudent" and "carefully designed."

In these reviews of a familiar text you can begin to see the kind of work done in a more formal analysis. These reviews use similar techniques across a variety of types of text — a memoir, an autobiography, a novel and a collection of poetry. We have seen that the reviewer's critical, formal voice is made up of the following elements:

- Use of literary or other specialist terms like Syms's "blurred boundaries between fiction, journalism, politics, and memoir" or Grekul's finding that Kostash's memoir was written in a "probing journalistic style" or Hardwick's "central characters";
- Inclusion of levels of detail and generality controlled by the length allowed, the greater the length the more detail;
- The finding of themes or issues in the reviewed text, wider general ideas that will interest the reader;
- For the longer types of analysis and evaluation, a significant amount of quotation or paraphrase is used for support and clarification of the theme found;
- Inclusion of relevant context; for instance, addition of facts about the author or period, or a comparison with other works not provided in the text itself;
- A careful and respectful approach to familiarity in the text; or, if it is a critical review, due attention paid to being accurate about the original through *verbatim* quotation; and
- In some reviews, a critical evaluation is put forward, based on the evidence presented.

A Close Reading of Joan Didion's "On Going Home"

Finding Levels of Generality

This brief study of book reviews is a good place to begin to discuss your own writing. Commentary is the gist of a book review. Reviews are usually based on finding a theme, a general idea, issue or claim, with enough supporting detail in the form of quotation or paraphrase to support the theme or claim. Although reviewers do not need to include extensive and expansive quotation, some specificity, as we have seen, is needed. Taking a page from the reviewer's method, a first step in writing a good paper is to read for both detail and theme — to cultivate close reading. Look for levels of generality first, these are especially useful in finding a theme that is grounded in the text. Our reviewers were good at this — they found themes in the works they analyzed. Unlike the memoirs we have studied, familiar essays are often about home life, travel or inner experience, but they can focus on a theme, (Montaigne's "Vanity," Dickens's "Houselessness") and they can thus include a general level, a claim, commentary on a wider, more comprehensive issue or problem. In your own close reading, begin by looking for the familiar essayist's own "reviewer" voice. Familiar essayists can also use a mixture of general and specific ideas. Grekul found that in Kostash's memoir, her outsider status enabled "her to provide compelling and controversial commentary." The author also comments and is alert for issues. Finding and using *authorial commentary* in a familiar essay can be a good first step toward formal analysis and it has the value of keeping you in contact with the work.

I will next explicate one of Joan Didion's essays, "On Going Home." My purpose is to show you how to build up an interesting theme from study of the levels of generality found in a familiar essay; that is, to show the value of a close reading based on authorial commentary.

Didion's essay is very well known. Even though it is about the most familiar of experience, family life, it is interesting, highly crafted, and difficult. The essay's point is somewhat hidden, enigmatic, hard to pin down. Didion begins "in media res" with no preparation or exposition — and her ending seems to trail off; we are left with many implications and a number of questions. Here is an excerpt from Didion's first paragraph:

> I am home for my daughter's first birthday. By "home" I do not mean the house in Los Angeles where my husband and I and the baby live, but the place where the family is, in the Central Valley of California. It is a vital although troublesome distinction. My husband likes my family but is uneasy in their house, because once there I fall into their ways, which are difficult, oblique, deliberately inarticulate, not my husband's ways. We live in dusty houses ("D-U-S-T," he once wrote with his finger on surfaces all over the house, but not one noticed it) filled with mementos quite without value to him (what could the Canton dessert plates mean to him?) (1)

"On Going Home" gives us some real problems in reading. Didion, like Montaigne, presents us with some intimate and troublesome details about family relationships. But how are we to respond to them? More than this, there is an underlying problem: What is this essay about? We are not told the theme. Nowhere can we find a simple introductory phrase like, "In the following I am going to focus on...." She is home for her daughter's first birthday, and at the end, we find an equally enigmatic reference that seems to refer to her daughter's future. She ends by saying, instead of giving her a home for her birthday, she will "give her a xylophone and a sundress from Madeira, and promise to tell her a funny story." (3) Where does the ending lead us?

We do have some possible guides: a consistent tone of unease infiltrates the whole essay; there are levels of voice to help us, and there is commentary. I began my close reading by distinguishing between the familiar and formal registers. Doing so helped me get to a problem Didion seems to be dealing with, and thus to a theme. These two voices in "On Going Home" conflict and align in a number of ways. As you will see, working with them gave direction to my analysis and became a good reading basis for what I hope could be a good explication of a difficult essay.

Didion uses the familiar voice in a number of ways. It includes the many references to herself (as marked by the pronouns "I," "me," and "mine") and her close awareness of her reader, as her careful explanations of the expressions she uses at home show us. These techniques, as well as a rich set of references to her husband develop an inviting familiarity in her descriptions — the customs, landscape, and lifestyle of her Central Valley family:

> I am home for my daughter's first birthday. By "home" I do not mean
> the house in Los Angeles where my husband and I and the baby live,
> but the place where my family is, in the Central Valley of California.
> It is a vital though a troublesome distinction. My husband likes my
> family but is uneasy in their house, because once there I fall into
> their ways, which are difficult, oblique, deliberately inarticulate, not
> my husband's ways. (1)

Beyond the more obvious deictic markers like "I" and "my," Didion's use of "the baby" is a clear instance of the way the interactions between formal and familiar voice can be developed in an essay. The definite article is one key — it is her particular baby, the one she knows well, (her name is Quintana) but she uses the careful language you would use to speak about family members to an audience; it is "the baby"; her first name is not used. She is careful to make her private life public in a way that is not damaging to family members. There is another modulation in the open, reader orientation we first saw with Montaigne. Look at the way Didion defines a personal meaning of the term "home" — as the one in Central Valley, not the one in LA. Again, no address is given, but we are invited in. In addition, she talks about her husband as if she were having a conversation with a friend about him or mulling him over to herself with a sympathetic reader listening in. These are examples of familiar language. But, as I began to understand these references, accept the point of view, and to move into Didion's familiar world through this inviting voice, I became aware of a counter thread. "It is a troublesome distinction" is not the kind of language I would normally find in everyday conversation, nor are the words "oblique" and "deliberately inarticulate." I began then to find two registers, one that was conversational and audience aware, and another that was more formal or analytical, more like the kind of commentary we found in the previous reviews.

Didion uses her formal voice often in the essay and develops it in a number of ways. For instance, we find it when she moves from the level of the details of her life at home in her two families to language about today's families in general. As we have discovered in the previous essays, the higher level of generality is a good key to a more formal register.

> Sometimes I think that those of us who are now in our thirties were
> born into the last generation to carry the burden of "home," to find
> in family life the source of all tension and drama. (1)

Using this more abstract language, Didion has made a claim about a much wider group than her own family, "those of us in our thirties." She has moved from her own experience to the general idea that her age group may be the last to have a deep sense of family belonging. This more formal claim is qualified with "Sometimes I think," but she has now added a note of wider significance. In this commentary, she proposes a general trend in society rather than her own, single familiar instance. If we are in our thirties or beyond, we may also find the general insight applicable to our life as well. Family life in general, as she says, is changing.

There are a number of examples of this general perspective. This is the voice she uses when she is *interpreting* or *explaining* her family situation to her reader rather than describing, presenting or evoking it through the familiar voice. In this explanation she often remarks on the differences between her two families and in doing so her language takes on a wider scope and becomes more precise, evaluative, and analytical, though this language puts her at a distance from both her husband and her relatives and it involves her in commentary about family life in general.

From Levels of Generality to Theme

In the first paragraph, I found a number of these general ideas and they helped me gain a better understanding of Didion's family situation. The essay seems to be about family life, but in some way there is a disjunction, an uneasy boundary at work. Piecing these general references together, hints of a core problem, perhaps a significant conflict, begin to emerge. I found it for instance in the idea that her husband does not understand her first family and they do not understand him. In the course of her essay, then, we should expect to gain some clarity about this problem, perhaps moving to a solution; or we should at least begin to understand *why* he does not get along with them and they with him.

Didion begins her exploration of this general idea with some details that show it clearly. Although her husband likes her family, he does not understand their ways of expression. For one thing, her mother, father, and brother use a "coded speech," referring to the effects of work stress in their real estate business: "people who have been committed to mental hospitals" or who have been "booked on drunk driving charges," and there is much talk about "property, land, price per acre and C2 zoning." And, conversely, Didion's brother cannot understand her husband's inability to perceive the advantages of a "sale-leaseback" (1). She has explained her husband's attitude through showing his misunderstanding of the *idiom*, the typical words and expressions, she and her family speak in her first home. These include terminology about real estate work and encode many judgments and specific kinds of knowledge and show the stress level in this business. Through her more detailed description, Didion has made clear one specific aspect of the more general problem. Her husband is having a specific problem with her Central Valley family—he simply cannot understand their specialized language.

This difference between his way and her family's way of expression is further developed. We come next to family customs. Here, though, her language becomes more clearly evaluative. She and her Central Valley family do *not care about* dust on the furniture, whereas her husband does. The *bric à brac* and other paraphernalia in the house, however, have definite meanings, though they are, like the real estate language, hidden from him. She says later in the same paragraph, "what could the Canton dessert plates mean to him? How could he have known about the assay scales, why should he care if he did know?" (1). There is an attempt at a neutrality here; her husband could not know of the significance of these items, and yet they are significant to her. By following this explanatory direction from generality to specific example you can probably already feel another aspect of the more general problem of family she might be exploring. What are the wider differences between these families?

From Modality to Evaluation

We have noted that evaluation is often carried through *adjectives*, and these are good ways to find submerged themes or positions. Didion evaluates the way her first family speaks at home when she says it is "oblique" and "inarticulate," which implies that she and her husband may use a more urbane or a more direct, perhaps a more educated, form of speech. Both Didion and her husband are writers and are likely to be sensitive to such differences in voice. Evaluative commentary can be carried by other means—it can, for instance, be found in *modality* as well as in adjectives. Modality is a sensitive register of a writer's attitudes and orientations. Likes and dislikes, opinions, and explanations are softened, qualified, or graded to show degrees of understanding, approval, or disapproval through modal verbs and related structures. The modal verbs are *"can," "may," "might," "ought," "should," "would," "could,"* and *"must."*

There is a good example of modality in Didion's discussion of her daughter's need for close relatives like aunts and uncles. At the end of the essay after her unsatisfactory meeting with her great-aunts, and speaking again of her daughter's need for a wider family, she says, "I *would like* to give her more" (3). Here she is showing her attitude quite directly: having an extended family is a good thing, though her positive evaluation is graded into a somewhat wishful attitude with the modal "would." The use of modal verbs shows that while she is pulled toward the older way, she yet realizes that it may no longer possible to have an extended family that is an active part of her life.

Another example of modal gradation occurs when she evaluates the difference between the two family generations with, "*Sometimes I think* that those of us who are now in our thirties were born into the *last* generation to carry the burden of 'home'" (1). She could have shown us a much more straightforward judgment without the "sometimes." If she were to have used only the adjective "last," as in "*We* are the *last* generation to carry the burden of 'home'" [my italics], she would have made a clear-cut statement that her first family is outdated, even old-fashioned, and that this family style is soon to disappear. This more severe judgment is however qualified with "sometimes I think"; perhaps at other times, she does not think this way. By using modality, she makes a more circumspect general evaluation and allows us to see her uncertainty. Didion is careful not to *overgeneralize* from her experience, and is also aware of the dangers of her own position as a writer. She is, after all, drawing her conclusions from a comparison of her own two families — their feelings and her relationships might be at stake or perhaps she is not willing to make such a wide general claim about her own generation with only this small amount of anecdotal support.

Generality and evaluative commentary with modalization is found in abundance in this essay. The more you focus on it, the more you will find that most of "On Going Home" is composed of a mixture of an interesting presentation of the ambiguities of Didion's home life using a familiar voice, general ideas about the different types of families, and carefully modalized commentary concerned with explaining and evaluating her two family situations. The commentary begins with the description of her husband's difficulties with her family and develops into a detailed comparison between the traditional style of family life she knew as a child and teenager and the more modern family life she is now living in. Through a close reading of Didion's more general commentary, we are beginning to find a theme.

We achieved this theme by reading Didion's essay for voice — trying to find distinctions in register between familiar and formal modes — and as we did so, we began to see that the essay was exploring a rich, interesting problem of current "family values."

Explication of the General Ideas in "On Going Home"

I can now use this close reading of formal and familiar registers to produce an explication — widening out these notes gleaned from a close reading, leads more easily to the first draft of an essay. We have found some wider and significant general ideas in this spare, yet precise familiar essay; an essay that at first reading was enigmatic, difficult, even obtuse. You probably now have the feeling that Didion is not just showing us the differences between the two families. She is also trying to find a wider framework through which to explain her conflicts. If she were to have written a more formal academic paper comparing modern and traditional families, she might have gone on to the final step and proposed a theory of the differences between a modern urban family and a more traditional rural or small town family. Here, she simply points to some possible explanations of the changes that were occurring in American family life in the 1960s.

There are hints of more specific issues. One of these more general explanations could have to do with the problem of gender in these two family types. Can we find a gender evaluation of the traditional family in her essay? At first, when discussing her brother's reaction to her husband, she, like Montaigne, uses the aphorism, "Marriage is the classic betrayal." She seems to use the phrase ironically, but we also can pick up some hints later that this phrase could have been meant seriously. When she looks at a snapshot of her grandfather, for instance, she says: "I smooth out the snapshot and look into his face, and do and do not see my own." (2) Is this a commentary about her own identity? I wonder what values her grandfather might have held that she *does* agree with and what values she *does not* agree with. Her grandfather was in some ways a pioneer, "surveying around Donner Pass in the year 1910" (2); perhaps he was even a significant historical figure. Yet it is somehow a flawed image of her grandfather; she cannot quite identify herself fully back there with him. There is a hint of problematic paternal authority. Was her mother "betrayed" in her own marriage? She hints again that such a betrayal was in some way the deeper structural cause of her malaise. Right after this comment, she also mentions that she and her mother were victims of "a guerrilla war" that "we never understood" (2) and later that her own daughter will be saved from the family "ambushes" (3) she suffered through. Perhaps she cannot make up her mind about her past because she was trapped in, and has been defined by, an early family power struggle in which she, as a female, was a secondary player in a male world, a world in which "guerrilla tactics" were necessary for her and her mother to survive. Could "marriage is the classic betrayal" (1) mean then that all marriages are deeply problematic, including her own and her mother's?

The final direction of her commentary and her comparison between the families might then show an illegitimate pattern of authority having to do with the significant men in her first family life — her father and grandfather. An interesting paper could be written that could recover this submerged theme and make a case that it was the real underlying problem of her first family. More research would be called for and this might lead you to other books and essays by Didion, or to biographies or further literary reviews. There are other possibilities, though.

Another general claim can be found in the almost sociological view of family life we find in Didion's interpretation of the kinds of fragmentation that have occurred since the days of her rural childhood.

> The question of whether or not you could go home again was a very real part of the sentimental and largely literary baggage with which we left home in the fifties. I suspect that it is irrelevant to the children born of the fragmentation after World War II. (2)

Is this another possible general answer to her search for the causes of the unease she feels at home? The conditions of typical family life have changed. The nuclear family of two parents and 2.5 children living alone and separate from other relatives had become the norm of North American life by the '60s. A more traditional, rural family life, with an extended close-knit group with relatives living nearby and a shared centre of work and common values, has been seriously eroded. Her return home, then, is a return to a past that is yet living but perhaps is on borrowed time. The whole nature of family relations has changed, and she is part of the change. It is now *the past*, and "going home" in this sense is a bit like going into a history book, only it is also her own personal history, and she can feel the change on her nerve ends. Another wider, more formal theme, then, could be that this older, more traditional form of the family is being superseded in American life.

Note again that a beginning explication of both of these more general explanations of family change came about through close reading of the familiar and formal voices. Can you find others? Perhaps, for instance, Didion is showing us a more philosophical stance. At maturity, each one of us is uncertainly poised between similar poles and must make choices like these. Is it the human dilemma? She might be asking whether she is wholly a part of a present situation or, perhaps, connected more deeply to the past, either a believer in or a doubter of her first family's values? Is there continuity with my family past, or have I grown beyond my childhood and finally superseded, grown beyond, the dependent being I once was? Does the self change so completely? Which self am I? Am I many selves, or do I have a deeper coherent identity that grew in my first home and that is my anchor in all change?

This brief familiar essay engages us deeply in the problems of modern family life and our roles in it. Didion does not approach her experience with a ready-made explanation. Like Montaigne, she flexibly applies a number of general explanations to her experiences at home as she develops her "assay," trying them on for fit as they come up. A paper can be written that follows up the question of which one of these explanations and evaluations is the most successful, or the one most in need of clarification.

Through study of the complex levels and types of authorial commentary like her use of general terms, analysis, modalized evaluation, and explication, we watch as Didion attempts to explain the conflict she is feeling about her two families. I have also noted that none of her explanations seem final, and none seem to lead her to decision or action. At the end do you think she implies a decision to finally leave the old family style — or is she still undecided about which is best?

Wrap-up to Didion

Such a precise description of family conflict automatically raises questions and almost demands a more systematic or general answer. With these thoughts about family power and social fragmentation, Didion is guiding us to her search for certainty, for a satisfactory explanation of her feelings through finding their deeper causes and reasons. I hope you can see that serious general ideas can surface in a very personal "familiar" kind of essay and that close study of voice and changes of register can be a good way to get to them. Didion is attempting to work through this feeling of fragmentation, of a painful separation from her roots. Her return home is not comfortable, and while the problem is not an academic issue for her, it is interesting to see how using formal language can inform a familiar essay with broad levels of significance.

Didion has commented on her use of the "I" pronoun, and why she has chosen to use it so extensively. For her it is based in recognition that subjectivity and perception are really all a writer has to offer. And that writing that is interesting is about things, facts, or highly specific details and the attitudes that come with perceiving them. She tells us in the essay "Why I Write" that she had trouble graduating from university (UC Berkeley) because she was not really interested in ideas, not because of an inability, but because her perceptions led her astray.

> I had trouble graduating from Berkeley, not because of this inability to deal with ideas — I was majoring in English, and I could locate the house-and-garden imagery in "The Portrait of a Lady" as well as the next person, "imagery" being by definition the kind of specific that got my attention — but simply because I had neglected to take a course in

Milton. For reasons which now sound baroque I needed a degree by the end of that summer, and the English department finally agreed, if I would come down from Sacramento every Friday and talk about the cosmology of "Paradise Lost," to certify me proficient in Milton. I did this. Some Fridays I took the Greyhound bus, other Fridays I caught the Southern Pacific's City of San Francisco on the last leg of its transcontinental trip. I can no longer tell you whether Milton put the sun or the earth at the centre of his universe in "Paradise Lost," the central question of at least one century and a topic about which I wrote 10,000 words that summer, but I can still recall the exact rancidity of the butter in the City of San Francisco's dining car, and the way the tinted windows on the Greyhound bus cast the oil refineries around Carquinez Straits into a greyed and obscurely sinister light.

Her point is not that ideas were absent, but that what was going on around her was paramount and more interesting in her memory. We have also found that Didion does include general ideas even in the most familiar of her essays, though she hides them a little. You should now be familiar with some of the ways of recognizing, finding, and using a sometimes hidden structure of general ideas and specific examples, when they are immersed in a familiar voice. Practice with this approach can help you come to a *supported* theme for your own commentary or response type of essay. The approach includes finding the base note in the familiar voice first, and then searching for a contrasting, more formal, register. This level of the familiar voice would include what I have called *authorial commentary*: an author's direct general or thematic statements usually accomplished by changes to a higher level of more abstract or general terms, uses of modality, and adjectival evaluations. Your next step would be to communicate your findings in a paper, showing your reader the problem you have found in the text, evaluating the two or more voices that allowed you to get to it, giving a range of examples to support your analysis and finally coming to a conclusion or solution, (or a carefully placed "non solution") about the problem.

Further Elements of the Familiar Voice

So far, we have recovered additional dimensions of the familiar voice from a number of literary reviews and one familiar essay. The voice uses the "I" pronoun and is rich in deictic markers or references to the reader, writer or their immediate contexts. Contractions like can't for "can not" or "didn't" for "did not" are used as they are the shortcuts we often use in everyday speech. The author's personality or situation is in the foreground. We know with some certitude that we are being given a true story through the lens of an individual perspective. The use of general language is minimized but present. If we look carefully we sometimes find wider commentary on the familiar situation or relationship. These may organize the essay and if this is the case we can more easily find a theme. Didion, for instance, hinted that her Central Valley family was slipping into history and the other type of life she has found was becoming the norm — though she did so as an implication of her reported conversations with her husband and with her aunts. Familiar essayists usually do not use specialist terms or quote from other texts to support their perceptions and insights. The focus of most of their paragraphs was on addressing and persuading an audience interested in close up and personal matters of relationship, family life, children, travel, or in exploring what other families or individuals living in widely different places might be like. Thus the point of view moves the reader to the narrator and the events he or she is involved in and only secondarily to an issue, analysis or topic. There is a range in this kind of style: at one pole it is highly personal and subjective perhaps even verging on the confessional; whereas, in essays with more general commentary, it can mix voices, or include formality. However, with its focus on perception, detail, relation and finding and describing an interesting situation, the commentary is usually secondary, and the familiarity and perception primary.

Study Questions

1. What other general claims or wide evaluations of modern American society can you find in Didion's brief essay?

2. In one of his telephone calls, Didion's husband recommends a trip to San Francisco or Berkeley to help her out of her malaise, but she resists and visits the family graveyard instead, only to find the old monuments vandalized. What do you make of this vandalism as a statement about old and new generations and families?

3. At the end of the essay, Didion shows her great-aunts' diminished awareness of her life. How does she take this change? What conclusion do you think she draws from it?

4. What are you gaining, what giving up when you use the more formal register in your own writing? Do you agree with Didion that perceptions are more interesting than ideas about perceptions?

5. What kind of familiar essay would you compose? What would be your theme? How would you solve the problem of the conflict between public and private concerns that Fawcett, Myrna Kostash, and Joan Didion seem to have resolved?

Check List

1. What kind of essay am I reading? *Familiar, formal, or story-telling (or narrative)*?
2. How can I tell whether it is a familiar essay?
3. What literary point of view is being used? *First person, third person, second person*?
4. What deictic markers can I find? *Me, mine, you, your, I, they, he, she, it etc.* (deictic markers refer to the participants in a dialogue and can point to ongoing events outside the text).
5. Are there many references to an immediate context?
6. Can I find authorial commentary?
7. Can I find three or more general ideas, issues, or themes?
8. Can I find many descriptions or perceptions that support the general ideas?
9. What is the most significant issue in this essay?
10. How would I support my close reading in a paper?

Key Terms

Register
The social level of language. It can also refer to a range from familiar language to formal language, or from idiomatic speech, or jargon to more "proper" speech that is careful with grammar and, in discourse, with pronunciation. Register is often used by writers to show the social level of the speaker.

Modal Verbs
The modal verbs are *"can," "may," "might," "ought," "should," "would," "could,"* and *"must."* They indicate nuances of assent, probability, or evaluation of an action.

Abstract terms
Terms like "gold," "goodness," and "narrative" are highly abstract in that they point to a class of specific items. They are the stuff of theory and the view from 50,000 feet.

Specific terms
Terms that are closer to facts, things, objects or events. Didion's "three teacups hand-painted with cabbage rose and signed 'E.M.'" is highly specific language. They are the ground-level view, the deep dive into detail.

General terms

Values are good examples of generalities; they are guides for action applicable to many situations. The term "traditional family" is general it points to the similar features of many families. But if you were to show, as Didion does, how these values uphold and show a deep respect for rural California life with its closeness to natural rhythms: "the things we like best, the yellow fields and the cotton woods and the rivers rising and falling and the mountain roads closing when the heavy snow comes in" (1), then you are now being more specific and concrete.

Authorial commentary

Those areas of a text where the writer proposes a wide general claim, or moves from specific language to wider, more thematic language. Commentary is inherently evaluative.

Verbatim quotation

Word-for-word quotation. If a quotation is enclosed in double quotation it indicates that this is an accurate, fastidious copy of the original. Single quotation can indicate a paraphrase and while not verbatim, it should be accurate to the author's ideas but in your own words.

Run in quotation

Verbatim quotation is set aside in double quotation marks as run into the text. It is then part of the text, but marked off as another voice. If the quotation is over 30 words, it can also be set off from the text through "block quotation." This does not require quotation marks as the change in speaker is evident through the changed margins and citation.

Idiom

The typical words and expressions used by a culture, a subculture or, in Didion's case a family. For instance, the lexicon of special words about real estate she and her Central Valley family speak in her first home, like "sale-leaseback."

Time line and plot

A time line is the simple development through time of the story, an evening, an episode, a lifetime in a novel by Thomas Mann. Sometimes the time line can flow in reverse as in a flash back, or forward as in a flash forward, and then return to the present. In contrast, the plot refers to the shaping of events by the author to show the working out in the life of a character or characters of a value, or a change in personality, viewpoint, or a decision. Such change can be used to make some thematic point by showing the development of characters in action.

Works Cited

Arnold, Matthew. "Wordsworth" *Essays in Criticism*: second series. S. R. Little-wood, ed. London: Macmillan, 1951, 73–96.

Didion, Joan. "On Going Home." *The Norton Reader*, Shorter 13th edition. New York, W. W. Norton, 2012, p. 1.

—. "On Going Home." *We Tell Ourselves Stories in Order to Live: Collected Nonfiction,* New York: Everyman's Library 2006, 125.

—. "Why I Write." *New York Times*, Dec. 5, 1976. Web. Dec. 5, 2013.

Grekul, Lisa. "Inspiring and Uninspired." *Canadian Literature*, 8 Dec. 2011. Web Nov. 27, 2013. (This review originally appeared in *Canadian Literature* #194 (Autumn 2007), *Visual/Textual Intersections*, 145–147.

Hardwick, Elizabeth. "In the Wastland." *New York Review of Books* (Online) 1996, Web. Nov. 20, 2013.

Hazlitt, William. "On Familiar Style" Essay XXIV. *The Selected Writings of William Hazlitt.* Vol. 6, *Table Talk.* Ed., Duncan Wu. London: Pickering and Chatto, 1998.

Shawn Syms, "Brian Fawcett, *Human Happiness*." *Quill & Quire*, Feb. 2012. Web. Nov. 27, 2013.

Further Reading

Didion, Joan. *Blue Nights*. New York: Vintage International, 2012.

Didion Joan and Darryl Pinckney. "On Elizabeth Hardwick (1916–2007)." *NY Review of Books* (online). Web. Dec. 21, 2012.

Follow-up interview by Emma Brockes from *The Guardian*, Friday, Dec. 16, 2005. Web. Nov. 27, 2013.

An additional essay-interview from the W.W. Norton Reader website: "Joan Didion 'On Going Home'" Web. Nov. 27, 2013.

3

The Formal Voice I, Coverage and Expertise

... the possibilities for amplification within essays seem to be bound-less — the many ways, for instance, an essay can pack narrative in-side itself, or meld it with any or all the other modes of discoursing: description, explanation, analysis, definition, argument. The fluid rhetorical textures so created have sustained the essay's liveliness, its capacity for renewal, from generation to generation. Then there is the variable timbre of essayistic prose — the human figure evoked by a particular way with language, a style — that we try to capture under metaphors like "voice" or "tone."

The essay as a form is "as idiosyncratic, as open-ended, as supple as any that has been devised in the language." (Lydia Fakundiny, *The Art of the Essay*, 6)

Sources

Nicholas Carr, "Is Google Making Us Stupid?" (2013)
Owen Gingerich, from the column "Wonders" in *Scientific American* (1996)
Stephen Greenblatt, "Shakespeare and the Exorcists" (1985)
Perry Link, "Does this Writer Deserve the Prize?" (2012)
Betty Rollin, "Motherhood: Who Needs It?" (1970)
Damian Tarnopolsky, *Books in Canada* review (1997)
Margaret Visser, "Feeding, Feasts, and Females" (1991)

OBJECTIVES

In this chapter, we will explore more formal essays on social issues. The goal is to help you build an approach to writing about this kind of essay through first studying a number of examples. We focus first on how to recognize the markers for this more impersonal voice and then propose a way to capture your responses to it, and this will help build your own academic style. These essays have a wider view than the familiar and anecdotal approach and in order to write well about them you will need to develop a method to work through their proofs and expertise. Our questions in this chapter will be:

- What makes up the formal voice?
- How do we construct a critical response that will make a good basis for a paper?
- What makes up a good close reading of a formal text?
- How can you can find and evaluate the range of *coverage* in an essay on social themes?
- How can you recognize *expertise* in essays and evaluate it?

In the *next* chapter we will continue to build on the above practice of close reading and effective writing, and will add *analysis, terminology,* and *definitions* to your repertoire.

Introduction

In the previous chapter, we studied the familiar essay. Essayists like Didion, used the first person singular point of view to write about their family lives, about what they suffered through or enjoyed while growing up, or about the peak or tragic experiences in their lives. Their range of familiar reference was interesting, and included many aspects and problems of everyday life we can all recognize. We also noted that the essay form allowed these writers to occasionally widen out from the familiar through commentary, to include criticism of social patterns, changes in groups, or resistant social attitudes in their evocations of familiar experience. Given the autobiographical nature of this kind of essay though, their focus was mostly on the inner aspect of such experience: the personal side of a trend in family change or the scarring emotional effects of a dysfunctional family. The ground note was the intimate, personal expressivity of the familiar voice.

The essays you will study in this chapter have another kind of focus and style. Their authors argue directly for change in our social habits and attitudes — changes in the typical ways of our life in society. They concentrate on areas of our shared experience like motherhood, the stereotypes that can sometimes shape our attitudes toward groups other than our own, on social power and its definition, or subjects like the drug laws, the effects of technology, underhanded business or customer relations practices. Essayists like Carr, Rollin, and Visser usually have their sights set on a wide kind of change for the general good. Sometimes, like Carr, they show us their personal experience of the social pattern that needs changing, but a dominant note is the formal, more impersonal style we first saw in Bacon's "Of Revenge." These essays analyze some of the "social fictions," the myths or defining social narratives that can shape our experience in hidden ways.

This more formal voice raises some interesting problems for you as a student writer. As I hope to show, your responses to these essays are likely to be more intricate and idiosyncratic than the more uniform formal voice allows. Can you yet incorporate a more familiar response to such essays in a university paper? As a student writer, you will be making judgments and adjustments to your own style, and you may wish to incorporate these formal elements in your own papers and discourse. But what about the advantages and intrinsic qualities and interest of the familiar voice we have just studied? I hope to help you make some stylistic decisions through this chapter. The formal voice has some powerful advantages and distinct limits.

Degrees of Formality

Social scientists are interested in subjects like those we are going to study in this chapter. Though they have a different overall approach, (based in qualitative or quantitative research), their work can provide us with a benchmark for an essay style marked by objectivity, impersonality and careful research. Their use of language is markedly different from the familiar voice. Sociologists and psychologists communicate in a style that is close to the reports of the physical sciences in an important way; their texts are *field oriented*. The way their disciplines are named in the academic world shows this field orientation. Titles like "The Social Sciences" or "The Behavioural Sciences" are often used in universities to describe the general areas in which departments of psychology, criminology, anthropology, or sociology are placed. Within these wide areas of professional concern, the subject matter extends far beyond an individual or familiar experience of social groups. However, *essayists* writing on such themes do not have to have the high degree of professional rigour and disciplined kinds of thought that are the hallmarks of a report in the social sciences. Many such essays are, though, supported with evidence, and their authors take a lot of care to cover the issue with a view to answering counter arguments or confounding facts.

Literary analysis and commentary also marks out a discipline or field. English Literature is an academic subject, but while some of the social sciences now inform literary approaches to creative texts, the field of literature has approaches, methods, rigour, and a lexicon of its own. Here is another example of commentary from the literary review journal *Books in Canada*. Damian Tarnopolsky is reviewing *In Search of Authority: An Introductory Guide to Literary Theory* by Stephen Bonnycastle (1997). After praising the book for its clarity and friendly manner, Tarnopolsky balances his positive review with some critical comments:

> This book opens up difficult areas for outsiders, but the accessibility comes at a price: the author cannot and does not wish to communicate their importance with the force and urgency a believer would bring. This leaves important subjects short-changed, for too many chapters have the unconvinced and uninspiring tone of someone just visiting. (26)

Tarnopolsky uses a number of contrastive techniques to show up the problem he has found with the book. A high standard of in-depth coverage is appealed to, and by this standard Bonnycastle's textbook on literary theory falls short. As we noted in the search for authorial commentary, adjectives, adverbs and idiomatic expressions are used to show the difficulties: for example, "first flaw," "do little more," "accessibility comes at a price," "unconvinced and uninspiring tone," "short changed," and "someone just visiting." These show a judgment, though we are not shown exactly how we are short changed or uninspired. Tarnopolsky places the book in relation to a standard of clarity, depth of understanding, and the author's *coverage* of the existing range of literary theory. The commentary persuades us by showing what is missing. The fundamental critical concept here is then *coverage*; according to Tarnopolsky, Bonnycastle simply does not include enough literary theory.

Critical judgments about essays on social or literary matters often rest on an exterior standard like coverage, and such evaluation can quickly involve other areas like overall philosophical or political position or values. Here is an excerpt from a longer and more robust review by literary critic Perry Link on the 2012 Chinese Nobel Prize award to the winner for literature, Mo Yan, (from the Dec. 6, 2012 *New York Review of Books*). The essay is titled, "Does This Writer Deserve the [Nobel] Prize?" Link begins with a discussion of Yan's first literary success in China, his novel *Red Sorghum*:

The main challenge for Mo Yan beginning in the 1990s was to find a literary voice that he could use in the long term. *Red Sorghum* had been a genuine breakthrough, but only because of the political situation of the 1980s, when Chinese writers could make their names by "breaking into forbidden zones." *Red Sorghum* had broken into two: sexual libertinism and truth-telling about the war with Japan. But by the 1990s there were fewer forbidden zones awaiting break-in, and those that did remain (the 1989 massacre, corruption among the political elite, and topics like Taiwan, Tibet, and Xinjiang) were so extremely forbidden as to be untouchable....

The voice that he has embraced has been called Rabelaisian, but it is even more earthy than Rabelais's.... Sometimes, but not always, Mo Yan's expression is ironic, and it includes flights of imagination that critics have compared to the "magical realism" of Gabriel García Márquez. (It is doubtful that Mo Yan has read either Rabelais or García Márquez; these are similarities, not influences.)

Mo Yan writes about people at the bottom of society, and in *The Garlic Ballads* (1988) he clearly sides with poor farmers who are bullied and bankrupted by predatory local officials. Sympathy for the downtrodden has had a considerable market in the world of Chinese letters in recent times, mainly because the society does include a lot of downtrodden and they do invite sympathy. But it is crucial to note the difference between the way Mo Yan writes about the fate of the downtrodden and the way writers like Liu Xiaobo, Zheng Yi, and other dissidents do. Liu and Zheng denounce the entire authoritarian system, including the people at the highest levels. Mo Yan and other inside-the-system writers blame local bullies and leave the top out of the picture. (paras 1–3)

What do you think of the positioning of the reviewer? The reviewing style is a bit like Astell's or Bacon's in that it reaches for a middle ground between rejection and acceptance, or at least seems to appear balanced. It is also not couched in anything like a familiar voice. Link takes care with the formal aspects of balance, coverage and an inclusion of facts about Mo Yan, and a comparison and contrast with other Chinese writers and traditions. There is no use of the "I" pronoun or many other markers of an immediate familiar context. Mo Yan and Lu Xiabo are seen from what is called the third person objective, or dramatic point of view often used by journalists and playwrights. This point of view is sometimes called "the fly on the wall" view as the author does not enter into the minds of characters.

Link's approach is directly evaluative and the *quantity* of his support gives his writing its objective tone. It is mostly concerned to provide the coverage needed to back up the commentary. In contrast to Syms in the previous chapter, Link includes summaries of much of Mo Yan's literary output, as much about him as possible in the space of a review. The review lists four of Mo Yan's books, *Red Sorgum, The Garlic Ballads, Big Breasts and Wide Hips, Life and Death are Wearing Me Out* and the reviewer goes back to the early Mo Yan works to begin an analysis that will show the growth (or limits) of these works — and his likely political perspective. If you read the whole review, you will note a balance between an overview and detail. There is more detailed coverage and research of the political context before and after the award of the Nobel, plus the contrasting theme with Liu Xiaobo. The space allowed for the review is about two and half tabloid size pages, or about eight, 8.5" x 11" typewritten double spaced pages. This additional space does not then constrain Link to such a high level of generality as Syms with his one page review; he includes some quotation of Mo Yan and other writers, though close reading based on analysis of the four novels is not included. Such detailed analysis would require much more space. The usual length of an academic article about literature is about fifteen to seventeen pages. Link's review is close to an academic article though it does not include a Works Cited, and only an occasional footnote. An academic book length work, (called a *monograph*) could easily be written on this theme of censorship, Liu Xiaobo and Mo Yan.

Coverage is also supplemented by another aspect of a critical review. Link includes a comparison of texts from other traditions and other writers. He positions Mo Yan in terms of some sign posts of two well-known literary traditions, Rabelais for the European, and Gabriel García Márquez for the South American. Rabelais developed a well know style of earthy satire and humour appearing early in France in the 15th century and his work *Gargantua and Pantagruel* marks a change to early modernism, folk humour and realism, and away from a moralist religious tone. Márquez, along with other South American authors like Jorge Luis Borges is founder of a style called *magic realism*. Link claims these are likely not known by Mo Yan; thus a gap has been found, and perhaps a lack of knowledge of the Western tradition as "these are similarities not influences." This is a way of further showing that Mo Yan is not a dissident. His milieu is (Rabelasian) Chinese rural life, which his work avidly evokes and, in part, critiques, but he does not touch on more dangerous territory of the censorship of literature practiced at the higher levels of Chinese political culture.

The review hinges on this comparison and contrast of Mo Yan with Liu Xiaobo, also a Chinese Nobel Laureate for literature, who was given an eleven year sentence in China in 2009 for the perceived political incorrectness of his work.

Interestingly, Link does not come out and accuse Mo Yan of complicity with an oppressive regime or that he accepts Chinese official censorship; he lets the work of contrast and comparison with Lui Xiaobo do this work through implication.

Another aspect of criticism is used to support this positioning, though this time the editor of the journal has helped. If you wish to know why we should give the reviewer our assent, Link's credentials are given at the beginning of the journal:

> Perry Link is retired from Princeton and now teaches at the University of California at Riverside. He translated China's *Charter 08* manifesto, published in these pages, and recently co-edited *No Enemies, No Hatred*, a collection of essays and poems by Liu Xiaobo. His latest book, *An Anatomy of Chinese: Rhythm, Metaphor, Politics*, will be published in January 2013. (3)

With this we can get a little closer to verification of Link's expertise. Link can translate Chinese into English, and likely has in-depth knowledge of current Chinese affairs and literature.

Despite the judgemental tone, you can see the care with which Link has positioned Mo Yan. The comparison with Liu Xiaobo takes into account the difficulty faced by both writers. Their human situation in China and its dangers are included, and though there is a definite weight given Lui Xiaobo, the humanity of both authors is allowed, touched on, lightly included.

Here is a non-literary example showing an additional type of such coverage and how an essay's focus can be on defining and the meaning of terms, in this case the difference between a planet and a star. Owen Gingerich from the column "Wonders" in *Scientific American* (1996) explains how the planet Neptune was discovered and recognized as a planet. Note the interaction of analysis with expertise in the history of science.

> For young John Couch Adams, a new planet figuratively swam into view when, as a University of Cambridge undergraduate, he wrote, "Formed a design of investigating ... the irregularities in the motion of Uranus which are yet unaccounted for; in order to find out whether they may be attributed to the action of an undiscovered planet beyond it...."
> Uranus had been discovered 62 years earlier, in 1781, by William Herschel. In 1843, with its period of 84 years, Uranus had not quite made a complete cycle around the sun since its detection. But a few "prediscovery" observations had turned up, whereby astronomers

had recorded its position under the assumption that it was a star. By the early 1800s those positions obtained before 1781 had become a problem — an orbit that could represent the "modern" observations simply didn't fit.

Adams was challenged to make sense of all the observations by postulating an unseen planet whose gravitational influence was perturbing the path of Uranus....

... The same sort of mathematical attack on the recalcitrant motion of Uranus had been undertaken by Urbain Jean Joseph Le Verrier of the École Polytechnique in Paris. D. François Jean Arago, director of the Paris Observatory, had suggested the problem to him, and by August 1846, Le Verrier had also predicted a position for the unknown perturber.

****

In the end the honors were shared, although naval Britain won out with the name "Neptune," after the mythological god of the sea, as opposed to the modern appellation "Le Verrier," espoused by the French, (who were also disposed to rename Uranus "Herschel"). (181–83)

In this explication of historical texts, we see a precursor to a formal analysis. There is a movement from a question, "how did the planet Neptune get its name?" to a short survey of "the historical record," which provides us with an answer and some clarity. Gingerich introduces us to how Adams came to his idea by quoting an excerpt from the original text by Adams, and then giving some background on the problem — in doing so he works back to 1781 and Herschel. That is, he summarizes some of the scientific history about Neptune. Gingerich has set the problem as one of naming and redefining. How was Neptune named when *two* astronomers, separated by distance and time, claimed the first discovery that it was a planet not a star? The solution was a name that was not tied to either discoverer, "Neptune." There may be a tacit approval of the sharing of the honours by both discoverers, but the essay is primarily descriptive and informative allowing the reader entry into the scope and types of history texts available on the topic. Coverage, then, like Link's approach, is front and centre as the method of this essay.

Further Elements of the Formal Voice

So far, we have recovered additional dimensions of the formal voice from literary reviews and an essay on a scientific discovery. The voice is "field oriented" and has a more objective tone; it uses the *third-person objective point of view,* and not the "I" pronoun; for instance "Adams was challenged," "the main challenge for Mo Yan beginning in the 1990s....", and "this book opens up difficult areas for outsiders." There are few, if any, deictic markers or references to the reader or the immediate context of the writer and reader. The author's personality and situation is held in the background. General language and abstraction are clearly present but so are specific or concrete details, and this relation organizes the whole of the formal essay. These essays are, in a word, *thematic*: Link, for instance, claimed that Mo Yan was not a dissident, Tarnopolsky that Bonnycastle did not include enough theory, and Gingerich that Neptune was named out of a dissension and was not a bad choice. These essayists used a lexicon of specialist terms like "Rabelasian," "magic realism," "perturber" or "orbital irregularities" plus direct quotation either from the texts they were evaluating or from supporting material. The focus of most of their paragraphs was on addressing and persuading an audience interested in literary or scientific matters and issues. Thus the point of view moves the reader away from the narrator, to an issue, analysis, or topic. There is a range in this kind of style: at one pole it is impersonal and almost scientifically objective; whereas, in essays on literary and social analysis, it can mix voices, or include some familiarity. However, with its focus on coverage and support of claims, the literary or other commentary is primary, and the familiarity secondary.

Evaluating Formal Language

In the following study of the formal thought found in essays on social themes, we will be looking more closely at the methods essayists use in order to support a claim. I have selected *coverage, expertise, analysis,* and *definition* and as these can be complicated matters, we will be doing so across the next two chapters. Getting to know and work with these formal methods provides you with a good opportunity to evaluate the quality of arguments and the advantages and disadvantages of the formal approach. After examining each example we will build a response to it.

Coverage

One of the primary features of the more scientific approach is its goal of significant coverage in range of samples or illustration. This feature is, of course, the basis of most kinds of proof. If you make a general claim, you must find wide and relevant support for it or illustrate its relevance in experience, research, or fact. Margaret Visser's popular essay "Feeding, Feasts and Females" uses this pattern of a claim supported by many illustrations in an interesting way. Her essay about the gender aspects of feasting is a telling instance of how a general claim about social life can be made credible — she supports her claim through providing numerous examples of feasts and women's roles in them. As social arguments are obviously about group behaviour, the wider the number of cases that support the claim, the more certain a claim about a social group is likely to be. Here are two excerpts from Visser's illustrations:

> An ancient Greek wife would not have been seen dead at a symposium.... Her honour was, and had at all costs to remain, unassailable: the legitimacy of her offspring, and the honour of her menfolk, depended upon it. It was all right for *hetairai* (courtesans) to mix with revelling and orgiastic males; they were shameless women, outrageous in their freedom and lack of *tenue*. A dining room was called an *andron*, "a room for men"; a woman eating there was a woman out of place, marginalized and unworthy of respect.... (2)
>
> Brewing beer is an ancient female preserve; and where beer is central to the economy and nutrition of a society — as it often still is in Africa, among South American Indians, and elsewhere — control over it naturally becomes a source of female power. It may link up with another commonly traditional female skill and responsibility: that of making and controlling the use of clay pots. (The ancient Greek god Dionysus — feminine is ['in' sic] so much of his nature — had power over both wine and over the area of Athens called Ceramicus, where pots were made.) The Newar women of Nepal must personally serve the beer they have made, even at a public feast. Among the LoDagaa of Ghana, a woman's good beer can turn her home into a beer house, a place where people gather to exchange news and gossip. She sells her product, and puts it out for her clients.... She plays a role rather like that of European society hostesses who used to keep "open house" or a "salon" on certain days of the week where people could collect together and socialize. The hostess of a tea party, like the LoDagaa breweress, must pour the tea. (4–5)

Visser uses one of the most basic forms of evidence — proving a general claim through collecting relevant, supportive illustrations or samples; and the bulk of her essay is devoted to this task. The example of Greek women begins her proof. It shows that women have been preparing feasts and men consuming them (and not preparing them) from ancient times. Note that her topic statement in the third paragraph restates her thesis, keeping it in the forefront of her reader's mind throughout: "brewing beer is an ancient female preserve." This subtopic is itself supported through three relevant illustrations. One focuses on the Newar women of Nepal; the second, on the LoDagaa women of Ghana. In the third, it is the European hostess at a tea party who is participating in an ancient and culturally widespread ritual controlled by women. Visser cites these examples to support her secondary theme about brewing, and it, in turn, supports her overall theme that there is a distinction between feasting activity allowed to men and women. In addition, she has made us realize that there is a lot of power and control involved in the production and serving of food and drink at feasts by women.

Visser uses many instances like these, but as they accumulate, they become the basis for her final, surprising conclusion that men in Western cultures are becoming increasingly socialized in what has traditionally (and worldwide) been a "woman's preserve." Women, as she says, have won in this area as men "in short...have become more like women" (525). Note again that the enumerating of instances is the key strategy for arriving at this conclusion and that a familiar note is present. Visser is engaged in her argument and clearly approves of the reversal of roles she sees occurring. The number of illustrations she uses has persuasive force. The instances add up and progress to a different conclusion than you might have anticipated, until at the end, we recognize that women do have power through preparing and serving feasts, so much so that during the course of the essay, we see women emerge from secondary roles and gradually take on active and primary roles and agencies through their feast preparation. Coverage, the working through of instances and examples, wide illustration of an idea therefore, can be an effective persuasive strategy.

Building a Critical Response to Coverage

You might have a number of initial feelings, insights, or other responses to this excerpt. There is, however, one general area from which your responses are likely to have been drawn. Your initial reactions are likely to depend on whether you feel included or excluded in the essayist's readership. As we have seen, finding a relationship with a text like this one usually depends on your ability to locate its context, authorial attitude, or audience. The way to this relation can be found through one of the text's *deictic markers*, namely the addressed reader.

To recap, *deictic* markers are the references a speaker or writer makes to the context of utterance, including the participants in the utterance — that is, other speakers or potential speakers and listeners or readers and their settings. A rereading of the excerpt from Visser's essay shows how few pronouns and possessive pronouns for herself and her readers she uses. "I," "me," "mine," "you," or "your" are lightly present. The point of view is almost wholly objective and third person, and it is reflected in her extensive use of illustrations drawn from many cultures and periods. She does, however, use other deictic markers for speaker, readership, and context that are often found in a more formal approach: the first person plural pronoun "we," the possessive plural pronoun "our," and the indefinite third person pronoun "one." Like the markers of familiarity, this more formal mode of address to an audience can also invoke a strong initial response.

Visser introduces a segment of readership through these pronouns both in her beginning and end paragraphs. In the first paragraph of her essay she states, "Ceasing to eat together is tantamount to divorce — or ceasing to 'sleep together,' as *we* still put it. *Our euphemism* is not merely coy." And she ends the essay with a clear reference to her readers, "Men who succeed and are admired in *our culture* must demonstrate that they have opted for finesse, sympathetic awareness, and self-control." The "our," "we," "our euphemism," and "our culture" are likely to have been made to address the English-speaking, likely Western, reader from Visser's perspective. It is hard to pin this very large audience down precisely, but we can say that if you feel excluded, then you are likely to have a skeptical view of her claim about progress. On the other hand, if you feel included, your response is likely to rest on your own similar experiences with cooking, eating, serving, and feasting or with gender or other differences that you have experienced that parallel Visser's claim.

On the exclusion side, you might, for instance, be part of the general culture she refers to but be a member of a particular segment of it. If you work as a short-order cook in a fast food outfit in Toronto, Visser's claim about being made more refined through your cooking skills might not make much sense to you. Your work might simply be tough, poorly paid labour, especially if you prepare rather than serve food. Would you have "opted for finesse, sympathetic awareness, and self-control" while slinging hamburgers? If not, you might not really feel part of Visser's "our culture." This does not necessarily mean you have to respond negatively. Her claim is general; you could very well begin to see her point despite the evidence of your own experience. On the other hand, if you feel strongly excluded (or that a significant segment of readership has been left out), you might want to pursue a critical evaluation.

Less skeptical responses could perhaps come from a "feast giver," preparing and serving a meal for a spouse's company president who might believe in the ethical issue about fairer work distribution and refinement that Visser raises. At first reading, then, there are two primary questions you are likely to ask: "Am I included in this discourse?" and "Does its claim meet with my own experience?" Study of the way the *deictic* markers for the formal voice are used can help you determine an answer.

While vital and necessary, this kind of initial response to the image of readership or audience in a formal essay is really a first step in evaluating a general claim like Visser's. Sometimes your feelings of exclusion or inclusion might be borne out by further thought, but in a more studied evaluation, you will likely want to revise and add a more reasoned examination to your initial insights. But how do you do so? And what is the value of this formal evaluation?

For one thing, such scrutiny of claims and the coverage used to back them up is basic to academic discussion and debate. Wide representative support is one of the dimensions of an argument you should first look for in an essay with a general claim like Visser's. If present, the argument can be judged effective on this level. Poorly supported claims, on the other hand, *overgeneralize* or claim ideas as more representative than they really are. Does Visser overgeneralize?

Her claim is highly general: "It has for most of history been common for men and women to eat apart, especially in public." "Men" and "women" are group nouns and highly abstract. Such general claims are in fact so high up on the ladder of generality that they are called *universal* because they attempt to say something about all of a group. In this case, because Visser includes the women of ancient Greece and the phrase "most of history," her universality of scope seems to include most of recorded time as well. Her related claims that there is a gender coding in how feasts are conducted concern all feast givers and feast participants world-wide through most of cultural history.

This high level of generality is shown in other ways. While more specific nouns and adjectives are found in the illustrations that support this claim, note that the *level of specificity* of Visser's language is not the same as the concrete expression we have studied in the familiar essay. She does not, for example, reach the detailed expression of perception we noted in Didion's essay, with its use of dialogue and the minutiae of episodic setting. Compare, for instance, Visser's level of language with Didion's. There is a high level of detail when, for instance, Didion lists the memorabilia of her childhood as in "Three teacups handpainted with cabbage roses and signed 'E. M.,' my grandmother's initials"(2). The following example from "Feeding, Feasts, and Females" is, by contrast, still high on the scale of generality:

> The *Newar women* of Nepal must personally serve the beer they have made, even at a public feast. *Among the LoDagaa* of Ghana, *a woman's* good beer can turn her home into a beer house, a place where people gather to exchange news and gossip. (5) [Italics added]

This language is about groups of women (Newar women and LoDagaa women) rather than individual cases. To write more concretely, say by reporting a specific feast in the Newar culture of Nepal that Visser herself might have attended on a specific day, would require many more details (and thus less coverage or perhaps a chapter on this illustration alone), which could prevent the reader from keeping her general claim in view.

This mid-to-high level of general language provides us with a way of critically evaluating Visser's strategy of evidence. You can now see that Visser has constructed a *sample* rather than used an all-inclusive approach, and she also has had to sacrifice a fine level of detail for the wider coverage provided by "cultures" and "periods." You can evaluate sampling strategies like this in two ways.

First, if you are doubtful of a claim, look for examples that do not fit — in research terminology these are called *confounding instances*. We can ask whether Visser's sample includes enough attention to cultures in which men do serve the food or brew beer or other alcoholic beverages or in which this gender distinction is not made or is more complex. In the novel *Things Fall Apart* (1958) by the Nigerian writer Chinua Achebe, for instance, the "tapper" or brewer of palm wine is male not female, though the warrior Obi culture he describes seems to have been maintained on the basis of other profound gender distinctions. Men grow and harvest the food in this culture, but they do not cook and serve it. Or, in terms of the last claim she makes, you might ask whether there really has been a significant shift in the willingness of males in Western culture to cook and thus become more refined in the way she claims. If you are skeptical, look then for exceptions or instances that "confound" the claim.

However, the essay does have a convincing number of supportive instances. There are about thirty-four illustrations for her claims, and Visser has obviously tried hard to include as many cultures as she could to support the universality of her thesis. This attempt at being representative is convincing.

But can we accept her claim on the basis of the *number* of illustrations alone? Coverage is a necessary component of a good argument. It is the ground note of all good research, and without it an argument can be seriously flawed. But in a more thorough evaluation, we should also ask *how* the facts were arrived at. How did Visser get her insights about the LoDaaga, or the Newar cultures?

We can also evaluate coverage by assessing the material and sources that *are* used rather than searching for confounds. We now need to look at the way in which her research has been conducted, at Visser's *method*, which will lead us into some research ourselves.

This level of evaluation of evidence asks questions like: Is she an expert? Where did she get all of this supporting material? Did she do the research herself? If so, what method did she use to get the facts she uses? If she did not do the research, what was her source of information? As you can see, obtaining this kind of information is made difficult because we have no introduction to her expertise or the research methods behind her essay. There is no bibliography, and she does not *document* all of her sources. Indeed, she rarely *cites* them through quotation or paraphrase. There are though a few gestures in this direction. Here is one of her literary illustrations:

in Thomas Peacock's novel *Headlong Hall* (1816), "the little butler now waddled in with a summons from the ladies to tea and coffee." (9)

Visser cites the novel through her quotation and documents it with an author's name, the title of the novel, and its date, but we do not have a page number or publishing information. It would be hard to find the quotation and its context in Peacock's novel. In a number of other instances, there is neither citation nor documentation. There is no indication in this form of the essay where Visser obtained her illustrations about the Newar and LoDaaga women. Again, were they based on her own research? Is she a trained cultural researcher and thus capable of finding out of this kind of material through field work? If so, when and how did she do it? How are we to judge these claims to fact if we do not know how they were arrived at? Answering questions about sources, methods, and authority requires some further digging.

Through library work and reading the introductions to some of her other writings, I first found that Visser was trained as a classical scholar at the University of Toronto. Her area of specialty is the cultural study of the rituals of everyday life like those practised around eating. In addition, she has published a number of books and articles on the subject. As she is a recognized social or cultural historian, many of her examples about other cultures might then very well be the result of her own research.

A second trip to the library catalogue showed me that Visser has written a number of books on the subject of daily eating rituals. Two of these, *The Rituals of Dinner: The Origins, Evolution, Eccentricities, and Meaning of Table Manners* and *The Way We Are*, deal extensively with the rituals of eating, and they are much more widely supported than the illustrations in our essay. In fact, through looking up the list of acknowledgements in *The Broadview Reader* (1992) from which the essay was drawn, I found that "Feeding, Feasts and Females" was taken from her longer work *The Rituals of Dinner*.

The next obvious step in my research was to read through parts of *The Rituals of Dinner* in order to track down and assess her sources. By reading relevant parts of the book, I found that the excerpt about the LoDaaga is documented as coming from a work by the anthropologist P. J. Quin, *Foods and Feeding Habits of the Pedi*, published in 1959 by the Witwatersrand University Press of Johannesburg, South Africa. Visser's claim then seems to be supported both by her training and by exterior (and seemingly credible) evidence arrived at by another expert. These claims are not simply opinion or hearsay, nor are they a reflection of her own personal experience; they have some footing in a recognized study. If I wanted, I could now go further in my evaluation and read on in P. J. Quin and his research.

Note that the date of the Quin text might indicate a confound. Because the work is over fifty years old, the techniques used in his study could be outdated, and the academic climate has certainly changed in South Africa since 1959. But, if we stop at this preliminary level, we now know a little more about where Visser got her information about African women and brewing beer, and we can at least accept her data provisionally, though full assent would have to wait for our assessment of the more completely documented and up-to-date research that confirmed her evidence. If the evidence is verified by further reading, it might well provide further support for her claim.

Careful scrutiny of these basic aspects of evidence (coverage and documentation) can uncover the methods of sampling or interpretation used to support a general statement in a more formal essay. In Visser's case, I found both authority on her part (university training) and a reliance on expertise (Quin) for some of her illustrations. As I have said, though, the lack of citation in this work is not necessarily a fault. The popular essay does not require the documentation procedures of a formal academic essay. Note as well that in this social-historical approach, familiar experience is used, but it is collected from people other than the narrator (they are called *subjects* or *participants* in the social sciences) and should include a wide enough range to be significant. I think that the range of samples Visser gives is impressive, and I lean toward being convinced, but I suspect that if I were to really bear down and study this theme, finding and assessing other experts and positions, there might be more confounding or ambiguous cases than she has shown.

If, by the way, sampling was used more widely and drawn from a whole region or city, then we would have a *survey* rather than a *case study* reliant on a number of representative individuals. In a brief evaluation like this one, you could assess Visser's essay as something like a preliminary survey (an "assay") of the gender aspects of feasting. Visser's essay, while more formal, is not quite on the level of a full academic article in terms of its assessment and research procedures.

I hope that you can begin to see one of the obvious values of the more formal approach. In giving up the immediacy of the familiar voice, we gain more certainty, a longer term reliability of general claims, a clear way of assessment, and discovery of many areas and aspects of an issue that we might have not considered. What do we lose? One thing is the fine level of detailed perception that we found in so many of our autobiographical essays; another might be the creative use of narrative devices like irony and character. In Visser's essay, I could sometimes hear a subtle tone of play with her audiences. Did you pick up, as I did, that there was something tongue in cheek and ironic about her style?

Expertise

Essayists who do not claim expertise in the field they are dealing with will often support their claims through proof drawn from authoritative sources like government statistics or from experiments or studies that have been done by well-known experts and scholars.

Note that the following excerpt by the literary theorist and historian Stephen Greenblatt in "Shakespeare and the Exorcists" (1985) bristles with scholarly references:

> Between the spring of 1585 and the summer of 1586, a group of English Catholic priests led by the Jesuit William Weston, alias Father Edmunds, conducted a series of spectacular exorcisms, principally in the house of a recusant gentleman, Sir George Peckham of Denham, Buckinghamshire. The priests were outlaws — by an Act of 1585 the mere presence in England of a Jesuit or seminary priest constituted high treason — and those who sheltered them were guilty of a felony, punishable by death. Yet the exorcisms, though clandestine, drew large crowds.... In 1603, long after the arrest and punishment of those involved, Samuel Harsnett, then chaplain to the Bishop of London, wrote a detailed account of the cases, based upon sworn statements taken from four of the demoniacs and one of the priests. It has been recognized since the eighteenth century that Shakespeare was reading Harsnett's book, *A Declaration of Egregious Popish Impostures*, as he was writing *King Lear*.[1] (94)

(*Recusants* were Roman Catholics who refused to attend Church of England [Anglican] services during this period of Protestant ascendancy in the sixteenth and seventeenth centuries). Greenblatt's scholarly style requires that he let his reader know where he obtained this recondite information, and he creates a list of his sources in the following muscular footnote found at the bottom of the page:

1. Samuel Harsnett, *A Declaration of Egregious Popish Impostures*, (London, 1603). Harsnett's influence is noted in Lewis Theobald's edition of Shakespeare, first published in 1733. On the clandestine exorcisms I am particularly indebted to D. P. Walker, *Unclean Sprits: Possession and Exorcism in France and England in the Late Sixteenth and Early Seventeenth Centuries* (Philadelphia, 1981). *King Lear* is quoted from the New Arden text ed. Denneth Muir (London, 1972). All other quotations from Shakespeare are taken from the Arden editions.

This is the kind of citation and documentation we did not find in Visser's essay. And you can probably imagine what her essay would look like if she had included it. For one thing, it would likely be twice as long. It would also slow reading down. It is again possible that the lack of documentation in the essay we read was a decision made by the publisher. An essayist writing for a popular audience will rarely use this more academic model of reference and will rely instead on a variety of other ways of indicating use of scholarly material or experts.

But while it makes reading more difficult, this kind of framing, citation, and documentation has an advantage. With this apparatus ready to hand, it is easier for the reader to assess the author's claims. If you needed to, you could follow through and track down some of Greenblatt's material in a library, whereas finding Visser's sources proved more difficult.

Essayistic styles of using documentation vary widely, and essayists can be as creative with them as any novelist is with narrative. In an interesting '70s analysis of images of motherhood in Western culture, "Motherhood: Who Needs It?" essayist Betty Rollin uses some of the features of a formal, sociological style but not others. She deploys a number of abstract terms, supports them with a range of samples, illustrations, and analysis, and uses expert testimony to develop a general claim that is close to the foundations of sociology. Her theme is that motherhood and the nuclear family that support it are not driven by instincts but are learned and culturally coded. But in support of this claim, you will not find a continuous use of the formal scientific register or an academic method of documentation. Rollin's style is much more familiar than Greenblatt's, or Visser's — and though she does not often use the "I" pronoun, the familiar voice is present because her diction is *colloquial*, full of the kinds of idiomatic speech suited to her popular audience. Her essay is addressed, and includes the reader through deictic markers that stress her feelings and her focus. This general essayistic attitude affects her use of experts as well.

If we first concentrate on Rollin's use of expertise it will show us another value of the formal style. After the opening paragraph, we come across a catalogue of experts in social science and many direct quotations, which are used to support her claims about motherhood.

> Motherhood is in trouble, and it ought to be. A rude question is long overdue: Who needs it? The answer used to be (1) society and (2) women. But now, with the impending horrors of overpopulation, society desperately *doesn't* need it. And women don't need it either. Thanks to the Motherhood Myth — the idea that having babies is something that all normal women instinctively want and need and will enjoy doing — they just *think* they do.

The notion that the maternal wish and the activity of mothering are instinctive or biologically predestined is baloney…. "Motherhood — instinctive?" shouts distinguished sociologist / author Dr. Jessie Bernard. "Biological destiny? Forget biology! If it were biology, people would die from not doing it." (1)

"When a woman says with feeling that she craved her baby from within, she is putting into biological language what is psychological," says University of Michigan psychoanalyst and motherhood-researcher Dr. Frederick Wyatt. "There are no instincts," says Dr. William Goode, president-elect of the American Sociological Association. "There are reflexes, like eye-blinking, and drives, like sex. There is no innate drive for children. Otherwise, the enormous cultural pressures that there are to reproduce wouldn't exist. There are no cultural pressures to sell you on getting your hand out of the fire." (2)

If motherhood isn't instinctive, when and why, then, was the Motherhood Myth born? … Originally, it was the word of God that got the ball rolling…. But in no time, supermoralists like St. Augustine changed the tone of the message: "Intercourse, even with one's legitimate wife, is unlawful and wicked, where the conception of the offspring is prevented," he, we assume, thundered…. And so, based on need, inevitability, and pragmatic fantasy — the Myth worked, for society's point of view — the Myth grew like corn in Kansas…. (3)

Rollin's use of expert testimony in the first quotation and her use of St. Augustine in the third provides an interesting essayistic mixture of formality and familiarity. However, this is not the style of citation you would find in a social science text, and it is not something found in the standard university term paper.

One clear difference from the academic style lies in the way Rollin cites her experts — her approach to scholarly support is *rhetorical*. Note, for instance, that there is a high degree of audience awareness in the imperative "Try asking most sociologists" (1). This is a more argumentative and reader-aware voice than Greenblatt's. Rollin often directly addresses her reader, and her way of handling quotations from experts has overtones of a dramatic dialogue — her experts almost become characters in a play: "'Motherhood instinctive?' *shouts* distinguished sociologist/author Dr. Jessie Bernard." In addition, this language is so close to gesture and action (e.g., "Forget biology") that you feel impelled to get engaged and respond as if you were in a vigorous argument or debate with the author. Her experts are standing there in the background like a squadron of troops that have been marshaled at the ready to defend her ideas (imperatives, questions, and assertions are called *speech acts* by linguists, and Rollin is certainly using *active* language).

In the case of the St. Augustine quotation, Rollin simply makes up a scholarly example, just covering her creativity with "he, *we assume*, thundered." Do you want to follow her assumption? What exactly did St. Augustine say? Her examples and analogies all show her high awareness of her audience — the readers of the '70s *Look* magazine in which this essay first appeared. Her audience is not scholarly. Rollin is not using a formal tone like Greenblatt's; she reaches out and engages us in an interaction that is very close to lively argument and narration. An audience of general readers is very much addressed and *acted on* in this essay, and her use of expertise is a part of her wider rhetorical strategy.

Building a Critical Response to Expertise
In Visser's, Link's and Greenblatt's texts, the deictic markers and the immediate context are muted, and emotional expression is placed in the background. These are more disinterested styles, and they focus on ideas and their proof. Rollin's rhetorical, active approach to an audience and language invites, (even provokes) a response from you. What is your reaction to the level of diction Rollin uses? You may like her debunking, dramatic, and "tough debater" style ("baloney," "try asking," "forget biology," "shouts," "thunders," and so on), or you may think it inappropriate for such a serious area of study and decision as motherhood and children. Which of the two styles, rhetorical or scholarly, do you prefer? Why do you think Rollin is using this style?

Again, as with coverage, in composing an academic response to an essay, you will want to evaluate not only your immediate response but the expertise and coverage used. As you have probably begun to realize, there are constraints of evidence in formal thought, and, as I have mentioned, one of these is a well-known procedure for allowing readers to check up on expertise. As we have noted, it would be out of place in the popular forum of a magazine, but the standard method of academic writing would include providing the titles of the articles, journals, magazines, or books from which quotations are excerpted and also giving other publishing information, including the publication date and page numbers on which the material appears.

Here is a good example of this procedure from a psychotherapy text, *Ethnicity and Family Therapy* by McGoldrick, Pearce, and Giordano (2005). Note how the quotation is introduced, cited, and documented. The author prepares her reader for the inclusion of the quotation at least four lines ahead of it and lets us know who will be speaking and his authority on this subject. The lead-in is part of a procedure called *framing*, and it is another hallmark of the academic style. (As a university student, you will need to get good at framing techniques — and it requires skill to do it well.) After the introduction and the citation, note how the quotation is documented for further reference:

> As Andrew Greeley, one of the few sociologists who has been study-ing ethnicity, has observed, future historians will be amazed that we have stood in the midst of such an astonishing social phenomenon and taken it so much for granted that we did not bother to study it.
>
> > They will find it especially astonishing in light of the fact that ethnic differences, even in the second half of the 20th Century, proved far more important than differences in philosophy or economic system. Men who would not die for a premise or a dogma would more or less cheerfully die for a difference rooted in ethnic origins. (Greeley, 1969, 5)
>
> Ethnicity remains a vital force in this country [the U.S.], a major form of group identification, and a major determinant of our family patterns and belief systems. (1)

This way of presenting an excerpt from another text is called *a block quota-tion*. The indentation stands for the quotation marks and signals a word-for-word transcription of the original. In addition, the excerpt from Greeley has been carefully documented — we can, with the aid of the References section in the back of the textbook, find the cited text through the page number. Note also that the careful frame shows us that the speaker has changed to Greeley and tells us what to look for in the quoted material — that ethnicity is a vital but often ignored social fact in current social science about the family.

But again, what is gained and what is lost when this formal procedure for the introduction of expertise is used? Can you see its value? One drawback is, of course, that you are no longer so free to do the kinds of things that Didion, Swift, Rollin or many other essayists do with language — the immediacy of perception and expression of emotion and the urgency of the claim are lost in the more academic style. It communicates restraint and a studied approach. On the other hand, the framing technique does allow you as a reader to access this expertise. You can now both find its source and assess and incorporate more dimensions of the claim in your response than the familiar style might allow. The authors have left Greeley pretty much to talk on his own without direct interpretation — the reader makes the connections. Note, though, that there is a positive evaluation (commentary) of Greeley as support for their position; he is one of the "few" sociologists studying this area of ethnicity and family therapy. And some urgency has been communicated: there should be more of this kind of study.

Here is another example of the more formal use of citation from a social psychology text that shows the highly disinterested tone and reserved attitude of the formal voice. Here providing information is the uppermost task, and immediacy, emotion, and the rhetorical, narrative, and familiar modes are left well in the background. The complete system of citation and documentation (in this case the APA, American Psychological Association) requires that the quotation and its documentation be backed up with a references page or a bibliography. The example is drawn from an overview of the development of psychotherapist John Bowlby's theory of attachment.

> The 1960s saw two important developments in the understanding of the psychological impact of loss. First, Bowlby was joined at the Tavistock [Clinic] by Colin Murray Parkes who undertook a systematic study of bereavement in adults which complemented and confirmed Robertson's (1952) earlier work with children (Parkes 1975). Second, the crystallisation of Attachment Theory provided a theoretical basis on which to understand these empirical findings.

This example, taken from Jeremy Holmes's *John Bowlby and Attachment Theory* (1993), uses a different citation procedure than the MLA style we have been using so far. The APA citation procedure is different in a number of ways, and the parenthetical notes in the text include the name and date. The excerpt itself is from a book that has a seventeen-page bibliography at the end. The full author names, titles, publishing information, editions, page numbers of articles, and dates of publication can be found there. This more detailed documentation allows the professional reader to track down the references to Robertson and Parkes. If you wanted to find out more about this phase in the development of Attachment Theory, or check the documentation cited you could do so quickly by finding the reference. One of the references in the bibliography looks like this:

> Parkes, C. M. and Stevenson-Hinde, J. (1982) *The Place of Attachment in Human Behaviour*: London: Tavistock.

Papers for a course in literature will likely use the MLA system. You should also note the differences with the MLA (Modern Language Association) style in which the date–name system of the APA is not used. If the name is not present in the text, it will be included in the citation, but the year is not required in the MLA approach. In MLA documentation, the parentheses usually have the name or the title plus the page, "Parkes often stated that.... (Parkes 54)." In the APA system, name and date as in "Parkes (1982) often stated that...." are most often used. Literary studies uses the MLA parenthetical approach, not the APA and both now replace footnoting as the method of documentation of sources. One advantage of both procedures is obvious: they openly present sources and invite scrutiny. This is part of a scholarly orientation in which all materials used in research are listed and made available to other scholars so that they can make a studied judgment about the findings produced through the research. After locating this and other references, the careful reader could begin to widen her understanding of the development of this theory in psychiatry. If she were interested in responding further, she might then also wish to evaluate Holmes's summation of Parkes.

Speaking of dates, another related criterion for the evaluation of the use of expertise is the *relevance* of the citations. With the documentation procedure in place, you can ask whether the research is dated or has been superseded by other, newer research. Note, for instance, that the date of Rollin's essay is 1970 and that expert thought about this bedrock issue of motherhood and women's roles in the family is sure to have been developed and significantly changed since her essay appeared. Perhaps, for instance, ideas like Bowlby's about attachment have now superseded instinct theories in the discussion of motherhood and child raising, or neuroscience and theories of empathy based in brain structure, now have precedence and thus at least in the academic world, the distinction Rollin makes may no longer be quite as relevant or dramatic as it was when she wrote her essay.

Nicholas Carr in "Is Google Making Us Stupid," shows another variation on this approach to coverage or support. At about the third page of this seven to eight page essay, Carr modulates from a familiar voice and the "I" pronoun to a more formal voice reliant on the inclusion of expertise, coming to a limited middle type of voice. After some anecdotal evidence from his own experiences that shows what the availability of Google has done to his memory and intellectual acuteness, he makes a gesture toward a more supported position.

> Anecdotes alone don't prove much. And we still await the long-term neurological and psychological experiments that will provide a definition of how Internet use affects cognition. But a recently published study of online research habits, conducted by scholars from University College London, suggests that we may be in the midst of a sea change in the way we read and think. (152)

Note the contraction, "don't" for "do not." We are yet marginally in the zone of the familiar and speaking voice; the formal voice rarely uses contractions.

Carr then summarizes the findings that came from the study, that researchers who used online databases of journal articles provided by the British Library for instance were exhibiting "a form of skimming activity." Online readers rarely returned to these articles to read them at depth. At this point Carr uses a block quotation that draws *verbatim* from this expertise. According to Carr,

> ...the researchers report:

> > It is clear that users are not reading online in the traditional sense; indeed there are signs that new forms of 'reading' are emerging as users 'power browse' horizontally through titles, content pages and abstracts going for quick wins. It almost seems that they go online to avoid reading in the traditional sense.

The quotation occurs on the third page of the essay, but it is interesting for another reason. It is not cited. There is no documentation at all for this block quotation, no mention of dates, the authors, or the journal in which the research was studied and no Work Cited page at the end of the essay. Like Rollin, we are then in a middle range of the formal style in which there is a gesture made to the necessity of a formal underpinning of anecdotal evidence through expertise, but we are not given any means for checking up on it, other than, perhaps, our own use of the Internet or a library data base.

The essayists discussed in this chapter have constructed arguments about our prevailing social practices and ideas; they have used coverage of evidence, illustration, a higher register or diction, and expertise, to clarify and support positions and to disprove countervailing claims. In these essays, familiar experience is at a minimum; there is an occasional reference to the writers' own situations, and given their more objective method, such reference is likely inappropriate. When familiarity does occur, it yet has use and interest, but we cannot rely on the higher level of certainty the full apparatus of formal thought would give.

Check List

We can now summarize the questions we have been using to build a response to this more formal kind of essay writing:

Coverage

- Am I included or excluded in the discourse and its context?
- Is the sampling or evidence used to support a general claim representative, or is it too narrow?

- Are there too many "confounding instances" that could undermine the given evidence?
- How has the evidence been arrived at? What method was used? Is the method and its evidence dated?

Expertise

- Is there a claim for authority or expertise on the part of the writer? If so, is it warranted? Is there a way to track down the training, professional standing, and publication record of the expert?
- How am I being addressed? Is the style of address (diction) appropriate to the subject matter? What are the benefits and drawbacks of the style being used?
- Can I check up on the evidence used, or is citation minimal or otherwise inadequate. How much documentation is there? If I can get to the source material, is the quotation, paraphrase, or summary of evidence accurate?
- If expertise is cited, can I find it through library research and evaluate whether it is in fact expertise, and, if so, whether it is relevant?
- Has the cited material been decontextualized, or is it an otherwise accurate or inaccurate reflection of the original?
- Is there adequate representation of an opposing point(s) of view? Or could the opposing point of view be characterized as "a straw man"?

Study Questions

1. What makes up the formal voice?
2. What are the advantages of the formal voice?
3. What are the disadvantages of the formal voice?
4. How would you evaluate an essay for its coverage?
5. How would you evaluate an essay for its use of expertise?
6. Which of the essays studied in this chapter most impressed you? Which the least? See if you can clearly state why you had this response.
7. Where would you place Rollin's argument today? What about Carr's?

Key Terms

Framing

The line of division between your own voice in a paper and another voice you have "borrowed" from a *primary* source, the work you are analysing, or a *sec-*

ondary source like a biography, history or critical analysis. An introduction to the source is then followed by a quotation or paraphrase, which is usually commented on. Typical markers: As Link says in "Does this Writer Deserve the Prize?"; According to Link; Tarnopolsky continues.

APA Style
The American Psychological Association Style. The citation and documentation style used in the social sciences.

MLA Style
The Modern Language Association. The citation and documentation style used in the humanities and literary studies.

Formal Diction
The level or register in a text. The usual range is from high diction to low diction. An author of a novel or short story will often vary diction to indicate a change in character. There is a quite specific diction used by essayists writing formal essays: no contractions, use of the indirect passive voice, a reduction of the "I" pronoun, fewer deictic markers, more third person objective narration, few if any figures of speech, or "play" with language. This voice is used in literary studies, but is not so severe in its restrictions as in the sciences.

Contractions
These are the shortcuts used in speech and in texts using the familiar voice. "Cannot" becomes "can't," "do not" is contracted to "don't," "should not" to "shouldn't" "you have" to "you've" and so on. The formal voice, along with more attention to detail and fuller coverage of evidence, rarely uses contractions.

Close Reading
Reading at depth with notes, and attention to detail. Ask whether you have understood each sentence. Building from your notes then ask whether you have a good sense of the overall theme. What general sentences and supporting details can you remember after your reading? Coverage, expertise, analysis, and uses of definition and terminology are places in the text where you can begin to sift and evaluate the proof and quality of thought of the essay you have read.

Theme
The topic of an essay. It is usually a general idea that is stated as a claim in the essay, and then supported with illustration, quotation or detail and the essay progresses.

Confound or **confounding instance**

A fact or other item of evidence that contradicts a claim, thesis or argument. A possible refutation of an argument or claim.

Works Cited

Carr, Nicholas. "Is Google Making Us Stupid?" *The Norton Reader.* Eds Linda H. Peterson *et alia.* Shorter 13th ed. New York: Norton, 2013, 150–159.

Gingerich, Owen. "Wonders" "Neptune, Velikovsky and the Name of the Game" *Scientific American Magazine;* September 1996, 181–183.

Greenblatt, Stephen. J. "Shakespeare and the Exorcists" *Shakespearean Negotiations: The Circulation of Social Energy in Renaissance England.* Oxford/ Berkeley and Los Angeles: OUP/U California P, 1988.

Link, Perry. "Does This Writer Deserve the Prize?" *The New York Review of Books,* December 6, 2012, Vol. 59, No 19.

McGoldrick, Monica, John K. Pearce, and Joseph Giordano, eds. *Ethnicity and Family Therapy.* New York: The Guilford Press, 1982.

Rollin, Betty. "Motherhood: Who Needs It?" (*Look* 22 Sept. 1970). *The Norton Reader.* Ed. Linda H. Peterson and John C. Brereton. New York: Norton, 2008. 369–377.

Tarnopolsky, Damian, *Books in Canada* Review: *In Search of Authority: An Introductory Guide to Literary Theory* by Stephen Bonnycastle (1997).

Visser, Margaret. "Feeding, Feasts, and Females." *The Broadview Reader.* Ed. Herbert Rosengaren and Jane Flick. Peterborough: Broadview Press, 1992. 347–356.

4   The Formal Voice II, Analysis and Terminology

... to return back to the primitive purity, and shortness, when men delivered so many things, almost in an equal number of words. They have exacted from all their members, a close, naked, natural way of speaking; positive expression; clear senses; a native easiness: bringing all things as near the Mathematical plainness, as they can: and preferring the language of Artizans, Countrymen, and Merchants, before that, of Wits, or Scholars. (Bishop Thomas Sprat, *History of the Royal Society*, 1667)

Sources

Jacob Bronowski, "The Reach of Imagination" (1967)
Rachel Carson, "The Obligation to Endure" *Silent Spring* (1962)
Gerry Coulter, "Jean Baudrillard and the Definitive Ambivalence of Gaming" (2009)
Stephen Jay Gould, "Evolution as Fact and Theory" (1981, 1994)
Marshall McLuhan, *Understanding Media: The Extensions of Man* (1964)
George Orwell, "Anti-Semitism in Britain" (1945)
Schumpeter, "The 'Breaking Bad' school" *The Economist* (2013)

Objectives

In this chapter we move forward with the discussion of the formal voice we began in chapter three, and will concentrate on two other formal methods, *analysis* and *terminology (definition)*. We will be exploring more objective and rigorous kinds of essay writing based on logical development, accurate reports and evidence. In our approach to increasing your skill in essay writing, we will study how writers develop a theme through *comparison* and *contrast* as this often engages analysis and terminology. A primary goal of this chapter is to help you improve your ability to evaluate more impersonal, complex, and higher-level arguments based on these logical-formal methods. And we concentrate on how you can work up a response to them that will pass scrutiny. You will need to know something about the more general academic procedures of analysis and uses of terminology because they occur in most academic essays.

Introduction

As we have seen, academic evidence typically appears in essays as expert testimony. We are now going to see how some of this expert knowledge is constructed. After we have explored this basic structure, you will see that you can make credible and useful evaluations even though you are not yet an expert in a field yourself. The persuasiveness of expert testimony comes from the respect we give to disciplined analysis and empirical research — in which results are based on scientific or logically based modes of analysis and observation. Such procedures were not always so highly regarded. At its inception in the 1600s, the "New Philosophy" of science, for instance, was considered dangerous and provocative. Both Bacon and Locke were suspected of atheism in an age when it was quite risky to forward the new approach. And not very much later, Romantic writers were dramatizing science in dystopian visions like Mary Shelley's novel about the ethically suspect "mad scientist" Victor Frankenstein. Science had to struggle to become accepted, but today, nearly three hundred years after Locke, Bacon, Newton, and Shelley, attitudes have reversed. We now give science and academic expertise based in it, a privileged place in explanations of events, though controversy yet surrounds this evaluation.

Calling science an "established model" is an understatement. The use of scientific technique has become so deeply ingrained in our thinking that our training in it probably begins at birth. The very first perceptions of a 21st century newborn raised in a culture dependent on modern technology, are likely to be of the antiseptic world of a hospital with its glittering array of medical instruments and white or blue-coated personnel. The store of our impressions of technology grows quickly as we use and come to understand the switches and control devices on the wide variety of machines and tools that surround us. Technical marvels like television, game computers, video recorders, word processors, cars, refrigerators, cellular phones, radios, central heating, and the Internet support us (and bedevil us) so completely now that they have surely become part of our transmitted culture, part of the way most children in the developed and developing countries grow up. The pattern has spread rapidly to affect most cultures and has become something of a universal norm among the middle classes and economic elites.

Likewise in the academic world. In the university generally, science and its realization in technology, have become a highly regarded approach to understanding both nature and humanity. Its methods, language, and instruments and the kinds of training found in its various schools now have the authority of an academic norm and they are used (and argued about) in almost all disciplines. The scientific method, as the '70s French sociologist Jacques Ellul was only too aware, is one of our most thoroughly established paradigms, though Ellul argues that we have glorified it far beyond its merits. Critical analysis of science itself is a focus in some of the following essays — and yet it is relied on extensively. Some accept the basic values of *empiricism* (the world view or philosophy of science) and call for changes *within* it; some wish to move away from this paradigm entirely. Two of our essayists, (Gould and Carson), are scientists themselves (in paleontology and marine biology respectively). Their arguments certainly rely on rational argument, much empirical evidence, and careful, logical analysis, and they rely on a style much influenced by scientific techniques and reporting in which terms are used and defined very carefully. We will in the following, study two of the basic structures of this approach, *analysis* and *terminology* in order to evaluate their essays and build effective responses.

In your assessment of these more impersonal arguments and positions, you will have to attempt to evaluate claims based on data and research. Usually this evidence is publicly available and presented in such a way that you could sift it through, find the evidence on which it is based, and, theoretically at least, make up your own mind about its conclusions. But how do you make a credible case for your judgment in a paper that is to be read by a critical audience? The list of experts Carson marshals for her arguments is impressive, and you might feel that there is no way you could judge them fairly. There are, however, some trustworthy questions you can ask of this kind of proof.

Analysis

Analysis is an important means of formal development in the essay on social, technological, or other more scientific themes; it again marks the difference between formal and familiar approaches. Analysis requires an impersonal stance, so it needs support that goes beyond personal experience. It can be used in many ways, from simply taking apart some of the implications of a general idea to making a full-scale attempt to describe, say, the economic causes of a world view.

There are a number of different types of analysis, but two are often used. *Causal analysis* gives evidence for *why* something is the way it is. This method concentrates on finding and proving causes or reasons for a social practice or on showing that it has a certain predictable effect. Race prejudice, for instance, could be found to be caused by a colonial past, or by perceived threats to economic status, or by imagined cultural differences, or, simplistically by a spirit of evil working through humanity. Here is an interesting example of *causal* analysis from Marshall McLuhan's *Understanding Media: The Extensions of Man* (1964). Discussing Lynn White's *Medieval Technology and Social Change* (1962) he notes that White

> ... explains how the feudal system was a social extension of the stirrup. The stirrup first appeared in the West in the eighth century AD, having been introduced from the East. With the stirrup came mounted shock combat that called into existence a new social class. The European cavalier class had already existed to be armed, but to mount a knight in full armor required the combined resources of ten or more peasant holdings. Charlemagne demanded that less prosperous freemen merge their private farms to equip a single knight for the wars. The pressure of the new war technology gradually developed classes and an economic system that could provide numerous cavaliers in heavy armor. By about the year 1000 AD the old word *miles* had changed from "soldier" to "knight." (163)

This *causal* analysis shows that an invention that might at first be considered historically insignificant, the stirrup, eventually helped produce (McLuhan uses "called into existence") a major change in social organization, the rise of the feudal system. Analysis of causal relations often leads to surprises or the uncovering of hidden relations and influences, but, even with as respected a theorist as McLuhan, we would have to ask whether this claim was adequately supported. Another main type of formal analysis is *structural or process analysis*; it tries to answer questions about *how* something works. Structural analysis can be used in a simple set of directions on how to build a model airplane or, at the other end of the scale, in a voluminous study of a complex institution like kinship.

Critical Responses to Structural Analysis
From George Orwell's, "Anti-Semitism in Britain" (1945):

> There are about 400,000 known Jews in Britain, and in addition some thousands or, at most, scores of thousands of Jewish refugees who have entered the country from 1934 onwards.....

I start off with these background facts, which are already known to any well-informed person, in order to emphasise that there is no real Jewish "problem" in England. The Jews are not numerous or powerful enough, and it is only in what are loosely called "intellectual circles" that they have any noticeable influence. Yet it is generally admitted that anti-Semitism is on the increase, that it has been greatly exacerbated by the war, and that humane and enlightened people are not immune to it. It does not take violent forms (English people are almost invariably gentle and law-abiding), but it is ill-natured enough, and in favourable circumstances it could have political results. Here are some samples of anti-Semitic remarks that have been made to me during the past year or two:

> Middle-aged office employee: "I generally come to work by bus. It takes longer, but I don't care about using the Underground from Golders Green nowadays. There's too many of the Chosen Race travelling on that line."

> Tobacconist (woman): "No, I've got no matches for you. I should try the lady down the street. *She's* always got matches. One of the Chosen Race, you see."

George Orwell's classic 1945 essay on racism, "Anti-Semitism in Britain," relies both on the kind of sampling we have already seen, and on a structural method of analysis for its support. Orwell first attempts to show that anti-Semitism is widespread, thus important enough to study; then he concentrates on finding out how it works. In order to understand it, we must see its role in a wider structure. This wider pattern or structure, for Orwell, is nationalism.

Because the Jewish population of England is small, the shocking anti-Semitic views Orwell lists are indefensible from the side of reason and fact; yet, according to Orwell, people yet hold them, often strongly. They seem anomalies, odd and disconcerting habits of thought, out of keeping with the other attitudes of otherwise rational, humane people. Seen alone, as isolated events in conversation, we cannot do much about them. However, Orwell proposes that they might be explained by relating them to a wider structure of belief. When irrational acts come our way, wider structures can provide an explanation and perhaps a method of amelioration. The structural approach has one clear benefit: if we can understand a phenomenon like anti-Semitism, then we might be able to do something effective about it. As Orwell implies, by examining the wider social structure of racism, he and his audience can make a first step toward change.

Building a Response to Analysis

To get to this kind of analysis, and to evaluate it, we first need to work with the deictic markers in the essay. There are a number of ways Orwell addresses the reader. Under the pressure of this more formal style, even the "I" and "you" pronouns become less personal. We can, however begin to form a response by connecting this more impersonal use of "we," "I," and the indirect "you" to our own ideas or experiences of anti-Semitism. One area from which we can bridge to our own experience is found in Orwell's image of the general reader. Most of Orwell's reader references are to a typical English reader of the 1940s. Note your response to the pronoun used near the end of the essay: "*we* are all more or less subject to believing that whole races or nations are mysteriously good or mysteriously evil" (7). You can ask whether your own experiences of nationalism or racism are being included or excluded here, or whether today *we are all* more or less subject to this tendency so equally — after all, which "we" is it?

If you are not English or were not in England during the 1940s and had a strong feeling of agreement with Orwell's essay, you will likely have made a comparison with a present "we," a context of social practice that you understand or have directly experienced today. Or, Orwell's general claim about nationalism might be something you can agree with on principle, and you can see the whole argument as still relevant to your own experience or ideas. On the other hand, your feelings might differ with Orwell's stance and his distance in time. Perhaps you feel that things have changed since then and that the disturbing examples he quotes would not be uttered today. Or you could feel that anti-Semitism is still alive but that it has gone more underground. While it is present, it could no longer be directly expressed as in these examples. You would not then feel much of an identity with these racist attitudes from war-torn England and would see the essay as fixed in its moment, a historical document, interesting for the value it has for gauging how much "we" might have changed. On the other hand, if your experiences are directly like these today, you might be feeling how racial attitudes have sadly remained the same despite changes in time and situation.

A more formal evaluation of this essay would depend on your assessment of Orwell's structural analysis. We can begin with two questions related to your initial response: Is it adequately supported? *And*, is it outdated? We get a clue from Orwell's terms for structure.

Analysis of structure can often be indicated through language of part and whole relations. What looks like an independent kind of belief is, through analysis, found to be a partial, dependent part of a larger structure, and the analysis shows that it makes no sense without this whole. Orwell concludes, "All I would say with confidence is that anti-Semitism *is part of* the larger problem of nationalism" (6–7) [italics added in this and following quotes]. The analysis of structures can also use surface and depth metaphors. Orwell uses them in his summary of the prejudicial remarks, "these accusations rationalise some *deep-rooted* prejudice" (2). And in summing up his first brief sample, he says, "Two facts *emerge* from them [the samples]" (2) and later that "Anti-Semitism is only one *manifestation* of nationalism" (7). Nationalism, at least of the flag-waving variety, does not seem anti-Semitic on its surface — though Orwell certainly can convince us that it might have this potential to be so. He recognizes that the part's relation to a whole is hidden and that analysis is needed to show it. Through his analysis, this wider structure of nationalism emerges, shows its roots, and is made manifest. But how do we judge this claim for such a structural relation between nationalism and anti-Semitism? We can begin our assessment with scrutiny of Orwell's proof and range of illustration.

In our attempt to assess this coverage, we can, to some extent, rely on Orwell's careful judgment of his own procedures — his own authorial commentary. We can detect this commentary first in his use of *modality* (we looked at this kind of qualifying language in Didion's essay in Chapter 2). When he proposes the wider belief structure of nationalism as a key to understanding anti-Semitism, Orwell's language becomes quite careful. "*It seems to me* a safe assumption" and "we are all *more or less* subject to" (7) [italics added], are ways of qualifying the scope of his general claim about the relation between anti-Semitism and nationalism. Later, he limits his conclusion about nationalism more formally: "In this essay, I have relied almost entirely on my own limited experience, and perhaps every one of my conclusions would be negatived by other observers" (7). Orwell is paying attention to the coverage rule of formal thought. He is recognizing that his claim is supported by the limited sample of anti-Semitic remarks he has been able to collect (and later in the essay some examples from literary works), and he is offering his analysis as a minimally supported hypothesis.

The word "perhaps" in the last quoted sentence is also a key. Orwell's analysis is better than an opinion because it is supported by some evidence, but at the end, he reminds us that the link he is finding between anti-Semitism and nationalism is yet speculative, close to an "informed opinion." The relation is evidently too complex for this one essay and its limited evidence to cover; it would, he reminds us, require much more research, analysis, and sampling to be held as a strongly proven claim. As the essay is clearly marked as a preliminary look at or an assay of the problem, then, we do not have to give our assent fully to its conclusions. However, the preliminary "essayistic" nature of the analysis gives you something to work with. It at least raises the question of completeness. If the sample is so small, are we getting a representative look at how anti-Semitism might work — is it really a matter of nationalism? Or, another dimension of the problem, are there other aspects of this structure that Orwell is not aware of or not including? There are a number of other well-known analyses of anti-Semitism. A brief comparison with one of them might help you gain a perspective on Orwell's preliminary analysis.

Child psychologist and psychoanalyst of discrimination Bruno Bettelheim also calls anti-Semitism a disease or a neurosis, though he means it in a much more literal way in "A Victim" an essay excerpted from Bettelheim's book, *The Informed Heart: Autonomy in a Mass Age* (1960). Such racial views are a very dangerous kind of hate-mongering, and nationalism is, in his theory, also part of the equation. But, in addition, he sees racial stereotyping arising though a set of complementary relationships in which both victim and victimizer play a role.

> Many students of discrimination are aware that the victim often reacts in ways as undesirable as the action of the aggressor ... victim and persecutor are inseparably interlocked. (1)

According to Bettelheim, stereotyping is best seen as a complex social relationship in which a dominant side is dependent on a complementary weak side and vice versa. The relation is not simply one way — it requires both to function. This redefining of the structure of racial prejudice has the interesting result that the social force of stereotyping could be broken if the victim decides not to participate in the codependency relation and not act out his or her side of what Bettelheim calls the "delusional creation" (3). If we were to compare the two essays we may in fact achieve a wider picture. Where Orwell is focused on the dominant side, Bettelheim adds the victim side to the equation and finds a complex social relationship.

In your evaluation, you might wish to ask what avenues of action are opened by each analysis? What would Orwell do to end stereotyping? What would Bettelheim advise? Another avenue of evaluation can be opened, then, if we ask whether *the whole of a structure* has really been uncovered in a structural analysis. Structural analyses can vary widely in their approaches, but they are also constrained by relevance (date) and the need for evidence. The more complete the uncovering of a structure by analysis, the more likely it is to have explanatory value. Ask whether the structural analysis is dated, whether there are enough examples to support the claim for a wider structure, and if this is not the case, also ask if the structural analysis is complete.

Structural Analysis in "The 'Breaking Bad' School"

In a marvellous and brief essay (from the regular column "Schumpeter") on the highly successful TV series "Breaking Bad" the Schumpeter column of the magazine *The Economist* shows the effectiveness of another type of structural analysis based on finding and supporting a strong parallel and comparison. According to the columnist, the TV series, which describes in realistic detail how the development of a successful criminal leads to his inevitable demise, has relevance to a wider structure: the formal and well-known techniques of developing a successful business. The essay describes "Breaking Bad" as a virtual textbook on the use of modern business techniques to gain success and wealth, and then to lose them:

> There are obvious reasons for watching "Breaking Bad": for once the Hollywood hype surrounding the television series is justified. But there is also a less obvious reason: it is one of the best studies available of the dynamics of modern business. A Harvard MBA will set you back $90,000 (plus two years' lost income). You can buy a deluxe edition of all five seasons of "Breaking Bad," complete with a plastic money barrel, for $209.99, or a regular edition for less than $80. (para 1)

The essay continues by drawing out the parallel and showing how an "enterprising entrepreneur," Walter White, a chemistry teacher finding himself condemned by a diagnosis of cancer, finds his "inner businessman" through the manufacturing of methamphetamine, a highly illegal, highly addictive, and corrupting drug. White, according to Schumpeter, follows the track of any successful businessman by making the best product (an illegal drug in this case) and by being obsessive about maintaining its quality. He also shows most of the characteristics noted by business analysts which define highly successful bosses. "William Thorndike of Harvard Business School (HBS) studied eight bosses whose firms outperformed the S&P 500 index more than 20-fold over their business careers. He found that they were all outsiders who brought fresh perspectives on their industries" (para 4). White, according to Schumpeter, is clearly such an outsider, and this fresh perspective (he began as a high school chemistry teacher) is clearly the basis of his success, plus he realizes over time what most of these successful bosses also realize: that maintaining a lucrative business, once the start-up period is over, is much harder and more risky than it looks. The parallel continues through the upswing of success and the downswing of tragedy and defeat at the end episode, "'Breaking Bad' is even sharper on the forces of destruction in business" says Schumpeter, (para 7). He shows in some detail the supply and distribution problems that develop and how his "work-life balance" suffers. The end paragraph clinches the claim, but also turns this structural analysis so that it suddenly works the other way. Not only does the series throw light on the "successes" of the illegal drug world when run by businessmen who bring fresh outside ideas and perspectives, it also shows how that world can give us insights about the business world itself. According to Schumpeter, Vince Gilligan the show's creator, "also holds a worrying mirror to the business world" (para 9).

In terms of building a response, to this essay we have noted that structural analyses can be judged on whether they are complete, or have indeed captured the correct wider structure. Can you find enough evidence in this brief essay to agree that the claim for this parallel is justified? Is the larger structure that is uncovered in business psychology a complete explanation? How much and what kind of further evidence, and the answering of confounding evidence would you need to accept this interesting, but lightly supported parallel?

Definition and Terminology

The last dimension of the formal voice we will study is terminology and its definition and re-definition. This means of development is extensively relied on by many formal essays, and can have profound effects on your responses.

Extensive defining of terms and use of a specialized terminology are not usually found in the familiar style. One advantage they have is that the coherency of an argument can be helped through stability of nomenclature. If you can define your terms and use them consistently, you are more likely to construct a logical argument. If your terms change meaning in the course of your paper, it can seriously weaken your claim. On the down side, a familiar or literary essay would be seriously cramped if it used the standardized language and conceptual consistency demanded in a scientific or other academic field.

To see what I mean, look at the following abstract taken from the article "Transpedicular Wedge Osteotomy for Correction of Thoracolumbar Kyphosis in Ankylosing Spondylitis: Experience with 78 Patients" in the medical journal *Spine.*

> This is a retrospective study of surgical correction of thoracolumbar kyphosis caused by ankylosing spondylitis.
>
> Objective. To report the surgical results of thoracolumbar kyphosis deformity corrected with transpedicular wedge osteotomy performed by a single surgeon at a university hospital.
>
> Summary of Background Data. There has not been a large series in the literature reporting on results of the Thomasen-type closing wedge osteotomy for correction of kyphosis deformity secondary to ankyl-

osing spondylitis, nor has two-level osteotomy of this type in one patient ever been described.

From 1991 through 1998, 92 transpedicular wedge osteotomies were performed in 78 patients with ankylosing spondylitis for correction of fixed flexion deformity of the thoracolumbar spine.

Results. The mean amount of correction for each level of osteotomy was 34.5[degrees] (range, 15[degrees]-60[degrees]). The largest amount of overall correction for a single patient was 100[degrees]. Most of the osteotomies (64 of 92) were done at L2 and L3. Fourteen patients with severe deformity required staged two-level osteotomy. Excellent and good results were obtained in 77 patients (98.7%) at the final follow-up. There was no mortality, nor were there any major neurological complications. (E354)

Terminology like "ankylosing spondylitis" or "thoracolumbar kyphosis" is probably at the limit of our understanding of specialized words. I certainly would have to reach for a medical dictionary to begin to find out what was meant. Even if I did get the direct word-for-word translation, it would still make for a limited understanding. On the one hand, these terms would not make particularly scintillating or interesting reading in a familiar essay (unless played for humour) precisely because they are not familiar. But, despite the difficulty, this kind of terminology reminds us of the value of specialized lexicon. I do not think you would want a neurologist or osteopathic surgeon treating you for the kind of back problem described who did not know the definition of these terms.

There are many levels of use of terminology. Essayistic uses of such terms and their definition are subtle and various, and they can be highly convincing. One way of proceeding is to redefine terms. We can sometimes find essayists using a definitional strategy in a hidden or assumed way. Here is the well-known mathematician and philosopher of science Jacob Bronowski in "The Reach of Imagination" arguing that the defining feature of humanity is our ability to imagine. His opening paragraph uses an effective kind of definitional approach though it is not named as such.

What goes on in the mind when we imagine? You will hear from me that one answer to this question is fairly specific: which is to say, that we can describe the working of the imagination. And when we describe it as I shall do, it becomes plain that imagination is a specifically *human* gift. To imagine is the characteristic act, not of the poet's mind, or the painter's, or the scientist's, but of the mind of man. My stress here on the word *human* implies that there is a clear difference in this between the action of men and those of other animals. (125)

One key that this is a definition is the highlighting of the term to be defined and then the placing of the term in a new category. Bronowski includes "human" in the general category of animals (we are unlike *other* animals), but he distinguishes us through our possession of the power to imagine something that does not yet exist. This placing of words in categories and then distinguishing them from other members of the same category is fundamental to definition. The new definition is also supported through a wide range of illustrations. In the course of his essay, Bronowski presents many instances of human imaginative powers at work in the history of science, citing many experts and studies, and he develops his definition by showing how each instance of imaginative breakthrough is beyond the power of even closely related species. Note then that definitions in essays can be built up over the course of paragraph development and can continue throughout the essay. Bronowski's "The Reach of Imagination" has a strong theme in which he explores an *extended definition* of what it is to be human — we are not "the tool using animal" we are "the imaginative animal."

We can find definitions supported by examples in abundance in essays, and they can be very persuasive. Definitions are one of the ways through which general ideas make their way most forcefully from writer to reader, and they are often used to establish or overthrow established and authoritative patterns of proof and thought. This degree of influence comes about because one of the important functions of scholarly argument is the reworking of the meanings of specialized terms or replacing them with other terms as research develops and new knowledge is constructed. Note as well that there is a persuasive or rhetorical structure in definitions. The definition "The human species is the rational animal," for instance, has the effect of summing up all of the cases and types of rationality in humanity, yet it excludes all of the actions and instances included in, say, a definition like, "The human species is the imaginative animal." In addition, you may disagree, many birds are tool users and also have some imaginative uses of their tools. This selectivity gives us a clue about how to evaluate definitions.

Redefinition in Rachel Carson's "The Obligation To Endure"

Another instructive example that shows how a scientist can use analysis and terminology, well combined in an essayistic approach is Rachel Carson's groundbreaking *Silent Spring* (1962). Carson's work began as a series of popular articles which were collected into book form. The collection gives us a good example of the difference between books and essays on science. Carson can afford a much more comprehensive overview and is thus closer to a "field approach" than Orwell. Yet even in this much larger form, her original essayistic style comes through in the many other styles and voices she includes.

In this influential work, Carson pointed out the general misuse of pesticides to control insects and the resultant pollution of lakes, air, and animal and human tissue by toxic chemicals. However, as a scientist appealing to a popular audience, she faced two fundamental problems. Her descriptions of the abuse of toxins in pesticides had to have scientific validity because, talking as an expert in her field, she faced a scientific audience, but she also had to move her lay audience to change their accepted perceptions of science as a neutral and always benign force in the world. She wished to initiate a change in government policy and to move her readers to political action to change the rules of research into chemical toxicology and the technology of its application to crops. Her style reflects this mixture of goals.

On the formal side, her coverage is shown in the clear, expansive range of sampling and experiment she gives. *Silent Spring* is rich in detailed reports and full of verified examples showing the effects of toxic waste on fish, the accumulation of toxins in fatty tissue in humans, and the widespread, often unreported, poisoning of animals. In general, *Silent Spring* emphasizes this approach, and the amount of supportive material is impressive. She can afford this large volume of evidence because she is producing a book, not an essay.

Including this amount of testimony would be difficult for a typical essayist. The "List of Principal Sources" appended to *Silent Spring* is twenty-nine pages long [longer than most essays] and includes material drawn from the sciences that study plant life, soil, air, water, and animal tissues. These articles are anything but imaginative or literary; sources like *The Journal of Economic Entomology, Science,* or *The American Journal of Veterinary Research* are rigorously scientific. Used to support Carson's general theme, they proved, in convincing detail, that then-current chemical methods of insect control were having dangerous side effects in many areas of the ecology. This richness of empirical example is one of the reasons the book had such an impact. It changed readers' attitudes to the widespread, uncontrolled spraying of insecticides on various crops because its hypothesis about the effects of pollution seemed so strongly supported by a mass of inductively researched and verified observations.

Nevertheless, in "Obligation to Endure" Carson uses the familiar and narrative voices extensively in addition to this inductive "full coverage" style. She speaks from her personal experience and uses brief but vivid narratives to convince her audience of the moral weight of her ideas. In terms of narrative, she opens with a story that pictures a future world without insects and, thus without birds and their songs, a "silent spring." In the same chapter, in line with her goal of changing public policy, you can see her using her rhetorical skill with both logical analysis and figures of speech:

> There is still very limited awareness of the nature of the threat. This is an era of specialists, each of whom sees his own problem and is unaware of or intolerant of the larger frame into which it fits. It is also an era dominated by industry, in which the right to make a dollar at whatever cost is seldom challenged. When the public protests, confronted with some obvious evidence of damaging results of pesticide applications, it is fed little tranquilizing pills of half truth. We urgently need an end to these false assurances, to the sugar coating of unpalatable facts. (5)

Note the figures of "tranquilizing pills" and "sugar coated" to position her opposition and her general argumentative structure. Carson's statement of highest level of generality is that ingestion of pesticides by mammals causes death, birth defects, and disease. Another lower level is that the evidence for massive pollution of our food and water sources by pesticides is overwhelming. The extensive range of evidence buttresses these claims and supports her frightening conclusion (highlighted through the figure of the "silent spring"): If we continue along this line, the ecology will break down and mass-scale human and animal health problems will follow.

Carson is also expert enough that she knows the power of terminology, that it can hide assumptions having far reaching effects on our approaches to the problems she is showing us. Note in the following her deft redefinition of "pesticide":

> These sprays, dusts, and aerosols are now applied almost universally to farms, gardens, forests, and homes — nonselective chemicals that have the power to kill every insect, the "good" and the "bad," to still the song of birds and the leaping of fish in the streams, to coat the leaves with a deadly film, and to linger on in the soil — all this though the intended target may be only a few weeds or insects. Can anyone believe it is possible to lay down such a barrage of poisons on the surface of the earth without making it unfit for all life? They should not be called "insecticides," but "biocides." (193)

The combination of coverage, expert testimony, changes in terminology, analysis, narrative, some familiarity, and rhetorical devices was clearly effective.

The work is now one of the bibles of the ecology movement, and has helped radically alter public policy on many areas of environmental pollution.

Each of Carson's claims can be argued with and further assessed along the lines suggested in our discussion. One way to assess them is through evaluating the dates of her research. A brief trip to the library showed me that these dates could be important. I found, for instance, a solid reference to Carson in a standard and more current work on pesticides, *Pesticide Application Methods* by G. A. Matthews (1992):

> Recent advances in plant breeding and genetic engineering to improve resistance of crop plants to insect pests and diseases will undoubtedly reduce the need to rely on the conventional pesticides, and incorporating resistance in crops to herbicides may make chemical control of weeds easier than at present. Nevertheless, there will still be a need to apply "pesticides" as a relatively easy and quick method of regulating an upsurge in a pest population. Such "pesticides" will not be the highly persistent, broad-spectrum organochlorines or similar products from the 1940s and 1950s, which prompted Rachel Carson to predict a *"Silent Spring,"* but will be increasingly pesticides which are more readily degraded and be more selective in their mode of action, so that they present less risk to the environment....
>
> The latest pesticides to be developed are generally far more selective and less toxic to humans if they are to be accepted by the registration authorities. (2)

One of the clues to seeing the argument behind the objective style came to me because I was unsure why Matthews had enclosed the word *pesticides* in quotation marks. It seems to suggest that he has read Carson enough to realize that he could no longer get away with using the term without the very negative connotation that they are really what she redefines as "biocides." If this is so, while we can detect a general influence of her work in this excerpt, Matthews has proposed something of a counter-argument of the "kind and degree" type. That is, he shows that pesticides are not the same as they were in the 1940s and 1950s; then they were organochlorines that did not biodegrade, and today they are regulated much more carefully. Do you agree with this submerged argument? Are there some hidden assumptions you can find? Who, for instance, is overseeing the regulation? What tests have been done on current "pesticides" to show that they are not harmful to humans and animals and in fact do biodegrade?

Gerry Coulter on Jean Baudrillard

The following Internet essay uses another redefinition strategy, this time of the meaning of the word "game." It is a summary of the work of one of the well-known postmodern theorists of the Internet, cyberspace and virtual realities and their meaning for culture, Jean Baudrillard. Coulter summarizes Baudrillard's thought about the term "game" and "gamer."

"Jean Baudrillard and the Definitive Ambivalence of Gaming"

1. Our Passion for Games

Some detractors treat electronic games as if they were a hard drug, but for Baudrillard (1979), the games are merely the equivalent of soft drugs. Like drugs, games fascinate us as much as they repel, and from the standpoint of Western reason, they arouse intellectual ambivalence (Baudrillard, 2002b). The game does this by leading us into an environment dominated by a mental surgery of performance — a kind of "plastic surgery of perception" (Baudrillard, 1993c, 49). Yet when we are in the game, we are also protected from "the brutalizing effects of rationality, normative socialization, and universal conditioning" taking place in the social (Baudrillard, 1993c, 67). This is a very important aspect of the ambivalence of digital games for Baudrillard — they originate in a society that is increasingly ambivalent about its future. The pleasure of the game is at best an uncertain and cool pleasure (Baudrillard, 1988). Baudrillard (1979) pointed to the artificial intensity surrounding the playing of digital games, but he found this to be not unlike that surrounding a person watching sports on television — and every bit as unhealthy. But we are too concerned with health; the gamer worries about boredom far more than obesity and death. It is better to be a gamer than a jogger in Baudrillard's world! The jogger — contrary to the delusional state he or she may be in — struggles only to exhaust and destroy the body (Baudrillard, 1993c). Joggers disappear in Baudrillard's world. The gamer, too, longs to disappear, but in an ecstatic disappearance from which he or she is eternally reborn in the next game (Baudrillard, 1990). The gamer fears only the dizziness induced by the connections — the lassitude of network man (Baudrillard, 1987). Gamers are viewed as immoral in the eyes of those who work to engage all of society in the production game. But the gamer is seduced by other possibilities and attempts to turn away from the order of production to an order of reversibility (Baudrillard, 1979). Reversibility for Baudrillard is the opposite of production, and gamers may be understood as an exemplary form of it. Ambivalence, however, is a two-way street: Ironically, the gamer is worked very hard by the game into a frenzied state of a will to mastery — mastery of what amounts to nothing as the game he or she masters becomes instantly obsolete (and soon "upgraded" or replaced by another new game). Games, too, are victims of fashion, and there is no greater game than fashion (Baudrillard, 1993a).

Note the way in which the word "game" has been reset to mean something a little more substantive than what we do with chess pieces or cards. In this view, games are becoming a way of life, the a way of escaping a reality that is boring, and deferral of a world of consumption in which many feel powerless. It becomes first a drug, then a necessary drug. Do you agree? If you are a gamer, Baurdrillard's theory may seem fanciful, too negative, and beside the point. Online computer games are, after all, highly imaginative, and are achieving the status of novels in many young minds; one can now compete for money, attend conferences, accrue as much status in some circles as Gretsky in his, or Atwood in hers.

Building a Response to Definition and Terminology

An initial response to the excerpts above is likely to come from the way in which Carson, Bronowski and Coulter signal their readership. Carson's language is a mixture of a persuasive, rhetorical style and a scientific style, and one way this is shown is through the type of audience recognition she gives in her first sentences — it is an audience of both average readers and experts. Coulter is clearly onside the redefinition of gaming given by Baudrillard's critique of the digital world, its ability to absorb our attention, and its drug status.

If you are *not* a marine biologist, a great writer like Orwell, or a media theorist, you can still participate in the discussion. You could for instance play the role of a "disinterested observer" who is not an expert but who would like to take on the challenge of trying to understand the basic outline of a specialist's discussion from its general interest or because it is related to other areas in which you are interested or knowledgeable.

Carson's prose also appeals directly to the non-specialized reader. Her references to this reader are a little hidden, but they can evoke a powerful response. You could be included in the following submerged references already quoted from the opening paragraph: "There is still very limited awareness of the nature of the threat. This is an era of specialists, each of whom sees his own problem and is unaware of or intolerant of the larger frame into which it fits," (197). There is again an implied reference to two segments of readers in this quotation; one is the specialist who is on the same footing as Carson, but as it is critical of this "era of specialists" the audience can include the general reader who is outside this field. The general reader is also not aware enough, and even if we are not such a specialist, we can, with Carson's help, also see "the larger frame."

We are likely to think that the more formal the essay, the more formal the required response. You probably feel at a disadvantage when confronted with expertise like Carson's. I am not a marine biologist and as a student you are not likely to be able to evaluate an essay like this one from the point of view of an expert, but as "lay readers" even in marine biology, and media studies, we can apply some general criteria about defining to help us evaluate how Coulter and Carson are using their terms.

First, Carson's and Coulter's terms are different types of definition. *Reportive* definitions, like those in dictionaries, list usage. For Carson the common usage of "pesticide" has grown much too vague to cover the threat she is seeing, and we need to reclaim the word and align it more carefully with the facts. What we sprayed on crops not only kills insects, its scope is much wider and more dangerous. The dictionary meaning of "pesticide" was in her day, out-of-date, the usage was no longer accurate and she stipulates "biocide." And for Coulter we are no longer taking into account the new meanings and scope that are now becoming used in the word "game."

The study of literature has a wide reaching specialist terminology and re-definition and inclusion of new terms is one of its areas of growth. Terms like "point of view" or "metonymy," "romantic irony" and "caricature" are specific to this field. "Diasporic subject," "subtext," "postcolonial," "diexis," "rhizomic," amd "simulacra" are relatively new additions. Another kind of definition is *essentialist*. It usually concerns the meaning of wide general terms like "power" "authority," "humankind," "love," "truth," "beauty," "the good," "the imagination" or "game" and requires a more extensive kind of defining. This is usually the type of defining that experts, especially in the humanities, are engaged in when they are constructing terminologies. When critics define a work's themes, they are often concerned with essentialist defining. If Camus' novel *The Stranger* is "existentialist" then we will need to know the definition of "existentialism" and perhaps how Camus' use differs from the term as used by, say, Jean Paul Sartre and you would be engaged in a critique of essentialist defining. A third kind of defining is called *stipulative* — where a word is provisionally redefined or a new definition is invented in the course of a work. Carson is pointing out the weakness in reportive uses of the word "pesticide" and proposing a new stipulative definition in her use of a new term "biocide."

Second, defining shares with all general language the dynamic of exclusion and inclusion we have been following in this book and we can judge most definitions this way. In a typical dictionary, a word is defined by first placing it in a general category and then differentiating it from other members of the same category. Here is a condensed example from the *Shorter Oxford Dictionary*; it is part of the entry for the definition of the word "gold":

> **Gold** (gould) [Com. Teut; OE. gold: — O'Teut *gul o: — pre-Teut. *gh-lto-, af. root *ghel-yellow (see Gall sb.[1]) 1. The most precious metal; characterized by its yellow colour, non-liability to rust, high specific gravity, and great malleability and ductility. Chemical symbol Au. 2. The metal as a valuable possession or as a medium of exchange; hence, gold coin; also, in rhet. use, wealth OE. 3. *fig* something brilliant, beautiful, or precious 1553. b. Gilding, **Merch.** V.II. VIII. 36. c. *pl.* Kinds of gold (*rare* 1683. 4. The metal as used to ornament textile fabrics; gold thread; as in *g. of Venice* etc. Hence textile materials embroidered with or partly made of this, ME. 5. Used with defining words in the names of kinds of gold, alloys, imitations of gold, etc. 1839.

In this example, gold is placed in the general category "metal" and then distinguished from other kinds of metals through adjectives like "most precious" and "yellow colour" or qualifying phrases like "non-liability to rust." Definitions thus have a particular syntax and are usually constructed from an alignment of genus and species (Latin *genus et differentia*), in which a general term is aligned with a modifier that distinguishes a more specific instance of this category. Sometimes this modification can carry through a number of sentences and lower level differentiations. Having found some of the features of typical definitions of terms, we can now discuss their evaluation.

With this background in mind, we can see that there are two basic ways of evaluating definitions. The first is to ask whether a definition is too inclusive or too narrow. If, for instance, we say that "soccer is a game played with a ball," we can see that the definition is *too broad* — it does not specify how soccer can be distinguished from other ball games like baseball or basketball. It is weak on the "species" side of the definition and includes too much. If, on the other hand, we say "a school is an institution that aims to teach children how to read and write," our definition is *too narrow or reductive* because many other kinds of skills and types of learning are taught in schools.

Definitions in essays can then be evaluated by sifting through the amount and kind of material they include or exclude and what they imply. When the definition is the major formal strategy, the essayist will often do the evaluation for us. In her well-known essay "Graduation," Maya Angelou finds a definition lurking behind superintendent Donleavy's speech. She could feel the confining, narrow, exclusivist definition of African-Americans implied in his glowing picture of her future. Donleavy defined African-Americans in terms of the kinds of jobs they could (and could not) expect after graduation; they would be restricted to being placed in the categories of day nurses, plumbers, and sportsmen. Angelou analyzed this definition as being far too narrow and disturbing and showed us another more inclusive and just definition that included jobs as poets, teachers, and university professors and that included black women. Didion also used definitions in a subtle way. While she was interested in defining her identity, she did not seem able to find a set of values and descriptions that suited her new situation, and we were left between the self-definitions given to her by her old and new families. Essayists, then, are aware of the power of defining their terms and use it extensively, either criticizing an old definition or claiming the power of a new one.

Stephen Jay Gould, "Evolution as Fact and Theory"

Terminology, and correct use of terminology is much used in the sciences. Scientific defining can, as in literary studies, also involve much complexity of interpretation. In the essay "Evolution as Fact and Theory" well-known paleontologist Stephen Jay Gould, comes to the definition of his terms about evolution and his counter argument gradually, after much work with the logic of his opponent's anti-evolution claim. You can see that *coverage* is used extensively as well as terminology in his argument. In the sciences, "induction" refers to the amount of physical and measurable evidence found for a hypothesis or claim made about the natural world. *Coverage* is then given a lot of credibility in the sciences, and it is the basis for defining terms. Gould is generally positive and supportive of scientific technique and the analytical methods by which science reaches its conclusions. You might say that he is an apologist for Darwin, and in many ways an apologist for the scientific method. Though he claims his own theories of evolution are not a type of "Darwinian fundamentalism," he reaches them on the basis of rigorous deduction from very well-established Darwinian facts like the fossil record.

Defining of terms in science involves logic. The deduction comes from the limits of coverage as a technique and his attempt to show the correct use of the term "evolution." In "Evolution as Fact and Theory," note that Gould's argument against creationism is a type of critique of false deduction (of the "valid reasoning but false because the premises are false" type). He first presents the opposition argument: "[according to the creationists] if evolution is less than a fact, and scientists can't even make up their minds about the theory, then what confidence can we have in it?" He then answers the question with inductive evidence (coverage) that proves the creationists' premises wrong. Evolution may be a theory and thus open to interpretation and debate, but it is "also a fact...."

Human beings evolved from apelike ancestors whether they did so by Darwin's proposed mechanism or by some other, yet to be discovered." He goes on to show that the current debate in science about evolutionary theory, fractious as it may be, nowhere implies that evolution did not occur. The redefinition of "evolution" does not really matter in terms of truth value — it is as stubborn a fact as any geological formation. Gould's argument finally rests on a summary of the collective evidence for evolutionary change and a general statement about how most science works:

> Our confidence that evolution occurred centers upon three general arguments. First, we have abundant, direct, observational evidence of evolution in action, from both field and laboratory. This evidence ranges from countless experiments on change in nearly everything about fruit flies subjected to artificial selection in the laboratory to the famous populations of British moths that became black when industrial soot darkened the trees upon which the moths rest.
>
> The second and third arguments for evolution — the case for major changes — do not involve direct observation in action. They rest upon inference, but are no less secure for that reason. Major evolutionary change requires too much time for direct observation on the scale of recorded human history. All historical sciences rest upon inference, and evolution is no different from geology, cosmology, or human history in this respect. We must infer them from results that still surround us: living and fossil organisms for evolution, documents and artifacts for human history, strata and topography for geology. (382)

This evidence is not fully documented, nor could it be, though we can safely assume it exists and that Gould could have presented it if called upon to do so. Gould's argument rests on a point about defining. The "inductive leap" is one of the strengths of scientific method, but there is always a gap in the amount of evidence. One cannot cover all instances. Thus definitions always fall short. We cannot include all the instances that support the definition of a term. This leaves open the possibility for variation in theory and for what Kuhn calls, "falsifi-ability of hypotheses." Gould, evidently, has been cornered into answering the creationists because they used his own theory of what he called "punctuated equilibrium" to prove that evolution itself was wrong. But they falsified the facts of evolution by mistaking them for his theory, or in other words, for mistaking them for a term — for them, his definition of "evolution" could be wrong and thus evolution as a whole could be wrong. They assign the whole scientific idea to the category of "interpretation," or definition of terms. However, evolution is, according to Gould, far more than theory — our explanations and definitions might be wrong (or inaccurate), but the facts remain. His reasoning is then fundamentally inductive (excuse the pun) and secondarily definitive.

One final point, this essay, with its strong support of scientific method and its evocation of the great name of Darwin, might have reminded you of some further implications. The debate about science and technology and their social effects, deleterious or benign, is very much with us. As you might have realized, its modern variations are actually quite old and derive from similar positions taken in the eighteenth century when science was just emerging (Swift, Locke, Montaigne, all touched on it). Today, philosophers of science are taking up the challenge posed by the sociological critiques above and presenting counter-arguments of their own. Oliver Sachs, Freeman Dyson, Daniel C. Dennett, and others have forwarded some persuasive views that defend science. You might wish to read some of their work to see where the argument is going today.

If you decide to do so, you will need to visit a library, or its website, or go through some preliminary research (say Amazon) to find some of the recent titles of these scientists. Looking up Daniel C. Dennett on your university library website catalogue search. It will likely give you a list of about eighteen titles. Which is the most appropriate? You will have to take out some of these books and look into them first, but there are about three instances of online texts, or "e-texts." These will allow you sift for relevance quickly, though you may want the physical books. Here is the table of contents from the library entry of Dennett's *Darwin's Dangerous Idea: Evolution and the Meanings of Life*, New York: Simon & Schuster, 1995.

> Tell me why — An idea is born — Universal acid — The tree of life — The possible and the actual — Threads of actuality in design space — Priming Darwin's pump — Biology is engineering — Searching for quality — Bully for brontosaurus — Controversies contained — The cranes of culture — Losing our minds to Darwin — The evolution of meanings — The emperor's new mind, and other fables — On the origin of morality — Redesigning morality — The future of an idea.

You could use this entry to develop an initial response you may have had to Gould's essay and begin to fashion it into a critical, evaluative response. And as you can see, defining of terms is yet very much with us; for science defining, and coverage (induction) are deeply connected.

Check List II

We can now again summarize the concepts and questions we have been using to build a response these additional aspects of the formal essay, analysis and terminology:

Analysis

- Has the context of utterance changed significantly since the essay was written? "Significantly" would mean that the change affects the general claim being made.
- How much support in terms of sampling or surveys can you find for the structure that is being claimed?
- If structural analysis is used, is it complete or are significant dimensions or parts of the structure left out?
- What larger structure is, in fact, being shown?

Terminology

- If highly formal language (a terminology) is used that is field oriented (part of a specialty), can I see myself as part of a more general speech community also engaged in the question?
- If definitions are used, are they too broad or too narrow?
- What are the wider implications of the definition(s) used? Do I agree with these wider implications? Can I find other works by the author in which these implications are more clearly stated?

Study Questions

1. How can you apply the higher level of formality discussed in this chapter to your own essay writing?
2. Now that you have seen some of the advantages of the formal voice, do you agree with your first answer to the question?
3. How would you begin an evaluation of Carson's *Silent Spring*? What do you have to do with the date of the work? Has the science of the ecology moved forward since then?
4. How much proof is required of you to support one of your own more formal claims?

5. The passages extracted from the essays in this chapter are, in the main, formal, abstract, impersonal. Can you find any familiarity in this selection of essays? Give examples.

6. Is Carson using a "middle style?" How would *you* describe the level of her vocabulary? For you, is it high, (formal) low, (familiar) or middle?

7. If you were to make your living writing formal essays, what subject matter would you write on? How would you support your claims in this more formal voice?

8. A repeat question, now with some more information. What would be gained and what lost if you included familiarity in one of your own academic essays? Would you have to seek permission?

9. Do you agree with the analysis of the series "Breaking Bad"? Can the drug business be so analyzed? Is there a more difficult, more entrenched structure like "poverty" that could also be brought in to the analysis?

10. What kind of formal voice have you been able to put together in the course of your reading of these two chapters. What are the elements of this voice?

Key Terms

Empiricism
The philosophy of science — the attitude toward knowledge that states that only what can be perceived and measured is worthy of the term "existence"; all other manifestations are the product of language or the human imagination.

Stipulative definition
In which a word is provisionally redefined or a new definition is invented in the course of a work. Carson is pointing out the weakness in reportive uses of the word "pesticide" and stipulates a new term "biocide" to replace it.

Essential definition
This type usually concerns the meaning of wide general terms like "power" "authority," "humankind," "love," "truth," "beauty," "the good," "the imagination" or "game" and requires a more extensive kind of defining. Such defining often comes into an essay when an issue or theme is being discussed, like the meaning of the word "existentialism" or "capitalism."

Reportive definition
Reportive definitions, like those in dictionaries, list usage. For Carson the common reportive usage of "pesticide" needs to be changed to "biocide," our current usage is incorrect. For Coulter our definition of the word "game" needs to be seriously redefined to include the online world and its set of skills.

Works Cited

Bronowski, Jacob. "The Reach of Imagination." *The Norton Reader.* Ed. Arthur M. Eastman. New York: W.W. Norton, 1992. (125–32).

Carson, Rachel. "The Obligation to Endure." In *Silent Spring.* Boston: Houghton Mifflin, 1962. (16–23).

Coulter, Gerry. "Jean Baudrillard And The Definitive Ambivalence Of Gaming" *Insomnia Essays.* Web. Nov. 27, 2013.

Ellul, Jacques. "Techniques." *The Technological Society.* New York: Alfred A. Knopf, 1967. (3–22).

Gould, Stephen Jay. "Evolution as Fact and Theory." *Major Modern Essayists.* Ed. Gilbert H. Muller. Englewood Cliffs, NJ: Prentice-Hall, 1991. (379–85).

Matthews, G. A. *Pesticide Application Methods.* 2nd ed. Oxford: Blackwell, 1992.

Orwell, George. "Anti-Semitism in Britain." *1945. England, Your England and Other Essays.* London: Secker and Warburg, 1953. Web. Aug. 13, 2007.

Shumpeter. "The 'Breaking Bad' school: The best show on television is also a first-rate primer on business" *The Economist,* Sept. 28, 2013. (64). Web. Nov. 8, 2013.

Sprat, Thomas. From *History of the Royal Society,* in Robert Demaria Jr. ed., *British Literature 1640–1789: An Anthology.* 1996. (402).

5 Literary Technique in the Essay

An artistic movement, albeit and organic and as-yet-unstated one, is forming. What are its key components? ... Randomness, openness to accident and serendipity, spontaneity, artistic risk, emotional urgency and intensity ... a blurring (to the point of invisibility) of any distinction between fiction and nonfiction: the lure and blur of the real. (David Shields, *Reality Hunger: A Manifesto*, 5)

Sources

Sasha Archibald, *Rumpus* (2013)
Maya Angelou "Graduation" (1971)
Hume Baugh "Fred Wah's Diamond Grill," in *Quill and Quire* (Sept 1996)
Melissa Chadburn, *Saturday Rumpus Interview: Dana Johnson* (2013)
Harold Rhenisch, "A World of Water" in *Out of the Interior: The Lost Country* (1993)
Charles Dickens, "Night Walks" (1861)

Objectives

When you finish this chapter you should be able to recognize and analyze the following elements of both the familiar and formal essay:

- *Highlighted language:* how verbal backgrounds and foregrounds are used to make words and phrases stand out and imply additional meaning;
- *Continuities in texts*: how cohesion markers point forward and backward as a text is unfolded, and how authors make and break this continuity;
- *Elements of figurative language:* how abstract and concrete terms and general and specific terms align to form figurative meaning in essays;
- *Types of figurative language:* how authors make old expressions new by using specific figures like simile, metaphor, and personification;
- *Variations in syntax and word order:* how regular word order can be altered for effect and additional meaning;
- *Elements of narrative:* continuing on from our first chapter we will further explore general and episodic setting, plot, point of view, characterization, motif, and theme; and
- *Close Reading:* a revisit in order to show how to read highlighted language closely in order to initiate and support a theme.

Introduction

As we have seen, along with its personal atmospheres, the familiar essay can include ideas with much wider application than the author's anecdotal or private concerns. We have found this more formal thought through a close reading of authorial commentary in the familiar essay, and we have studied the claims and their support in formal essays, but you can read for more general significance through other means. Both familiar and formal essayists use language in many creative ways and these can also forward wider issues and themes. Linguists call the language we are going to focus on, *highlighted* or *foregrounded* language; it is the kind of language that defamiliarizes our everyday usage, gets our attention, and makes us focus on implications.

Three types of this highlighting we find easily in most essays are *figurative language, markers of continuity,* and *markers of discontinuity.* In addition we continue our analysis of the *narrative voice.* It also requires additional attention; as we know, essays can have a story-like quality which calls into play many of the terms of literary criticism.

Figurative language is made up of combinations of abstract and concrete words shaped into verbal patterns like *metaphor, allegory, symbol, simile,* or *personification.* Through such figures, (loosely called *imagery*), language can be made to imply or "figure" additional meaning through picturing an abstract or general subject visually or through other sensory means, and our task as critical readers and writers is to find, interpret and gather proof for this additional meaning.

Syntax or *word order* can be used in a wide variety of ways to "disorder" the conventions of the usual sequencing of words. This is done to get our attention, or add significance, or indeed to disrupt expectation. When well-done, disruption of word order can be persuasive. It can catch us unaware and convince us to agree with a claim. But by analyzing and unpacking the way essayists produce unusual sequences of words, we find a neutral point. If we can see the basis of the persuasion, we can then evaluate it in order to support our dissent or agreement, or to ask further questions.

Continuity or coherence in essays can be formed through transitional devices, through the repetition of words, through specific references backward and forward in a text — textual linguists like Roger Fowler call this *textual cohesion, progression or themeatization* (61). An essay's forward motion and persuasive power are formed from these means. They are a principal type of essayistic highlighting, and finding them and analyzing them is a very good way of arriving at a theme, and of recognizing their value in your own writing. Continuities can also be deliberately broken through juxtaposition and surprise endings.

Narrative is the most persuasive form of highlighted language in the essay. As a narrator, the essayist will use all of the figurative, transitional and syntactical devices we will next study, and many others. But narration strives for a more thorough attempt at persuasion, often asking us to participate, as we would in a short story, in other, fictional minds and existences with full psychological detail, in dramatic events and precisely rendered contexts, in outcomes that have the weight of the ending of a short story. The forms of essayistic narrative are diverse, but we can begin to analyze the ways they get our attention by unpacking their basic elements like *plot, characterization, setting,* and *theme.* The essayist's use of such devices, usually reserved for fiction, is as diverse as figuration, continuity and syntactical variation.

Figurative Language

One would expect that highly individualized writing like the familiar essay would use a kind of language close to the author's experience and perceptions. In his essay on the essay "The Singular First Person," Scott Russell Sanders puts his finger on the familiar essayist's approach. "It is the *singularity* of the first person — its warts and crochets and turns of voice — that lures many of us into reading essays, and that lingers with us after we finish" (37). One of the familiar essay's key expressive devices, its most engaging "warts and crochets and turns of voice," is figurative language. There are a number of figures in Sanders' own phrasing — metaphors are catching.

Recognition of a figurative passage is probably now second nature to you, but slowing down and reading it closely in order to get its precise meaning may not be. The following discussion is designed to help you increase your skill in the close reading of this highlighted language; it can help you find themes, ideas and significance as figures of speech can appear in most types of essay.

A useful structure to show how figurative language works is to see it in terms of foreground and background. Figurative language is "foregrounded" or "highlighted" usage; it is prepared for in prose by a dominant background of literal use. Highlighting occurs in the repetition that forms a pattern, or through the disruption of a pattern. In the previous personal essay, "Night Walks," Dickens comes upon the following insight about London at night. We know immediately that the first sentence of the second paragraph is meant figuratively.

> (para 1) The month was March, and the weather damp, cloudy and cold. The sun not rising before half-past five, the night perspective looked sufficiently long at half-past twelve: which was about my time for confronting it.

> (para 2) The restlessness of a great city, and the way in which it tumbles and tosses before it can get to sleep, formed one of the first entertainments offered to the contemplation of us houseless people. (Dickens, "Night Walks")

We know that "the restlessness of the great city" that "tumbles and tosses before it can go to sleep" is meant figuratively. The effect of this metaphorical language comes about because it is unusual *in context.* Just before the figurative passage, we have two sentences that are *literal* — that is they are meant to be taken with the obvious single meaning. "The month was March, and the weather damp, cloudy and cold" and "The sun not rising." These are more factual and straightforward phrases that would likely not strike a reader as worth any extra attention, except perhaps for the Dickensian syntax — "The month was March" rather than the short form, "It was March." They predicate something about the world that we all share as subjects.

The next paragraph is clearly different from the first. Dickens is changing the pattern he used in the previous sentence. In the first there is an objective world of winter months, events like winter weather and dampness and there is a subject who experiences them and makes statements (predications) about them. The next paragraph blends what was separated. In this new use, a mass of people and things (the great city) acts like a person or subject (they act as if they were "I" narrators). Can cities be restless or toss and tumble in their sleep? As a preparation for the figurative passage the first paragraph is the background;

it makes the second paragraph stand out and become foreground. It does so because its language is unusual in relation to the first; it inverts a pattern. "Tumbling and tossing in sleep" is a phrase usually applied to humans or at least to other closely related living things — dogs and cats, perhaps. The phrase has been transferred to the much larger entity "London" in order to describe its disturbed night atmosphere. This *highlighting* produces an extra dimension of meaning. What though is it? What does Dickens mean?

To answer we need first to find the differences between metaphor and simile. A simile compares things, usually quite different things and uses the words "like" or "as" in the comparison. For example, in describing a room in which torture is used, in a well-known poem on political torture, Margaret Atwood says of the torture room, "It stinks, though; *like a* hospital,/ of antiseptics and sickness"[my stress] — (Margaret Atwood, "Footnote to the Amnesty Report on Torture," ll 14–15). Atwood keeps the two worlds of a hospital room, and a torture room distinct and separate, noting some very specific parallels through the simile. A metaphor on the other hand compares two things or events directly with no "like" or "as" between them. Dickens's figure tells us not only that there is a restless London night life but also that the city can exactly (no "like") act as our personal, subjective life of sleep and dreams does — cities have an equivalent turbulent night-mind as well, and with Dickens as our guide, we will experience it. The metaphor is interesting and has potential; it can lead us to an insight about London and its social layers. Even our personal night turmoil, Dickens could be saying, can have wider social meaning; perhaps my own troubles are a microcosm of the wider night world of the city. London at night may not be the calm place his reader might have thought it to be. London may open a night dream existence at least the equal of our singular dream experiences. An exposition of this night world could be further developed that is a parallel to the personal dream world. You can see that this reading leads us to the rest of the essay; the reader can now try to find if it is accurate and supportable. The essay in fact offers a number of disturbing encounters and shows us clearly that London never sleeps, is restless, in turmoil, has a potential for crime and homelessness. And that in the Dickensian London, as in our own cities, day time is dependent on a nightly labour of deliveries, sorting of goods, and the hard work of night shifts. There is a restless city dream world. We also use another metaphor to describe it; we call this work period the "graveyard shift."

These examples of foreground, middle ground and background can now begin to show us how analysis of highlighted language can help us get to significance. We may have found a theme — a relation between Dickens's own dark side and the dark side of London, or perhaps the first steps to a paper on

Dickens's politics, his fight for the poor, as shown through both through the figurative language of this essay and the textual cohesion it provides.

Textual cohesion is easy to find in this essay. We have been introduced to a thematic word, "houseless" that shows up first in Dickens's phrase "to the contemplation of us houseless people." Dickens will use the word often in the essay; it accumulates meaning to the point that, as we have noticed, it will move from its grammatical status as an adjective, to a proper noun, the name of a character, "Houselessness." This is a form of highlighting, and is a primary means of keeping a text on track through references to past uses. A repeated term or phrase can point forward or backward, (technically forward reference is called "cataphoric"; reference backward like this is called "anaphoric"). In this case it builds meaning, but is defined first through its status as an adjective; the reader can follow the process by backward reference, and its focus provides us with the theme of the essay, the stress, crime, alienation and poverty of London.

We find figurative language in the formal voice as well. Here is a more formal blog review of *Unruly Voices: Essays on Democracy, Civility and the Human Imagination* (2012) a collection of essays written by Mark Kingwell. The reviewer for the literary blog *Rumpus* is Sasha Archibald.

> Kingwell's style is to gather glittery scraps from the cultural miasma swirling about him to punctuate his arguments, such that individual essays are as meandering as the breadth of his corpus. A representative essay on the virtues of not-working mentions in short order Occupy Wall Street, Cary Grant's character in *Holiday* (1938), Bertrand Russell, the Third Reich, Thomas Carlyle, J.M. Barrie, Noël Coward, Jeremy Bentham, Serbo-Croatian War, the Iron Law of Oligarchy, Guy Debord, the author's disgust with Ivy League schools, and this is a very partial list. His references are highbrow, lowbrow, and entirely left field, as when he considers the side effects of his experiments with Prozac with a particularly Canadian idiom: "I was finding it harder to — how can I say it — put the puck in the net." When Kingwell castigates another writer for "banal delivery" the implication is clear: banality is one writerly sin he is loath to commit.

As you can see, the paragraph is heavy, perhaps over-weighted, with figures. In its evaluation of Kingwell's style, it begins with a statement of his procedure: "to gather glittery scraps from the cultural miasma." Again we have metaphor not simile. There is an immediate effect, we can see an action like gathering something up from the ground easily, and "glittery scraps" could be the detritus you can find in the street or the gutter. This imagery takes something difficult, a writer's style and reduces it to a manageable level — though at some cost. Can you determine the reviewer's evaluation from this language? Note the number of figures of speech: "highbrow," "lowbrow," "left field," "put the puck in the net." The evaluation also focuses on the lack of cohesion of Kingwell's style — showing how it develops through *digression*, and *discontinuity*, not cohesion, through its clashing variety of topics in a small space. Would you say the writer was clearly against or clearly for Kingwell's collection of essays? Are you intrigued enough to go find and read them from the overview given in this review? Once you have seen the significance of the metaphors, and the analysis of cohesion, you are more free to agree or disagree. What is the "cultural miasma" Archibald refers to?

Here is a good example of another type of highlighted language from the same blog accomplished through both syntactical variation and familiarity. It is taken from the January 5, 2013 *Saturday Rumpus* introduction to an interview of writer Dana Johnson by reviewer Melissa Chadburn:

> My first writing mentor in college was Dana Johnson. She is the author of a short story collection, *Break Any Woman Down*, and recently released the novel *Elsewhere, California*. Although she was my mentor, it wasn't until after reading her latest novel that I really felt I got to know her. It's true that sometimes you can learn more about people from reading their fiction than their non-fiction.
>
> I came across *Elsewhere* because I recently assigned myself the frolicking task to read every bildungsroman I could get my hands on. As a bi-racial woman who has resided in multiple class settings, it's been hard for me to find a coming of age novel that I could relate to. I wanted a simple and complicated coming of age story.
>
> Then I met *Elsewhere*'s Avery–young, black Dodger-loving, South LA-West Covina-Hollywood Hills-living, upward-mobility-having, SPAM-eating, drug-addicted cousin-loving, Italian boyfriend-possessing, Shaun Cassidy-obsessing Avery. And immediately I felt that I had arrived. On the page, I found me, young and struggling.
>
> I've been struggling in that I identify with this novel so much. Identity is such a big and important theme for me. Even more so as a woman of color, even more so as a woman that grew up belonging to one class and is now residing in a different class.
>
> There is so much wonderfully complicated turf explored in *Elsewhere, California* that I felt lucky to snag Dana Johnson during her winter break for an interview by email.

A *bildungsroman* is a novel of growth of character — it means literally an "formation novel" or novel of education and growing up — the development from youth to maturity of a hero or heroine. This essay is not so much an evaluation as a celebration of the author and the effects she had on the reviewer's own "bildung"; it has familiar elements itself and is loose and conversational in construction. One element of this familiar style is the number of contractions like "don't" for "does not" or "I've" for "I have." Note also the way in which adjectives are piled up in the third paragraph. The bunching of noun phrases together in such a dense way is interesting. Like the straightforward "background" language in which figures of speech are embedded and thus stand out, this example also has a background of simpler phrasing with fewer adjectival modifiers. What is communicated in this difference? There is an "all-at-onceness" about this language and it communicates a personality the reviewer has identified with — the character Avery in Johnson's novel *Elsewhere*. The adjectives gradually, and with some persuasive force, position the writer for the reader. Each is a mini-picture of an event or aspect of two lives that merge — the writer and Avery. Would the procedure of identification work for a reader in Duluth Minnesota, the town of Exeter in the UK, Or in Kingston Ontario? It may, if the reader could put in other markers than those the writer used and thus get something close to the significance. How would you position this procedure as a way of writing a more academic essay?

Here is another review, in a slightly more formal register of Fred Wah's Diamond Grill, by Hume Baugh in *Quill and Quire*, for Sept. 1996:

> Fred Wah's *Diamond Grill* is a small gem of a book. Wah refers to the book as a "biotext"; the publisher calls it both "biofiction" and "biography." Wah denies that it contains "true stories but, rather, poses or postures," and this echoes a line from the book's epigraph: "When you're not 'pure' you just make it up."

The metaphor, a "small gem of a book" forwards a neat piece of evaluation and is done with economy; the phrase is something of a cliché, but sometimes clichés can be effective. It begins the review and gets our attention with little background except its position in an initial sentence. We expect subject-object predication, but we get a figure of speech. Highlighted language is easy enough to point out and recognize through the idea of foregrounding. It has other features useful for getting to issues and themes, and forming a response.

Figures are composed of *concrete* and *abstract* terms in which a concrete parallel is used to explain the abstract term. Language is abstract if it refers to a *class* of people or things or to ideas and mental events; that is, abstract language is general language. Formal language is rich in abstractions. "All men are mortal" places humanity in the class "mortal," and "marriage is the classic betrayal" is an abstract (general) expression that places marriage in the class of "classic betrayals." "Heat" and "redness" are also abstractions — can you perceive, (touch, see, hear, smell, taste or feel) "heat in general" or "redness in general"? The general term in the Wah review is "book" and the reviewer has made it more concrete by putting it in the categories of "small gems," something you can visualize easily which helps us realize its value.

On the other hand, a word is *concrete* if it refers to a specific perception, to things that the speaker is directly sensing. "Students at Simon Fraser University average 25.78 years of age" is more concrete than most of the previous examples of abstraction, though not by much — the sentence still describes things mathematically and thus abstractly. But, "she wore a candy red bandana with a French lace border and an Irish square knot" is concrete because it refers to something you can perceive. You will have a hard time *seeing* "redness" in the world, or an average of 25.78, but you can visualize a particular red bandana. Concrete words refer to immediate experience and perception, and they are a favourite means of expression in the familiar essay as they are in most creative prose. In the antiwar novel *Regeneration* (1991), the English novelist, Pat Barker has one of her characters say, "You want perception, you go to a novelist, not a psychiatrist" (164). And we should add that the good essayist, like the good novelist, is expert at getting language to communicate both perceptions and their deeper meanings through intricate, detailed description, cohesion and disruption of cohesion, and figures of speech.

Metaphorical language combines the two kinds of language. In our Dickens example above, an abstraction, "a great city," is combined with concrete language "the way it tumbles and tosses before it can get to sleep." Again, foregrounding can happen in many different ways. Didion's commentary was sometimes carried through concrete descriptions that had extra, more abstract meaning. The image of her husband writing "D-U-S-T" on the tables of her home will stay with me for quite some time — it concretely represents the more general idea of a clash between her old and new family values. He made the idea of difference really stand out through the capital letters he printed in the dust. They are figurative because they imply a lot about him and what he might have thought about this old-fashioned, somewhat chaotic California family. However, allowing us to understand ideas and abstractions through concrete images is only one use of figurative language.

In her well-known essay "Graduation," Maya Angelou uses many figurative expressions, but they show us her personality and immediate emotions. We see heightened language when she describes the intensity of her expectation of the graduation to come in her small Stamps Arkansas school. Here is an example from this essay:

> The wind of our swift passage remodeled my features. Lost tears were pounded to mud and then to dust. Years of withdrawal were brushed aside and left behind, as hanging ropes of parasitic moss. (14)

What feelings and meanings do you think she communicates through these figures of speech? My first impression was that she has thrown herself into an imagined future and freed herself from an unhappy past. The figure of the past years of withdrawal as "ropes of parasitic moss" requires me to work harder. On the idea or abstract level, it could suggest that if we do not give up our memories of defeats or abuse we have suffered, we will be choked and weighed down or stopped by them. This could be its general significance. But this figure has many overtones. It also helps me feel the deepening sense of expectation she has of a better life to come. Can you find other connotations? What must her life as a younger child have been like? What precisely does she mean by these "years of withdrawal" figured through the simile (note the "as") of parasitic moss? Such emotionally loaded similes can be the basis for a response to an essay because it opens up so much. You could write an interesting paper that explicated the memory behind the figure "as ropes of parasitic moss" at some depth, perhaps some further research in the book from which Angelou's essay has been drawn, *I Know Why the Caged Bird Sings*, is called for.

Explication Through an Analysis of Metaphor

In *Out of the Interior*, a series of familiar and poetic essays by the British Columbia writer Harold Rhenisch, there is a great deal of figurative language. Since Rhenisch is a poet, he naturally tends to use figures of speech — imagery is one of his primary ways of conveying his attitudes, evaluations, and ideas. The collection of short *vignette* essays tells us about his upbringing on an orchard in British Columbia's Similkameen Valley. Problems of finding an identity and coming to his own values separate from those of his parents are evocatively placed before us in a concrete language that is the mainspring of the text. This text also requires a response from us — in fact, (like Didion's "D-U-S-T") these complex figures demand explication.

I can find a number of interesting general ideas operating in these mini poetic essays. Rhenisch, for instance, points up old European ways (his parents emigrated from Germany and started the orchard) and how they affected both his childhood and the way this part of North America was colonized and also how these old values are passing out of our cultural life. But these general ideas are communicated through his vivid, hands-on descriptions of this British Columbia landscape and of growing up on an orchard and working with his father. His descriptions are highly figurative. Here is an excerpt from the first essay of the collection "A World of Water":

> My father had small hands. They were the thin, clumsy hands of his mind. Some days they were hot and red, the nails ground down into small, delicate hooves. Some days they were white and cold and afraid. Through those hands he saw the world. When his eyes settled on an apple, a Macintosh, white with wax and yeast, that whole day before him drained immediately down out of the air and through his nerves into his hands, and they tried to grab it. In this way he attempted to make some sense of his world of things.
>
> In spring, with the light like saffron in the air, a thin wind fusing the sage pollen with the heat off the shale, he would walk out into the bright fields of dandelions under the trees.... When the trees at last flared into bloom, he would sit in the cool basement, poring over spray charts. Calibration rates, pounds per acre. Guthion 59% WP, Malathion, Thiodan....
>
> My father's hands always looked helpless, feverish, burning away the cold of the Uncle Ben's Malt Liquor — a green beer with a green plaid label: "A maverick too!" he'd say, looking up, bloodshot. His eyes would be small then, and such an ozone-blue they seemed to be chips of lapis lazuli, dug out of a damp, muddy barrow. They gave no appearance of usefulness. They did not seem eyes a man could see with, or through which an entire day could flood, filling his body with a late spring afternoon of pink-edged apple-blossoms, and icy rain sinking off the snow-choked peaks of the valley wall. They gave only one impression: of terror, of a god living there who did not need them to confront the world, but who was saddled with them and was utterly terrified of what he saw. My father's eyes were an extension of his body, of the energy in his chest with which he met the world, hardly needing to draw a breath, and, most of all, a reaching forth of his hands. (1–2)

This prose is a complex field of figures, facts and implication. Rhenisch's perceptions of orchard life and his family are presented in such a concrete way that we can almost see, touch, taste, and feel them along with him. Through this language we can sense the landscape and enter into his life, his emotions, and his attitudes. I can, for instance, feel the orchardist's struggle with the seasons, the muscular resistance of the trees with their constant need for pruning, picking, and spraying, the frustrating breakdowns of machinery that occur during harvesting, the old-country values and character of his parents, and, over all, the open freedom of the Similkameen landscape. While there are almost no abstract references or direct general claims to guide us to the abstract point of these passages, this language has been heightened such that through a close reading, we can find complex evaluations, feelings and commentary.

There is a good example of figurative language at the beginning with the metaphor of Rhenisch's father's hands. One way to begin an explication like this is to carefully note the way in which the figurative passage is prepared for. We first get "My father had small hands." This is straightforward, literal language, non-figurative; it is familiar and easy to understand. In the next sentence we have something quite different. "They were the thin, clumsy hands of his mind." The second sentence is unusual, different from the first, because we do not habitually think of the mind as having hands. In this foregrounded language, the metaphorical linking of an abstract noun "mind" and a concrete noun "hands" makes the sentence harder to read than the first sentence. We are aware that the mind cannot literally have hands, but we can also equally feel that a strong and understandable meaning has been intended. But what is it? We are required to slow down and interpret; we cannot simply stay on the surface.

For me this highlighted (metaphorical) sentence pictures Rhenisch's father's practical attitude to the world around him and shows the devotion of this man to his work and place. But in order to support this initial thought, I will need some more evidence from the text. First there is the noun, "hands." The "thin, clumsy hands of his mind" metaphor could be telling us that Rhenisch's father's thinking is "hand-like." Some other references in the text help support this reading. The paragraphs quoted above do show us that his mind seems focused on grasping the quality and health of his apples, figuring Guthion rates of flow or training his son to prune trees. Since these are a orchardist's hands, they are likely to be used in hard, physical work. His thinking is then likely to have the same quality — it is also physical and practical, perhaps a bit calloused. At this point, Rhenisch seems to be saying that his father is a man who is entirely committed to his work, who "thinks with his hands," and that this kind of thought can be powerful.

On the other side, the details of this metaphor might have a more critical message. They might, for instance, tell us that his father's mind does not work well with other more refined and difficult levels or dimensions, say of abstract thought or expression of feelings, or with creative ideas, or poetry. I can gain some support for this reading if I now work with the adjectives in the metaphor. As we have found with Didion's essay, adjectives are good clues to points of view and general ideas because they evaluate and show degrees of involvement, like assent, dissent, or contrast. These "hands of his mind" are "small," "thin," and "clumsy." You can probably begin to see my direction here. My struggle to find an interpretation of this complex figure of speech is already leading me to a theme that might be developed in a response to the collection as a whole. Through the use of these evaluative adjectives, I am beginning to think that there is an implied contrast in this figure between "large," "full," "flexible" things of the mind like poetry, reading, philosophy, and art, and the "small," "thin," "clumsy" "powerful" kind of mind wholly concerned with requirements of running an orchard.

There is further support for this idea at the end of the excerpt. What do you make of the interesting figure that appears at the end, where his father's eyes have become so blue they seem to be "chips of lapis lazuli, dug out of a damp, muddy barrow"? What kind of figure is this? Is it a metaphor or simile? In the language of anthropology, a barrow is an ancient, thousands of years old, grave, and *lapis lazuli* a semi-precious stone, usually blue and sometimes found in such sites. What does this comparison between a precious stone and his father's eye accomplish? Is Rhenisch seeing them as wise and as ancient as older civilizations say the Celts or Vikings, but also, again, more than a bit uncaring and physical? If so, they might be similar to his "thinking hands," which are also small and clumsy. Could they be contrasted with other kinds of eyes — for instance, with eyes that are sensitive and easily read or eyes that are "the windows of the soul"?

You can likely now see that this collection of figures holds complex meaning and commentary. The idea of a barrow and the description of the eyes as lapis lazuli could describe a man who is living an ancient kind of life, someone who is close to the earth and its forces, perhaps someone whose type could have existed in pre-industrial cultures. I find something poetic in the figure. Rhenisch's father's mind is, I think, the kind of mind in which trees, water, apples, weather, and air are realized through touch, memory, and action rather than through books and formal training. At the end, his father seems to have become an ancient and primal force. His eyes "gave only one impression: of terror; of a god living there who did not need them [eyes] to confront the world" (1). Now the eyes seem hardly attached to modern life at all; the connection is to something like the primal survival responses of humanity, responses that are eons old. Perhaps his father's kind of mind with its hand-like thinking and its ancient eyes goes much deeper than a modern, educated mind.

Rhenisch's brief essay has provided us with a good example of how to use figurative language to come to general ideas and themes. Through the explication of his figures of speech, we have begun to uncover a complex character study of his father — though we would need some other support from the text to help us with this reading. But rather than "talking about" roles or the conflict between old and new world cultures or the differences, fear and respect he feels for his father, Rhenisch creates the impression that we are there, looking through his eyes, feeling the textures and depths of his perceptions, participating with him in his struggle for an understanding of his parents and their life. He accomplishes this connection by using one of the dimensions of the familiar essay that distinguishes it from academic prose — its figurative language. The American poet William Carlos Williams had a rule that in modern poetry there should be "no ideas but in things" ("A Sort of Song"), and his dictum is very applicable to these essays. Didion, Angelou, and Rhenisch seem to delight in the ways that language can evoke things or make a particular place and time swim before our eyes or allow us to feel along with them; and ideas and evaluations are implied in this kind of language.

You may very well disagree with my reading (it is not yet developed and fully supported) and find another attitude altogether in this highlighted language. But when you develop your explication of figures, you should first be able to show the highlighting through a description of its unusual aspects.

As well as the types of figuration like metaphor and personification, you can also describe and find additional meaning in unfamiliar uses of syntax, unusual combinations of nouns or verbs, parallel constructions, contrasting adjectives, or fresh uses of idiom and phrasing. In these cases you also need to support your reading with a number of other instances that have a similar set of implications. Look for *patterns* of unusual language. See if you can find a consistency in their evaluations and attitudes throughout an essay. I have managed to find an issue and an interpretation from Rhenisch's use of this kind of language. But most of our authors have made their evaluations and commentary more meaningful through vibrant figures of speech and a consistent kind of usage of them.

How would you define, and explicate the figurative language in the following excerpt from the Rhenisch essay?

> Around him even the house would tremble as she smelled the change on the wind, and she would rise to it, unsteady on her legs. Each year for a few weeks she would come to life, at blossom time, when the air would smell of the water pouring like a river up through the roots and then out through all the new leaves of the trees, then she would collapse again, like a dry insect casing, into the gravel. (1)

This is another, complementary set of evaluations about a parental figure. The farmhouse at spring blossom time is seen as a female being coming to life.

The figurative description of the house is at least as unusual as the metaphor describing Rhenisch's father's hands. Yet it goes in the opposite direction from our first metaphor where a human being becomes thing-like. This is a good example of *personification* in which a non-living thing is animated and given human (person like) qualities.

Given the concentration on describing differences between father and son, it would be likely that this female house is a figure for Rhenisch's mother — she is often mentioned in other essays in this collection as a quiet person who rarely left her house. This maternal figure is more affected by spring than the father, who seems to work against nature rather than being revived by it as this personified house seems to be. The female figure, linked to the house, also has a closer connection to the seasons. And there is the further image of her acceptance of natural life and its rhythms when she collapses "like a dry insect casing" (1) after the first rush of spring is over.

These readings of metaphor and personification could then clearly lead to some wider themes about gender and role. In this family situation, the mother figure seems to be more receptive to nature but also more dependent, pulled and pushed and left by forces around her. She is also more hidden, she exists in the background and is strongly associated with domesticity and home. The father is the outside, active agent, tangling with the world. In my reading of these figures of speech, we are being shown some old-world, European values about roles and family life. Both of Rhenisch's parents immigrated to Canada from Germany after World War II, and if the figurative language is consistent in the directions we have so far found, gender roles were clear cut in this farm life. But I think you can see that I have now begun to develop a reading of the passage through my analysis of its figurative language.

The Essayist as Narrator

So far, we have been using the instances of highlighted language we find in the essay like continuities and discontinuities, unusual syntax, and literal and figurative usage to find a likely area for analysis. We have found these to be places where our depth of reading is likely to increase and where our engagement is intensified. We will next look at how *narrative* is used in familiar essays. This is necessarily a more global or overall approach to the essay as we focus on the essay's use of other genres like short stories.

As we have seen with Dickens, narration offers some clear opportunities for explication, for arriving at a theme for a paper; that is, it is an open invitation for you to respond and comment. It allows commentary because narrative is often used in the essay to express attitudes and values powerfully and to persuade us of general ideas and themes and because it is highly participatory. Often these values and general ideas are not overtly stated.

It might at first be hard for you to see how familiar essays could use narrative. Surely narrative implies that essays should be fictional; narrators tell stories; familiar essays are about the real life of their authors; and formal essays are about facts or statistics or theories—we may think that formal essays are not supposed to use fiction at all. To explore this question, we will begin with a definition of narrative and then add more elements to this basic framework. Afterward, you should begin to see how narratives and essays might fit together.

"Narrative" is a complex critical term. The word is complicated because while narratives are primarily fictions, the best narratives are "almost real." The literary critic will typically distinguish narrative from *acting* as in a play. In a play there are usually characters moving in three dimensional space who act out a plot. In narrative, usually one person, the narrator, *tells or writes down* a narrative. Another feature is its diversity. Narrative can be found in almost all communicative situations—in a conversation with a friend, in a sermon, in a TV news report, in the report of a physics experiment, in a therapeutic encounter, or in the most complicated Dostoevsky novel—and to complicate things further, actors in a play can also compose narratives and often do. Narratives are a universal way of organizing discourse, and they are found in all cultures and periods we know of. They should then be found in essays; it would be unusual if they were not.

It is rare however to find an essay that is wholly narrative. We already know that the essay is a hybrid of genres. If you remember Dickens's essay, it is obvious that familiar essays are not like scientific reports, journal articles, or the boiled down paragraphs that we find in a Reuters news brief. Such reports are *discursive* (reasoned or intellectual) styles that cannot use storytelling extensively and must stick primarily to chronologies, lists, descriptions, summaries, and other more objective structures of development to report events. On the other hand, essays often blend these discursive styles with narrative. In order to understand this additional pluralism of modes, we will have to study the structure of narratives more closely.

The fully developed narratives we find in novels and short stories are some of the most complex uses of language we have. The following is only a brief outline of their structures. Narratives are composed of the following elements:

- The *narrator,* who will tell the story from one of several *points of view.* The traditional types are: first person, first person limited, third person limited, third person omniscient, and third person interfering, though there are others. In the first person there is extensive use of the "I" pronoun and one focal, narrating consciousness. In third person points of view, the narrator is either *hidden* or *intrusive,* and "he," "she," or "it" are the primary pronouns. Some critics distinguish between *external* and *internal* narrators who have or do not have access to the characters' thoughts.

- There is also an *intended reader* for most narratives: children of a certain age for a fairy tale, adults who have a literary or educated background for the novels of say Henry James, Fumiko Enchi, Michael Ondaatje, Charlotte Brontë, or Dostoevsky. Critics have further broken this readership down into "real" readers — the audience that actually bought the work and read it, "virtual" readers — those whom the writer intended to read it, and "ideal" readers — those who would understand everything that a writer wrote perfectly.

- Narratives also include a *setting* of some kind. The setting can be both *spatial* and *temporal*, and either *general* or *episodic*. The general setting sets the scene of the whole story (as in a novel that begins with "Toronto in 1895 was finally becoming an interesting city"). Episodic setting focuses on a more specific locale as the story progresses (e.g., "He was there when she finally awoke in St. Paul's hospital room W45 on Saturday morning at two a.m.").

- A narrative will usually be constructed around a *plot*. The plot is distinguished from the *story line* or *time line,* which merely describe the sequence of events. Plots vary a great deal, but most involve a sequence of events in which we begin with an introduction of the principal characters (the exposition), usually a *protagonist* (the hero, or lead character) and an *antagonist* (the villain or the competition for the lead). Then follows a complication of relationship or event that develops to a conflict, a rise in action to a crisis where one side or the other is dominant, and an ending with a *resolution, peripetea (reversal),* or *dénouement* (the *Freytag diagram* of rising tension to crisis and resolution is the standard model). In comic plots, the reversal is from bad to good; in tragic plots, from good to bad. Narrative plots can also be complicated through subplots and backward and forward shifts in the time line. In addition good writers delight in breaking these rules and in defeating all literary conventions about plot by beginning at the end, or coming back to the beginning at the end, (the film *Pulp Fiction*).

- As we have seen, essayistic narratives have *characters,* and some of these can be typical or *stock characters*; though the more interesting stories involve *ambiguous* or *complex characters.* The "I" pronoun point of view lends itself, as we have seen with Swift, to the possibilities of mimicry and, as with Dickens, self-exploration, that is, with seeing the self as a character.

- Most narratives will also be based on a principle of repetition of images or words in which we can detect a *motif*.
- Lastly, we will have direct or indirect ideas, values, or principles that are realized or told in the narrative — that is a *theme*.

The essayistic use of narrative, however, does not usually engage full-scale deployment of all these structures. In the familiar essay, the language used to tell of the self and of familiar experience lends itself readily to storytelling, and often the short story seems the prevailing model of organization, but it is usually mixed with other modes of discourse: direct reporting or a more formal analysis, critical evaluation, or other kinds of discursive language.

How can narrative analysis be a way of explication and developing a paper? Let's first compare the opening of an essay with the opening of a well-known story. I have chosen an obvious fiction, Lewis Carroll's *Alice's Adventures in Wonderland*, and will compare it with the opening of Didion's essay.

Here is the opening to *Alice*:

> Alice was beginning to get very tired of sitting by her sister on the bank, and of having nothing to do; once or twice she had peeped into the book her sister was reading, but it had no pictures or conversations in it, "and what is the use of a book," thought Alice, "without pictures or conversations?" (25)

Here once again is the opening of Didion's essay:

> I am home for my daughter's birthday. By "home" I do not mean the house in Los Angeles where my husband and I and the baby live, but the place where my family is, in the Central Valley of California. It is a vital although troublesome distinction. My husband likes my family but is uneasy in their house, because once there I fall into their ways, which are difficult, oblique, deliberately inarticulate, not my husband's ways. (1)

If I were to ask you which of these is the story and which the essay, your first response would probably be that the first is the obvious story — you know that the speaker is a storyteller because Lewis Carroll is describing an imagined episodic setting using the third person omniscient point of view. He is describing a fictional character, the lightly comic protagonist Alice, and he can show us Alice's thoughts directly. Didion, on the other hand, is reporting real experiences that must have happened to her first hand, and while she is using the first person and talking directly about herself and her close relatives, she can only guess at the thoughts of the other people she is describing. Unfortunately, "On Going Home" does not fit so neatly into these contrasting categories of "discursive" or "fictional" either. We must quickly make our contrast between them more complex because Didion uses some basic narrative techniques very similar to Carroll's.

If you look carefully at Didion's opening, you will see that there is a first person narrator, an intended reader (probably a relatively serious, perhaps literary, audience); there are general settings (Central Valley California, Los Angeles) and shifts in episodic settings (her house and its interiors, her aunt's house, and the family graveyard), though we think these settings refer directly to a real context of utterance rather than a fictional one. There is also a plot, and it is propelled by a submerged conflict between her husband and her family, though it is not resolved but simply drifts off at the end. In addition, we have found a theme: the difference in family styles and Didion's uncertainty about her role and identity in marriage. "Birthdays," "plants," and "home" might be repeated elements with implied meanings or motifs. Beyond these more obvious similarities, moreover, there are more subtle narrative elements, which allow us to analyze the essayistic narrative more closely.

The narrative basis for the development of Didion's essay becomes more apparent when we analyze the *verb tenses* she uses. And these markers are a very good way for you to uncover and explicate the subtle narrative structures of essays. While the events that occurred in her parents' house during her stay there have probably happened in the past, Didion does not consistently stay with the past tense. For example, she begins to describe the last phase of her stay with "Days pass. I *see* no one. I *come* to dread my husband's evening call" (2) [italics added]. The *general present tense* (also called the *historic present* or *narrative present)* is one of the important markers of a narrative. Here it dramatizes the difference between home identity and new family identity by shifting it into the "directly before the eye" feeling of "I see no one" and "I come to dread" rather than the more distant feeling of "I saw no one" and "I came to dread."

The use of this tense allows us to be there along with her, participating in the process of her perceptions and thoughts as they occur, though we know that at the time it was written these perceptions must have been in the past and that there are gaps in the presentation of the time sequence. Like the narrator in *Alice in Wonderland*, then, we come across an ongoing event that is "directly before us" and are guided by a narrative time line that has been actively shaped by the writer into a plot designed to increase our focus on the significant events. Also, as in the description of Alice, we have been allowed into a world of private thoughts, of a self-assessment, that is usually kept out of the direct observations of reporting. The number of these tense markers show us that narrative is the primary way of organizing the personal experiences recorded in Didion's essay.

You might want to note how many examples of the narrative present tense there are in "On Going Home," (e.g., "I *am* home for my daughter's birthday" [1], I *go* aimlessly from room to room," "I *decide* to meet it head-on and *clean* out a drawer" [10], or "I *kneel* beside the crib and touch her face" [3]).

Narrative in Angelou's "Graduation"

The historic present is only one way in which tense can be used in essayistic narratives. Maya Angelou in her essay "Graduation" uses a variation when she opens her essay with the sentence: "The children in Stamps [Arkansas] *trembled visibly* with anticipation" and when she uses past progressive verbs like "Large classes *were graduating*" and "The junior students who *were moving*" (10) [italics added]. The progressive aspect joins an auxiliary verb (verbs with an addition of to be, to have) with an "ing" form of the main verb (I *am [now] going* to the store) and can be used in all the tenses. But the progressive aspect also has the effect of focusing on a precise moment, or series of events, in time. One example: think of a cell phone conversation in which in answer to the question, "Where are you now?" you say, "I *am* on the Second Narrows, *driving* home" or to answer the question yelled from another room, "What is the cat doing?" you reply, "He is *helping* himself to the butter again." Again we have the same sense of being there along with a narrator, watching a process or an event unfold before our eyes, and we are being introduced to the story at a particular point in this process. These modifiers and verb phrases allow the reader to enter the events described. We catch up with an ongoing process and expect the story to unfold, continuing from this moment, and we will participate in it as it goes along to its climactic (or unresolved) ending.

In both cases, the time schemes are not those that would be used by a reporter or a scientific recorder, who would probably have used the simple past tense consistently to tell us what *happened;* for example, "In the summer of 1945, the children in the school in Stamps *graduated* from the seventh to the eighth grade." By using the progressive aspect, "were graduating," and related adverbs, "trembled *visibly,*" Angelou can render the moment and the subtle atmospheres of mental states and feelings, and we participate in the observer's perceptions in a way that is usually edited out of a journalistic or more academic style. Essayistic narrators, like other narrators, use time flexibly and creatively. Angelou's use of progressive tenses and adverbs focuses our perceptions and allow us to catch the merest tremble of anticipation along with her as it occurs. This again is a *narrative technique* rather than a practical, objective recording of a past event or chronology. We cannot then really talk of such essays as "non-fiction" because they use many storytelling devices rather than the reporting style we would find in a newspaper or the logical thematic development of an academic article.

As we have seen in our exploration of narrative elements, plots can vary a great deal, though most describe a sequence of events in which the relationship between protagonist and antagonist develops to a conflict and there is a rise in action to a crisis where one side or the other is dominant, and an ending with a resolution, *peripeteia* (Greek for reversal), or dénouement or decrease of intensity. How can we use this narrative structure to explicate Angelou's essay "Graduation"? We can find quickly that as an essay, it has a strong narrative quality. We have noted the progressive aspect, but the whole essay is structured like a short story in which a dramatic climax comes at the end. Plot development is a strong feature of her text. Throughout "Graduation," there is a steady increase of tension; it reaches its peak during Donleavy's speech and then comes a relaxation and something of revelation. The strong narrative quality comes from Angelou's careful work with tenses and other temporal markers so that the day of the graduation and its damning speech become the focal point of the essay.

Let's work with the time line first. After setting the scene of the graduation in the first few paragraphs, Angelou begins her narrative with some strong and dramatic tense markers for beginning a story — emphasis has been added to the following quotations to indicate these and other markers:

> In the Store *I was the person of the moment*. The birthday girl…. *I was going to be lovely*. A walking model of the various styles of fine hand sewing (13).

She next uses nouns and verbs that focus on the sense of time passing that will lead from this moment up to the climax. The tension of expectation is steadily increased through these means. Some examples include, "*The days had become longer* and more noticeable," "*During that period* I looked at the arch of heaven so religiously" (13), and "*The weeks until graduation* were filled with heady activities" (14).

When the graduation day arrives, Angelou again actively shapes our sense of time. We begin in the morning, quickly progress to evening, and then finally enter the period of the ceremony itself. "Little children *dashed by out of the dark* like fireflies," or "Amazingly the *great day finally dawned*," and finally "The school band *struck up* a march and all classes *filed in*" (16).

After this point the temporal setting is compressed to one dramatic moment, the time it took Donleavy to give the speech:

Not one but two white men came through the door off-stage. The shorter one walked to the speaker's platform, and the tall one moved to the center seat and sat down. But that was our principal's seat, and already occupied. The dislodged gentleman bounced around for a long breath or two before the Baptist minister gave him his chair, then with more dignity than the situation deserved, the minister walked off the stage....

He said that he had pointed out to people at a very high level that one of the first-line football tacklers at Arkansas Agricultural and Mechanical College had graduated from good old Lafayette County Training School. Here fewer Amen's were heard. Those few that did break through lay dully in the air with the heaviness of habit.

He went on to praise us. He went on to say how he had bragged that "one of the best basketball players at Fisk sank his first ball right here at Lafayette Country Training School."

The white kids were going to have a chance to become Galileos and Madame Curies and Edisons and Gauguins, and our boys (the girls weren't even in on it) would try to be Jesse Owenses and Joe Louises....

He finished, and since there was no need to give any more than the most perfunctory thank-you's, he nodded to the men on the stage, and the tall, white man who was never introduced joined him at the door. They left with the attitude that now they were off to something really important, (the graduation at Lafayette County Training School had been a mere preliminary).

The ugliness they left was palpable. An uninvited guest who wouldn't leave. (17–19)

Note the number of evaluative adjectives and the metaphor of ugliness as the "uninvited guest" in the last sentence, signaling Angelou's understanding of the implications of the speech. This speech changed her life and rearranged the expectations she had had for her future. But more to our point about narrative, Angelou's timing, her placement of Donleavy's speech at this late place in the essay, resembles the plot technique of *peripeteia* or the reversal of fortune (in tragedies, from prosperity to ruin) that occurs in many narratives. But what does she gain by structuring a reversal of expectations in this way? And what can it tell us about the relation between the theme and the narrative structure? How can we use this idea about *peripeteia* to explicate the essay?

As we have noted, we have been prepared for the graduation ceremony by many chronological markers that give us a gradually quickening sense of time passing. But these markers also stress the depth and continuity of community expectation. Angelou lingers over the preparatory events and makes them meaningful as the beginning of a stage in growing up. The ceremony will be a reward for all the work that has been done, and the time scheme gives us a chance to look at the conditions around the ceremony, for instance, to see clearly that the black community as a whole is engaged in making the ceremony work and has invested a lot of hope in it. The sense of expectation these uses of narrative give rise to is intense, and the reversal at the end renders the impact of racism with full emotional force. It dramatizes the wider general idea that the educational system in Angelou's childhood was deeply biased. Feeling this race bias at this climactic moment changed Angelou's attitudes significantly, and it was a first step toward her identity with black poets and culture. This narrative tense structure and the *peripeteia* thus communicate a significant theme in the essay.

Even though it may seem less developed, Didion also uses a narrative structure. The chronology is more open, and the time line is intermittent rather than continuous. We are generally progressing forward, though there are brief flashbacks to her childhood, and the episodes are broken up, often with no indication about how much time has passed between them. In fact, most of the time markers are in the narrative present tense, which builds a deepening sense of the unchanging quality of her life there, of her situation as static, and the fixed quality of her feelings. In contrast to Angelou, Didion's ending is ambiguous — there is no resolution or climax. Where we might expect a decision for one kind of family life or the other, we find a deliberate trailing off. While the narrator has achieved some insights, the loose ending gives the impression that the emotional conflicts invoked have not really been resolved. In its own way, then, Didion's narrative sequence is just as finely crafted as Angelou's, but the narrative technique is used to give a very different emphasis to the ideas — it highlights the *non-resolution* of the family conflict.

The patterns of narrative in the essay are many and varied — we have only seen two here — but we can say that they are not constrained to the typical Freytag diagram of introduction, rise in tension, climax, dénouement. Narrative patterns, as Didion and Angelou have shown us, can be much varied for effect. And they can be the basis for a good explicative essay.

Summary

As we have seen, the modern familiar essay can have a strong literary quality as well as including serious analysis and other formal elements. In it, "issues" can be directly discussed as in commentary or presented as dramatic conflicts between characters or in narrative structures using the historical present tense, carefully designed plot lines, or *peripeteia*. The language of the familiar essay tends to be concrete and figurative rather than abstract, and ideas and judgments are often found in its narrative sequences (its use of historical present and a general plot structure), as well as in metaphors, personifications, similes, or other kinds of foregrounding. The notions of "authorial commentary," "formal and familiar voice," "literal and figurative language," "narrative and discursive technique," "plot and time line," and "concrete and abstract language" have allowed us to see the active combining of voices authors use in this kind of essay and their narrative techniques.

Probably one of the most engaging aspects of the familiar essay is its *polyphony:* the familiar essayist blends and contrasts voices and their registers. Like Montaigne and, modern essayists Didion, Angelou, Rhenisch, Laurence, and Orwell work with words as if they were making up a voice collage, experimenting with combinations of prose and poem, abstract ideas and narrative, subjectivity and objectivity; in this kind of writing, no single voice is dominant for long.

Familiar, Formal and Highlighting in The Internet Essay

The Internet's use of the essay breaks down neatly along a line of familiarity and formality. In relation to styles like email, Wikis, blogs, Facebook, Twitter and Linked In, the online *essay* has begun to differentiate itself as one of the ways in-depth information, rather than conversation or familiarity, is delivered through the web, and is becoming something of its formal voice. Social media like Twitter and other chat rooms are now one of the most popular *familiar* forms likely in the world, after, say, conversation itself. Twitter's reduction to 140 character sentences and hash tags is the textual online equivalent of a continuing multi-person greeting like, "how's it going?" or a group request like "what's it all about?" plus all the short responses.

If we want more information, and a more formal-analytical approach online, we go to web sites organized much like three column print magazines for the news, for opinion, and for serious discussion. *Wikipedia* has an essay-like form, but some serious differences from an essay. Can you find them? Are the authors experts? How much coverage is there? What kind of review has each article gone through? Is there consistent analysis, terminology, coverage, or expertise? Can you find them? Most of the larger print magazines like *Macleans, Time, Walrus, Wired, Salon, The Atlantic Monthly, the Economist, Harpers,* and *The New Yorker* have built extensively supported (and well visited) online sites; like their print counterparts, they rely on well-crafted essays. Are they like the essays you are writing? How are they different? Many of the established broadcasting networks, BBC, *Deutsche Welle,* CBC and CBS, NBC and Global, all have well stocked websites that rely on forms of text related to essays.

These sites also have a number of features recognizably different from print versions. Clearly their use of multimedia like video and audio clips, is one of these, but the most telling difference is their ability to link immediately through ip addresses to other web pages and other essays. This feature puts a new slant on what in the academic essay is called *citation* —the recognition of sources — and on the richness of what is called *subtext* —references to a wider number of texts and discourse in which a particular text is embedded as a comment, rebuttal or answer. Here is an example of how <u>linking</u> can change the landscape of secondary source referencing:

The following is taken from the site, "Ask MetaFilter" This site is blog-like,and the following is a excerpted from a posted question: "Who are the great essayists of our time?" Here are a few responses, (note we have underlined the links):

> I have a soft spot for <u>George Saunders</u>. Here are some <u>essays</u>, and here's a short story, <u>Sea Oak</u>, and here's <u>an excerpt</u> from another.
> posted by <u>marxuyh</u> at <u>10:27 PM</u> on November 16, 2006
> I really really like Frank Rich.
> posted by <u>vitxx90</u> at <u>10:28 PM</u> on November 16, 2006
> *****
> Interpreting both "present day" and "essayists" liberally:
> John D. MacDonald (d. 1985).
> John Leonard.
> John Le Carre.
> *Baffler*-era Thomas Franks.
>
> The repellent Clotaire de Rapaille.
> posted by <u>Phrooxed182</u> at <u>10:39 PM</u> on November 16, 2006
>
> I used to enjoy <u>P. J. O'Rourke</u>, although he hasn't written anything sharp for a number of years. posted by <u>KimG</u> at <u>12:14 AM</u> on November 17, 2006
> *****
> Kurt Vonnegut and Bill Hicks.
>
> Vonnegut definitely spent time doing formal essays. He's best known for his novels but if you strictly require essayist status, he qualifies.
> ****
> Seconding Joan Didion. No original suggestions, tragically.
> posted by <u>ptto</u> at <u>12:46 AM</u> on November 17, 2006

Note how the links are used to connect directly to the posters' choices for the best essayists. Multiple links to the essays are given but no quotations and no proof for the evaluations offered. It is left to readers to go to the link and draw their own conclusions. Unless oversighted by a patient webmaster, these links break quickly, though they have the advantage of "instant citation." How long do they last, and what is their value? Here, for instance is the link to P. J. O'Rourke. After a bit of digging you find only an excerpt from his publisher:

The Baby Boom
By P. J. O'Rourke

Board games and card games were for rainy days, and if it looked like the rain was never going to stop, we'd get out Monopoly. Despairing of its page upon page of rules, we'd make our own. This is how both Wall Street investment strategy and Washington economic policy were invented by our generation. We also invented selling "Get Out of Jail Free" cards to the highest bidder.

The 1960s was an era of big thoughts. And yet, amazingly, each of those thoughts could fit on a T-shirt.

Chloe lived in exotic Massapequa, Long Island. I came east by motorcycle with the idea of Chloe riding pillion to a "Woodstock Music and Arts Fair," which, according to a poster in a record shop back in Yellow Springs, Ohio, was "An Aquarian Exposition" featuring "Three Days of Peace and Music." I pictured something on the order of a wind-chime sale with evening hootenannies and maybe a surprise guest appearance by Mimi Farina.

We get a taste of O'Rourke's style. In our terms, these are examples of the familiar voice. Though there is perhaps, a gesture to formality. The most interesting part of this form of citation, though, is the way the link font is coloured. It is a form of highlighting, of showing in a tactile — visual way, further implications and resonances of meaning. Like metaphor, simile, and quotation marks, this is another way of calling attention to a word or meaning. The additional significance appears materially present, seeming to have the power to give any word or phrase substantial weight and behind it, through the figure of the web, a potential ocean of infinite, supportive reference; though, it is only a potential ocean. Do you see this as a form of aliasing, or is it trustworthy? Sometimes, as above, the links are not much more than advertising.

Study Questions

1. What is the plot of Didion's "On Going Home"?
2. Find the time line in Angelou's "Graduation."
3. Analyze the following figures: define them as simile, metaphor, or personification.

   "Love is a red, red rose"
   "My father had small hands. They were the thin, clumsy hands of his mind."
   The web and cyberspace

4. How would you position Melissa Chadburn's syntax in terms of voice? Could you use this adjectival procedure as a way of writing a more academic essay? What does this tell you about academic or critical writing?

Key Terms

Subtext
References to a wider number of texts and discourse in which a particular text is embedded; the primary text will then act as a comment, rebuttal or answer, or further question.

Bildungsroman
"Bildung" in German can mean either culture, formation or education. This literary term is usually applied to a novel of growing up or character formation from youth to maturity. Thomas Mann's *Buddenbrooks* is a bildungsroman, as are *Jane Eyre*, and *Catcher in the Rye*.

Concrete and abstract terms
Abstract terms refer to ideas, mental events that cannot be sensed directly; they have no physical referents. Examples: success, democracy, the good, beauty, capitalism, (any word ending in "ism" is abstract). A concrete term is usually based in perception and can be visual, tactile, auditory, kinesthetic, gustatory, or olfactory. Examples: *Gold ring, rough, tiny ant, red bandanna, freezing, stinky.* Such concrete language is used to present or show a perception rather than "talk about" it.

Compare:

"But even in the realist text certain modes of signification within the discourse — the symbolic, the codes of reference and the semes — evade the constraints of the narrative sequence." (Belsey 105)

and

"It stinks, though; like a hospital,/ of antiseptics and sickness." (Atwood)

Discursive style

Reasoned or intellectual styles that cannot use storytelling extensively and must stick primarily to chronologies, lists, descriptions, summaries, and other more objective structures of development to report events.

Syntactical variation

We can see that Dickens uses this kind of variation when he repositions an adjective, coming before a noun, as a proper noun. The term "houseless" is thus made much more significant.

Continuity and discontinuity

These are the twin results of textual coherence. On the continuity side, continuity is advanced through cohesion markers like a single word or phrase repeated at specific times in a text. Two forms of this cohesion or continuity are prevalent, *cataphoric* and *anaphoric* reference. A repeated word for which we must wait for adequate meaning via forward reference is cataphoric. A repeated word that builds meaning through reference backward is anaphoric. Once in place, textual coherence can be broken for effect. Expectations of a certain balance between subject and predicate can be broken through reversal of subjects and predicates, sudden leaps forward or backward in a time line, juxtapositions of speech and reverse endings are examples of textual discontinuity.

Simile

A figure of speech based on likeness rather than equation. An image in which one thing is compared with another and the "as" or "like" is stated, not denied, in the comparison.

Metaphor

From the Greek for a transference or carrying of something from one place to another. A figure of speech which is not a comparison but an equation. In a metaphor disparate things, situations, or events, are seen as equal.

Personification

The giving of an abstraction, an inanimate object, or a quality, human dimension and aspects. "The moon is no door. It is a face in its own right," from Sylvia Plath's *The Moon and the Yew Tree.*

Works Cited

Angelou, Maya. *I Know Why the Caged Bird Sings.* New York: Bantam, 1971.

—. "Graduation" in *The Norton Reader*, Eds. Linda Peterson *et al.* Shorter 13th ed. New York W.W. Norton, 2012. 10–19.

Archibald, Sasha. *Rumpus.* blog review of *Unruly Voices: Essays on Democracy, Civility and the Human Imagination* (2012) a collection of essays written by Mark Kingwell. Web. Jan 6, 2013.

Atwood, Margaret. "Footnote to the Amnesty Report on Torture," in *Two Headed Poems*, Toronto: Oxford University Press, 1978, ll 14–15.

Belsey, Catherine. *Critical Practice.* London: Methuen, 1987.

Barker, Pat. *Regeneration* (1991), London: Penguin, 2008.

Baugh, Hume. "Fred Wah's Diamond Grill," in *Quill and Quire*, (Sept 1996).

Carroll, Lewis. *The Annotated Alice: Alice's Adventures in Wonderland, Through the Looking Glass.* Introduction and Notes by Martin Gardner. New York: Meridian, New American Library, 1960.

Chadburn, Melissa, *Saturday Rumpus Interview of Dana Johnson.* Web. Jan 5 2013.

Dickens, Charles. "Night Walks" from *The Uncommercial Traveller.* The Project Gutenberg EBook of *The Uncommercial Traveller*, by Charles Dickens (#23 in series by Charles Dickens) Web. September 1, 2011.

Didion, Joan. "On Going Home" in *The Norton Reader*, Eds. Linda Peterson *et al.* Shorter 13th ed. New York W.W. Norton, 2012. 1–3.

Fowler, Roger. *Linguistic Criticism.* Oxford: Oxford University Press, 1986.

Rhenisch, Harold. *Out of the Interior.* Vancouver: Ronsdale Press, 1993.

Sanders, Scott Russel. *Aurora Means Dawn.* New York: Bradbury Press, 1989.

—. "The Singular First Person." *Essays on the Essay: Redefining the Genre.* Ed. Alexander J. Butrym. Athens Georgia: U Georgia P, 1989. 31–42.

Shields, David. *Reality Hunger: A Manifesto.* New York: Knopf, 201, 5.

6   Narrative and the Literary Essay

There are countless forms of narrative in the world. First of all, there is a prodigious variety of genres, each of which branches out into a variety of media, as if all substances could be relied upon to accommodate man's stories. Among the vehicles of narrative are articulated language, whether oral or written, pictures, still or moving, gestures, and an ordered mixture of all those substances; narrative is present in myth, legend, fables, tales, short stories, epics, history, tragedy, drama [suspense drama], comedy, pantomime, paintings (in Santa Ursula by Carpaccio, for instance), stained-glass windows, movies, local news, conversation. Moreover, in this infinite variety of forms, it is present at all times, in all places, in all societies; indeed narrative starts with the very history of mankind; there is not, there has never been anywhere, any people without narrative; all classes, all human groups, have their stories, and very often those stories are enjoyed by men of different and even opposite cultural backgrounds: narrative remains largely unconcerned with good or bad literature. Like life itself, it is there, international, transhistorical, transcultural. (Roland Barthes, *Introduction to the Structural Analysis of Narratives*, 79)

Sources
Joseph Bronowski "The Reach of Imagination" (1967)
Maia Joseph, "Wondering into Country: Dionne Brand's A Map to the Door of No Return." *Canadian Literature* (2007)
Henry James, "The Art of Fiction" (1884)

Anne Halkett, *The Autobiography of Lady Anne Halkett* (1677)
Virginia Woolf, "The Death of the Moth" (1942)
Charles Lamb, "Dream-Children: A Reverie," *The Works of Charles and Mary Lamb* (1823)
Alice Munro, "The Peace of Utrecht" (1976)

Introduction

The essays we will study next are recognizably literary. They use most of the features of the narrative voice we have worked with: figuration, plot, characterization, point of view, theme, and setting. But they do so in some interesting, sometimes challenging ways that demand a special kind of reading. We will now gather together the various approaches to the familiar, formal and narrative voices we have explored in order to build a depth response to essays that use narrative most richly. And we move from simply recognizing *coverage, expertise, analysis,* and *terminology* to showing you how to actively use them in your own writing. We are then on our way to building a method, a successful way of writing about the essay as a literary genre.

Objectives

Through the following examples of the literary essay and its related form, we will,

- introduce you to the essay as a literary form through in-depth study of well-known examples from the past and the present;
- use the voices and evaluative concepts we have developed so far — coverage, expertise, analysis, and terminology — and apply them to writing about the literary essay;
- ask what is gained in the use of literary strategies and procedures in the essay and find some answers;
- explicate such essays using literary features like figuration, point of view, characterization, plot; rising action, complication, climax, and resolution;
- begin discussion of current, more modern and postmodern forms of the literary essay, some now residing under the title "creative nonfiction."

Narrative in the Modern Essay

There are number of reasons for approaching the essay as a *literary* genre. Essay writers outside the university feel much less constrained by rules like the exclusion of "I" narrators and careful support of general ideas; they are writing for a literary public and use narrative as freely as poets use metaphor, imagery, rhythm, and the other potentials of "creative language." In this chapter, we focus on examples of this more full-scale essayistic narrative. I am especially interested in the way essayists use devices like *point of view* and *characteriza-tion* to speak about their lives as stories and to seek change or to solve personal or social problems thereby.

Sometimes, narration in the essay is a straightforward matter, much like a memoir or biography, in which a historical or contemporary figure is introduced and discussed. We have no trouble recognizing that such an essay presents an episode in a story about a real life. In this case its value is the increase in our understanding that narrative gives us. But the essay can also play with more interesting use of character and point of view. In these cases, we are no longer sure whether the character described is real or fictional. The author can allow us, for instance, to follow the transition from his or her life to a story, from reality to fiction, from self to character, or their reverse. In these essays, as we will see, the development of a character can be hidden by the narrative point of view such that we cannot tell immediately whether the mode is fact or fiction. The narrative picture thus becomes complicated by its intersection with an essay's "non fictional" status. I hope to show you that what is striking in such essays is the framing of these literary potentials and transitions so that in the course of reading, we become aware of them.

Literary theory about narrative shows us it can be interwoven in an essay in a number of ways. It exists on the micro-level so to speak: that is, it appears in typical grammatical forms, as we found in previous chapters. We found story-like tenses (the progressive aspect and general present) in both Didion's and Rhenisch's essays. But essayistic narrative can also be developed into a full-scale use of a fictional plot like a short story, with the inclusion of "made-up" char-acters and "made-up" events. One of the best known examples from the past is Jonathan Swift's "A Modest Proposal" of 1729, in which the narrator is a terrible fiction, but very close to the truth. And as we have seen, Erika Anderson's ren-dering of a close call in a New York subway station, "Man on the Tracks" show us how a skilful essayist can apply the "I" or first person narrator to work up an event and allow the reader to experience it along with her. The way reviewers and critics handle this kind of literary procedure, the balancing act between real event and fiction, is part of the theoretical landscape in literary studies today. We need a guide in this problematic area, and in the following we will include some critical studies and borrow some of their critical lexicon.

The Literary Essay's Relatives: Autobiography, Biography, and Memoir

We need first to bring up an issue about genre briefly before we move into our discussion of the literary essay. There is a similarity between the essay's fam-iliar voice and the voice we find in a *memoir* or *autobiography*. These forms are closely related to the elements we found in Montaigne's familiar "essai" because they also do not have to develop systematic general claims or use a consistent method of analysis. They are also close to narrative styles. The following example is drawn from Lady Anne Halkett's *autobiography* of 1677. As Roland Barths reminds us, it shows how narrative technique can be used in any form, and it will help us to clarify the difference between an essay and memoir, biography or autobiography. This difference is being challenged by essayists and theorists today, but we need to see it in established practice before we can evaluate its new forms and shapes.

Lady Anne Halkett

In this excerpt from the autobiography of Lady Anne Halkett (1622–1699), we witness a story told by an intensely Royalist partisan in the English Civil War. In it, Halkett is actively helping the future James II of England ("the duke" in the following) to escape his capture by the parliamentarians; the future James II is under house guard by his opponents but there is a chance for escape. There is no mention of general ideas and no formal analysis — Halkett is simply describing an exciting event and using narrative technique to do so:

> All things being now ready, upon the 20th of April 1648, in the evening was the time resolved for the duke's escape. And in order to that, it was designed for a week before every night as soon as the duke had supped he and those servants that attended His Highness (till the earl of Northumberland and the rest of the house had supped) went to a play called hide and seek, and sometimes he would hide himself so well that in half an hour's time they could not find him. His Highness had so used them to this that when he went really away they thought he was but at the usual sport. A little before the duke went to supper that night, he called for the gardener, who only had a treble key besides that which the duke had, and bid him give him that key till his own was mended, which he did. And after His Highness had supped, he immediately called to go to the play, and went down the privy stairs into the garden, and opened the gate that goes into the park, treble locking all the doors behind him. And at the garden gate Colonel Bamfield waited for His Highness, and putting on a cloak and periwig hurried him away to the park gate, where a coach waited that carried them to the waterside, and taking the boat that was appointed for that service, they rowed to the stairs next the bridge, where I and Miriam waited in a private house hard by that Colonel Bamfield had prepared for dressing His Highness, where all things were in readiness. But I had many fears, for Colonel Bamfield had desired me, if they came not there precisely by ten o'clock, to

shift for myself, for then I might conclude they were discovered, and
so my stay there could do no good but prejudice myself. Yet all this
did not make me leave the house though ten o'clock did strike, and
he that was entrusted often went to the landing place and saw no
boat coming was much discouraged, and asked me what I would do.
I told him I came there with a resolution to serve His Highness, and
I was fully determined not to leave that place till I was out of hopes
of doing what I came there for, and would take my hazard. He left
me to go again to the waterside, and while I was fortifying myself
against what might arrive to me, I heard a great noise of many as I
thought coming upstairs, which I expected to be soldiers to take me,
but it was a pleasing disappointment, for the first that came in was
the duke, who with much joy I took in my arms and gave God thanks
for his safe arrival.

This is an interesting slice of autobiography and of English history — we feel
some of the stress of being the friend of a hunted king in the English Civil War.[1]
Two clear narrative methods can be found in the excerpt: event selection and
point of view. Note the emphasis on chronological development; the exact date
at which the escape occurred is pinpointed first, "upon the 20th of April 1648,"
and the narrative's development moves from this point forward, working out the
events of one evening. Narratives are all about time, but it is subjective time, of
development related to the point of view of the narrator or character. Halkett
is showing the events through an "I narrator" lens that orders and compresses
time to portray a dramatic episode in her life.

In his essay, "Introduction to Narrative" Paul Hazel states the case neatly.
Narrative time is subjective, a function of the needs of the narrator:

> This subjectivity, this point of view of the narrator shapes every ele-
> ment of the narrative. The psychological weighting of time is itself
> reciprocally related to the processes of:

---

1   James II was born in 1633, so would have been 15 years old at the time of Halkett's narra-
    tive. After this came the civil wars, the beheading of Charles I, (1649) and the Interregnum,
    (1642–1651) then "The Restoration" and the accession of James's brother, Charles II, to the
    throne. At Charles II's death in 1685, James II [the Duke] did in fact become King of England,
    only to be deposed in 1688 for sticking, against fierce opposition, to his Catholic beliefs. His
    throne was eventually given to William of Orange, his Protestant son-in-law and nephew.
    James II was considered a threat to the Protestants as it was feared he would bring Catholicism
    back into England and reinstate it as England's religion. For Protestant England, he became
    a symbol of the royalist Catholic cause, [the epithet, "The Pretender" was used against his
    son — next in line for the throne]. Halkett uses narrative technique to effectively show us the
    dangers of supporting an heir to power already targeted as a possible threat.

1. Event selection. No matter what actually went on "in reality" only those events necessary to the narrative should be included. The choice of events — what is actually deemed necessary — relates directly to the point of the narrative, what message the narrator is trying to express. The effectiveness of this choice can be measured against criteria such as coherence and internal consistency.

2. Event sequencing. Events need not be narrated in the order they happened but can be recombined in an infinite number of ways (many of which may be medium specific). As Jean-Luc Godard has said, the narrative must have a beginning, a middle, and an end, but not necessarily in that order…. The selection of events, the relative importance attached to each, and the way in which subjective time is managed are all entirely dependent upon the point of view of the narrator.

A narrative is a re-presentation of reality from a particular perspective. It is a whole, an internally consistent, self-contained unit of expression; reality reconfigured in order to create meaning. (2)

With Halkett's autobiography, the temporal forward motion, an order something like a mini-plot, is highly selected and highly sequenced. After showing the preparation for the escape, it rises to a climax at the end; in between are moments of deception, peril and revelation and after the climax, where there is doubt whether the ruse has worked, we have a happy conclusion, and a final *dénouement*, a resolution and settling down of the emotion. Halkett selects events, and sequences them from her point of view to show what she needs to show. Using the first person or "I narrator" she is a witness to, and participates in this dangerous rescue of a courageous and clever king. Her point seems to be the wiliness of "the duke" and her loyalty to him under duress. Such narrative techniques often appear in the essay to highlight specific facts and events in dramatic ways. But essays, because of their brevity, usually remain episodic and they can have many other contents, notably as we have seen a general idea or theme.

Note, then the limits of Halkett's narration. We do not see the creative freedom of the novelist or short story writer who can enter into a character's thoughts and feelings, or juxtapose other characters, or shape a theme through multiple character developments and conflict. Narrative in this excerpt is used in a restricted way — the description is crafted like a story, but shares ground with a report of news as it presents some exciting facts and a time line, (dates, events and places) though from a subjective point of view. We can also compare this essayistic approach with a memoir: a memoir is also concerned with facts and accuracy, but looks more to the author's life from the subjective and emotional sides, the inner life of the narrator, though a memoir-like element can be detected, with Halkett's feelings and attitudes toward the conflict also present. Again, though the difference has to do with length. The essay cannot cover the whole of a life in the detail and inner richness required of a memoir or a complete autobiography.

We are though entering a discussion about the wavering line between fictional accounts found in novels and short stories and narratives like Halkett's about the events that occur in memoirs and autobiographies. It is a line much explored through the critical term *literary nonfiction*, or *creative nonfiction*. While the event occurred in history, we have noticed fictional elements in the Halkett example — the time line is carefully organized in order to show the setting, a wily king, a dangerous complication, the risky position of the narrator, and a resolution. It is a good mini-story as well as a true historical event.

The autobiography and memoir are much longer than the essay (remember the link to the word "assay") because they are collections of the major episodes of a lifetime. Halkett's autobiography, from which the excerpt is taken runs to about 21 volumes.[2] There are other differences. We do not find, for instance, the interpolation of aphorisms from classical authors that Montaigne experimented with in his text; nor do we find a general proposition that is proven in the essay, or a bibliography of supportive reading. That is an autobiography or memoir is not likely to be so resolutely focused as is an essay; it is rarely organized around a general theme like "Vanity," or "Revenge" though part of it might be, and sometimes you might wish it were.

"Narrative" as Literary Term and Essayistic Method

How does criticism handle narrative in the essay? Here is a critical essay showing an analysis of a memoir written by Canadian poet Dionne Brand. The critic is Maia Joseph and the excerpt is found in the literary journal, *Canadian Literature* (2007):

> Dionne Brand's memoir, *A Map to the Door of No Return: Notes to Belonging*, can be read as an elliptical, poetic meditation on a short passage by Eduarde Galeano[3] that Brand cites twice: "Im nostalgic for a country which doesn't yet exist on a map" (qtd. in Map 52, 85). Brand's desired "country," her imagined space of belonging, is not Canada, despite her formal citizenship. Her reflections on her experi-

2 See Moody, http://www.jimandellen.org/halkett/CastOut.html
3 Eduardo Galeano is a Uuruguayan writer and journalist, born 1940 in Montevideo. His most well-known works include *Open Veins of Latin America* (1971) and the *Memory of Fire* trilogy of 1986.

ences as a black woman and diasporic subject repeatedly exceed the boundaries of the nation as she explores the possibilities of diasporic community, political community, and artistic community. Nonetheless, just after she recounts the experience of reading Galeano in the silence of late night, Brand takes an imagined journey across Canada:

> In cities at 4:45 a.m., Toronto or Calgary or Halifax, there are these other inhabitants of silence. Two hundred miles outside, north of any place, or in the middle of it, circumnavigating absence. For a moment it is a sweet country, in that moment you know perhaps someone else is awake reading Galeano. (53)

As she muses on the possibility of a "country" where she might belong, Brand remains keenly attentive to the country she calls "home" (64, 77, 79). She brings the concept of impossible origins that informs her experience as a descendant of African slaves to the definition of Canadian identity, arguing that in the discourse on national belonging "[t]oo much has been made of origins" (69). She goes on to criticize what she describes as "the calcified Canadian nation narrative" (70), contending that national identity has been "drawn constantly to the European shape in its definition. A shape … which obscures its multiplicity" (72). She also challenges the reliance on narratives of origin by Canadian immigrant populations, suggesting that such a tactic simply produces a mirror image of its national counterpart.... (69)

There is an interesting inclusion of the term "narrative" in Joseph's article. This is a more in-depth analysis than say a review or a book report; it is about seventeen pages long. Joseph engages a strong theme of Brand's memoir, the criticism of the predominant "calcified Canadian nation narrative." The narrative of Canada is not inclusive enough and to Brand, our accepted narratives of origin, of how Canada came into existence, are, first, not as significant as we have made them out to be and second, exclusivist. "Narrative" is here present as a literary term, a critical concept, but one that is not so stable as the reader may have thought. It is being re-defined. Brand, according to Joseph, sees the current definition as a problem, and she shows how Brand is attempting to demystify the national narrative through paying more attention to cultural diversity and less attention to the myth of European and dominant culture sources. Note also the use of the terms "diasporic" and "diasporic subject" by Joseph to help in this redefinition. A defined national narrative is examined critically because it does not include many diasporic subjects. In its noun form a *diaspora* is the spreading of peoples from their homeland to other parts of the globe, usually done in response to poverty, colonization, or warfare. *Diasporic subject* is the particular shape of an identity formed through this experience.

Attention to narrative as a term and use of newly introduced terminology clearly shows one of the features of this critical essay about a memoir. We can though go a step further than Joseph. Even though Brand's text is a memoir, you can see it has an essayistic quality in its mix of generalities about narrative and the imagined experience of a trip to "Two hundred miles outside, north of any place." In Brand's text, as Joseph finds, narrative is talked about abstractly, theoretically, but her experience is also enacted as story, she is also imagining a better narrative. See if you can find the differences between Brand's use of "narrative," and what Halkett enacts in her story. Halkett does not include this essayistic quality — this critical overtone of a term or form. We can find a similar critical cast in Joseph Bronowski's approach to narrative.

In his classic essay, "The Reach of Imagination," (1967) mathematician, scientist, playwright, and literary critic, Joseph Bronowski uses a number of miniature narratives. He presents the history of Galileo's discovery of acceleration but also makes it a well-crafted short story in itself. We can easily find the plot. The plot is made up of a heroic *protagonist* (Galileo), a rather forbidding *antagonist* (the Church), and a dramatic conflict between them in which Galileo appears to lose but really wins. In addition, we are given some imaginative dialogue. The conflict also has the typical narrative structure (the event selection) of *rising action, complication, climax,* and *resolution.* We are introduced first to the antagonist and protagonist. Galileo is our hero, and the authority of the classic texts, backed up by the church, is set against him. Note how Bronowski (like Brand) is very much aware, and makes us aware, through a question, that he is communicating a story rather than a more objective historical account of Galileo's experiment.

> Let me find a spectacular example for you from history. What is the most famous experiment that you had described to you as a child? I will hazard that it is the experiment that Galileo is said to have made in Sidney's age, in Pisa about 1590, by dropping two unequal balls from the Leaning Tower. There, we say, is a man in the modern mold, a man after our own hearts: he insisted on questioning the authority of Aristotle and St. Thomas Aquinas, and seeing with his own eyes whether (as they said) the heavy ball would reach the ground before the light one. Seeing is believing. (4)

Galileo sounds more than a bit legendary here; he is the hero in a story we are likely to have heard when we were children or in school. After an introduction of the adversaries and a reminder about how old the story is, the reader is quickly brought to the essential struggle — two conflicting explanations of gravity and acceleration of mass. But the narrator shows that we have misread the story. Like Brand's critique of "the Canadian narrative," he does not accept the established myth of Galileo. Instead, he criticizes our older reading for being more than a bit inaccurate. According to Bronowski, Galileo likely did not perform the experiment he is credited with; it was an imaginative experiment not a real one. With this rereading, an old story becomes fresh and interesting. The essayistic nature of the narrative is clear because you can also feel Bronowski's *critical awareness* of the story-like aspect of his illustration — he knows and he makes his reader know that this is a narrative account, and a revision of an older narrative. He certainly seems, however, to take a delight in using this device and at the same time critiquing it. Bronowski is acting both as story teller and as literary critic. During the most dramatic moment of the conflict, we are brought into an imaginative, lively reconstruction of Galileo's thoughts:

> .... the eye that Galileo used was the mind's eye. He did not drop balls from the Leaning Tower at Pisa — and if he had, he would have got a very doubtful answer. Instead Galileo made an imaginary experiment in his head,...
>
> Suppose, said Galileo, that you drop two unequal balls from the tower at the same time. And suppose that Aristotle is right — suppose that the heavy ball falls faster, so that it steadily gains on the light ball, and hits the ground first. Very well. Now imagine the same experiment done again, with only one difference: this time the two unequal balls are joined by a string between them. The heavy ball will again move ahead, but now the light ball holds it back and acts as a drag or a brake. So the light ball will be speeded up and the heavy ball will be slowed down; they must reach the ground together because they are tied together, but they cannot reach the ground as quickly as the heavy ball alone. Yet the string between them has turned the two balls into a single mass which is heavier than either ball — and surely (according to Aristotle) this mass should therefore move faster than either ball? Galileo's imaginary experiment has uncovered a contradiction; he says trenchantly, "You see how, from your assumption that a heavier body falls more rapidly than a lighter one, I infer that a (still) heavier body falls more slowly." There is only one way out of the contradiction: the heavy ball and the light ball must fall at the same rate, so that they go on falling at the same rate when they are tied together. (4)

Although silenced in his own time, the heroic Galileo wins in the end by using his powers of imagination and analysis to construct a more accurate explanation (itself a miniature story) and thus prove the established authorities false. Galileo eventually overcomes the dogmatic reliance on Church-approved Aristotle and Aquinas, and with this climactic explanatory feat, the modern science of physics, at least the physics of moving bodies and projectiles, is born. The climax and resolution of the conflict occurs in the achievement of the new explanation when Galileo perceptively and once and for all shows the mistake in the old way. Note also that Galileo's conversation is narrated — with dialogue markers like "said Galileo," "Suppose" and "Very well," he is reproducing Galileo's speaking voice.

Both of these are pretty straightforward critiques of a known story by retelling it in another way. Bronowski uses a similar technique in his descriptions of Einstein (5) and Newton (6). Together, they show the power of the essay to make an accepted cultural narrative a little suspect, or to retune our image of these great scientists (and the importance of their science) as more imaginative Western culture heroes. Nevertheless, all told, this is a limited use of both criticism and narrative. The narrative technique is secondary to the proving of a more general claim about the imaginative nature of science, or the lack of acceptance of diversity in Canada. But Brand and Bronowski show the potential of narrative technique for characterization, dialogue, and plot, and have thereby criticized the older versions and remade myths into newly entertaining, more accurate or more fair narratives.

First and Third Person Narrators

We can now unpack some of other features of narrative that can be at work in the essay. We have looked at plot, character and timeline — the temporal or event aspects of narrative. But literary point of view itself can also come into play in essays. Essayists consciously and deliberately tell stories as they develop their ideas, and the stories they tell are usually secondary or illustrative, thus usually told from one of the third person points of view. But this is not always the case, when they use first person narration, determining which "I" it is can become quite a challenge.

Before going on to discuss essayistic first-person narrators, we need to explore some standard definitions of literary point of view drawn from literary criticism and make a step toward a more sophisticated use of this terminology. How is point of view related to plot and character in narration in an essay? In the following discussion we add to your store of literary terms, and the goal is to show you how these terms can be used in analysis of a literary essay, (these terms are of course applicable to other genres of literature).

The plot of a novel or short story is not simply the *timeline*. Rather, it refers to the shaping of events by the author to show the working out in the life of a character of a value, or a change in personality or a decision or to make some thematic point by shaping the development of character in the action. Hazel showed us that any narrative event is "subjective"; it is shaped by the intent of the narrator. The great Victorian novelist, critic, and essayist Henry James also felt strongly that plot, (the unfolding of events and action) and the psychology of character interact. In one of his well-known essays on the novel, "The Art of Fiction" (1884), James maintained that incident (action) and character are intimately related. The emotions, insights, and inner changes in a character and the events of the plot are an organic whole and cannot be separated out.

> When one says picture one says of character, when one says novel one says of incident, and the terms may be transposed at will. What is character but the determination of incident? What is incident but the illustration of character? What else do we seek in it and find in it? Is it an incident for a woman to stand up with her hand resting on a table and look at you in a certain way; or if it be not an incident I think it will be hard to say what it is. At the same time it is an expression of character. (431)

James is proposing that a good storyteller will arrange the incidents of a story to further our understanding of a character and that when a character has an important insight or change of attitude, or makes a decision, this is as much an element of the plot as is the description of physical action. We see in James's criticism a focus on our inner life and subjectivity and the use of narrative fiction to explore human psychology. According to James, narratives are not necessarily just about action or heroic or sensational events; the better narratives show subjective changes, changes in ideas, values, attitudes, emotions, or beliefs.

James is well known for his uses of a particular novelistic point of view. His mastery of the *third-person **limited** omniscient narrator* is shown in novels like *The Golden Bowl*, and *Portrait of a Lady*. In these novels, the point of view is third person: that is, the narrator controls our vision of all change and events. But the point of view is not the same as that of the standard, third person omniscient narrator; it is more self-effacing, more objective. The narrator is very much in the background, we get very little commentary. In addition we can see only into one character's mind. This central character is then something like a focus or, as James called it, a "centre of consciousness" through which we can see the events and "overhear" the other characters and through which we participate in the plot.

This "centre of consciousness" idea comes clearly into play with first-person narrators. Here is one example from fiction that should also give you more of a grasp of point of view before we go into the issue of its use in the essay. It is taken from the opening paragraph of Alice Munro's brilliant short story, "The Peace of Utrecht":

> I have been at home now for three weeks, and it has not been a suc-
> cess. Maddy and I, though we speak cheerfully of our enjoyment of
> so long and intimate a visit, will be relieved when it is over. Silences
> disturb us. We laugh immoderately, I am afraid — very likely we are
> both afraid — that when the moment comes to say goodbye, unless we
> are very quick to kiss, and fervently mockingly squeeze each other's
> shoulders, we will have to look straight into the desert that is between
> us and acknowledge that we are not merely indifferent; at heart we re-
> ject each other, and as for the past we make so much of sharing we do
> not really share at all, each of us keeping jealously to herself, thinking
> privately that the other has turned alien, and forfeited her claim. (191)

Can you hear this voice? In this first-person account, the point of view limits the focus to one mind and its perceptions — the narrator's. She then operates as a "centre of consciousness." The point of view is also *limited first person* narrative. Why "limited"? As the story unfolds, the reader becomes aware that neither Maddy nor the narrator can be trusted wholly and that the truth about the relationships must be reached through our own analysis of their partial truths. Much as in "real life" we must interpret what people tell us and assess their narratives. This type of narrator is also sometimes called an "unreliable" narrator.

Going the next step and applying these terms to the essay we are going to find that the difference between an essayistic narrative and a fictional narrative is quite subtle and hard to pin down. Both forms can use the elements of narration, control of time through plot, characterization, and literary point of view. You might have the feeling that there is no real reason why the first-person limited point of view could not be pretty much the same in both genres. Can the essay accomplish similar kinds of views, of self-delusion, insight, doubling, masking, and revelation, or present similar limits and entangle its readers in interpretation like a Munro short story?

The "I" Narrator in Didion's "On Going Home"

Didion's essay begins in a way that is strikingly similar to Munro's story: "I am home for my daughter's first birthday" (1). Munro begins, "I have been at home now for three weeks, and it has not been a success." One difference becomes evident though: Didion orients us very quickly to place, time, and relationship. She comes out and tells the reader where we are, Central Valley California. But while she handles the setting differently, the *point of view* she uses is very similar. But this is not a fiction — this essay is spoken by a real, not a fictional, person, Joan Didion, and about real, non-fictional persons, her husband, daughter and relatives, at least so it seems. The problem we now face is that this may be Didion's point. There is a delicate play of identity and difference between a first-person limited "I" of a fiction and the real "I" of a memoir or autobiography.

You might well ask why an essayist would use an "I" point of view that is like a "made-up" character. Didion's essay is a good example of the possibilities. From the beginning, I had the distinct impression she was using the first person point of view as the narrator of a short story might use it. I decided that she might be employing it to get a grip on her dilemma about her identity. Using the fictional possibilities of the "I" narrator, she could see her past self and her married self as somewhat separate from her current centre, as imaginative constructs or as roles, masks, or personae — that is, as something like *literary characters* in a short story. As we have seen with the critical awareness of "narrative" in an essay, point of view can function in similar, doubled way.

The "I" narrator speaking the story would then become a focus around which other selves or versions of the self could be seen and evaluated — much as we are required to do in Munro's fiction. Using the literary device of the limited first person, Didion plays with the idea of observing her other selves as roles or as made up of social expectations, not quite so close to her central identity.

The episode where she differentiates herself from her grandfather's photo is a good example of this kind of plurality of perspectives. In it, she plays out the conflict between her role as member of her "first family" and her identity as an independent woman with her own family. Another case occurs when she visits her great-aunts. The feeling that her childhood self has become a character in a story is quite apparent, though here the narrative seems to be made up by her aunts:

> I go to visit my great-aunts. A few of them think now that I am my cousin, or their daughter who died young. We recall an anecdote about a relative last seen in 1948, and they ask if I still like living in New York City. I have lived in Los Angeles for three years, but I say that I do. The baby is offered a horehound drop, and I am slipped a dollar bill, "to buy a treat." Questions trail off, answers are abandoned, the baby plays with the dust motes in a shaft of afternoon sun. (2)

The picture of her younger self as seen by her great-aunts (or Didion as the child they knew) slips in and out of focus here. It is partly recognizable and partly mixed in with memory and mistaken identities so that it becomes slightly un-real. Didion might be a little worried that an image she took for granted is slip-ping from her control, she is becoming a character in someone else's narrative, and a mistaken character at that. She is acting something like a literary critic of her aunt's narratives, correcting mistakes, showing them as being out of date. But we are in a complicated area. As author, Didion has constructed our access to this conversation with her great-aunts. Through point of view, she is control-ling the expression of this narrated version of herself and its unreal quality. We are seeing it through her spare, evocative description. There are a number of Didion's selves explored in this essay, a number of characterizations by others that might make up parts of her identity — mother, wife, daughter, sister, niece. What is the point of this exploration of these other selves? Are they trustworthy?

I surmise that the writerly centre of consciousness, the "I" narrator, gives Didion the chance to see these various "selves," to sift through them and come to the central feature or to explore how much of what we are is determined by social expectation, how we fit and do not fit into the characters given us by others or by society as a whole. After we subtract what has been given us by others in the creation of our identities, is there anything "left over"? For critic Shirley Neuman narrators in essays can "turn themselves into the creations of their own fictive discourse." You might be able to see why Didion uses this liter-ary device of point of view, why she might want to view herself as a story-like character. This creative "essayistic" use of point of view gives her an opportunity to work out a conflict between the self she can feel as her own and the selves given her by others. In the end the tension between the various selves does not seem to be resolved — none achieves dominance, but I think some forward progress has been achieved. She is experimenting with narrative point of view in her essay, and through it some kind of wisdom may have been reached and in which we can share. At least the problem has been described clearly: What is the range of roles offered me? Which one of these characters, asks Didion, is me?

Didion has here worked out an interesting critical view of fictional character, essayistic form, and self. She makes us aware that narrative is an organizing feature operating strongly in our lives; it is found in "literature," and also in what others say about us.

Coverage and Expertise in Writing About the Literary Essay

In this discussion of essayistic first-person and third-person narrators we have explored some standard definitions of *literary point of view* drawn from liter-ary criticism and we have focused on the relation between point of view, plot and character in narration. With luck, we have added to the depth of your understanding of literary terms and you have seen how these terms and their redefinitions can be used in analysis of a literary essay.

We now turn from such narrative devices to include the other categories of formal evaluation we have worked with so far. In an evaluative paper say on an essay like Carson's or Visser's on scientific or social issues, *coverage* and *expertise* were the other methods we found for organizing an evaluation or building a response. What though about your own writing? The same criteria can come into play in your own essay composition. In terms of coverage, we can certainly say that if the major outline, facts, or issues of the text you are dealing with are not mentioned or included in your work, then your writing can have the "just visiting" quality already mentioned as a fault. Seriousness of approach comes from close reading, and whether you can show your understanding of the whole of the work. And in a student paper on a literary essay, expertise is usually available in most university libraries, and the methods and style through which this secondary material can be incorporated in your essay are well known. The Modern Language Association (MLA) style of documentation and citation is the standard "rulebook" for inclusion of expertise, so it is best to know and understand these rules and guidelines. In the following analysis of an "I" narrator in Lamb's "Dream Children" note the use of literary terminology, analysis, coverage and expertise.

The Familiar Voice as Mask: "I" Narrator in Charles Lamb's "Dream-Children"

The literary experiment with narrative, self, point of view, and character appeared quite early in the development of the modern form of the essay, and essayists of the Romantic Period, were likely the originators. As Didion and Anderson were to do 190 years or so later, Charles Lamb, (1775 – 1834) discovered some of the literary potential of the "I" narrator in "Dream Children" (1822). Lamb gives the familiar voice an intriguing twist. The dimensions we have discussed so far — point of view, plot, character, exploration of role, and critical awareness — are all present in this essay from the far past. At the end, we realize that the narrative we were introduced to is not quite what it seems; behind it, we find an acute psychologist of dreams at work.

To see this, we will need some background. I will rely on two works about Lamb for my analysis of "Dream-Children": George L. Barnett's biography *Charles Lamb*; *Charles Lamb & Elia*, edited by J. E. Morpurgo, and *English Romantic Writers* by well-known romantic critic, David Perkins. From reading in these works, I learned that Lamb's essays were very popular and appeared in a number of literary magazines. *The London Magazine* was one of the best known.

According to Perkins, Lamb was a member of the first generation of the English Romantic writers and a friend of Samuel Taylor Coleridge. He was well enough liked by his literary acquaintances that he makes an appearance at the end of Coleridge's conversation poem, "The Lime Tree Bower My Prison," where he is referred to as "My gentle hearted Charles" (670–672, n. 519). This poem, written in 1796, also alludes to a tragic incident in Lamb's life that has relevance to my reading of "Dream-Children." His sister Mary, who today would be diagnosed as suffering from a severe kind of schizophrenia, became deranged and stabbed their mother to death. She spent some time in a hospital for the insane after this, but Lamb eventually persuaded the authorities that Mary would be better treated at home. He spent his life caring for her; he taught her to write, and she helped him in his writing. He never married, perhaps so he could care for his sister, though in his youth, he had romantic designs on a young lady named Ann Simmons. His courtship was, however, unsuccessful, and Ann married another man. Lamb spent his working life as an accountant for the East India Company, and his biographers attest that his essays were likely a release from the tedium of his job (Barnett 28–35).

According to Perkins, "Dream-Children: A Reverie" is one of a number of essays Lamb wrote under the pseudonym "Elia," (671). In them, he creates a world of fictional beings who are thinly veiled portraits of his colleagues at the East India Company, his poet friends and writers, and his small family. The pseudonym signed at the end is a clue that the point of view used in the essay is to be seen as a literary *persona* or mask.

We do not see the full reach of the mask at first because Lamb has hidden it well. He begins with an account of a playful discussion with his "little ones" in which he will tell them stories about relatives they have never seen. Lamb's story seems, at first, to be light and whimsical; he will not be discussing ideas but will stay, literally, on the familiar level.

> Children love to listen to stories about their elders when *they* were children; to stretch their imagination to the conception of a trad-itionary great-uncle, or grandame whom they never saw. It was in this spirit that my little ones crept about me the other evening to hear about their great-grandmother Field who lived in a great house in Norfolk. (691)

Note again the critical awareness of narrative — the idea that there is a value in audience awareness, and we are entering a genre or type of storytelling in this setting and with this audience; here we have Lamb showing us an example of the typical contents of a "children's story." Becoming part of Lamb's audience, we might be captivated by the familiar scene and settle in to watch a play-ful description of children charmed by fantasy and how they seem to mimic stories or to find moral lessons in them easily. But soon we find that mixed in with this playful, light, familiar voice there is an undercurrent — another more serious note can be heard. While Grandmother Field was once "the best dancer … in the county" (691), she died of cancer. There are also allusions to Lamb's lameness and to his difficulties in courting "Alice W — n," whom the children call "their pretty dead mother" (692). A realistic and tragic portrayal of a life and experience is unfolding underneath the surface level of storytelling with children around an evening fireside. In fact, Barnett is reasonably sure that this blanked out name is an allusion to Ann Simmons, the object of Lamb's failed courtship, (29) whose "bright hair" seems to be referred to in the essay (Perkins 693). And after the children request that the narrator talk about "their pretty dead mother" (that is, after his projected marriage to Ann Simmons), Lamb abruptly makes this secondary, more realistic theme the central focus:

> … when suddenly, turning to Alice, the soul of the first Alice looked out at her eyes with such a reality of re-presentment, that I became in doubt which of them stood there before me, or whose that bright hair was; and while I stood gazing, both the children gradually grew fainter to my view, receding, and still receding till nothing at last but two mournful features were seen in the uttermost distance, which, without speech, strangely impressed upon me the effects of speech: "We are not of Alice, nor of thee; nor are we children at all. The children of Alice called Bartrum father. We are nothing; less than nothing, and dreams. We are only what might have been, and must wait upon the tedious shores of Lethe millions of ages before we have existence, and a name." (693)

Lamb has suddenly changed his perspective, his point of view, and his text is no longer familiar in any sense. With the eerie disappearance of the children, we wonder, momentarily, what kind of a surreal world we are in. Then, the narrator "wakes up," and we find he has been dreaming. The effect of "Dream-Children" turns on the abruptly changed relation between fact and fiction, dream self and real self, narrative first person point of view, and essayistic-critical point of view. The reversal or *peripeteia* at the end puts us in the place of the children. We are now the ones who have been captured by a skilful narrator, a teller of tales, who has constructed a story for us complete with characters, a climax, and a first-person limited point of view. Like Swift's "A Modest Proposal," and Didion's "On Going Home," "Dream-Children" is a good example of narrative and creative use of point of view in an essay. "Alice" and "John" are not the names of Lamb's real children; he had none that we know of. They are skilfully drawn characters in a narrated dream episode and, this essay has a real surprise ending, it acts on us as a well-crafted short story does and it also makes us critically aware of the power of storytelling.

This essay shows us again the literary possibilities of the genre and how subtle this essayistic use of point of view can be. We begin with the conventional familiar voice, someone talking to us in a person-to-person, open, and friendly way as Montaigne did. We have no reason to doubt this voice, and we accept the narrator's description of a fireside scene with almost no reservation. Then, we drift seamlessly into the comfortable world Lamb is describing. In reality, we have simply been given a narrative framework — and part of the delight of this essay is the way in which it shows us how much of our reading is dependent on the expectations we have of genre. We readily accept the convention of an "I" narrator who will be telling children a story, and as we look or listen over his shoulder, we have some strong expectations about what kind of story it should be. But this expectation is disrupted by the intrusions of the other more realistic and seemingly inappropriate voice until at the end the whole convention we have put into place, along with the set of expectations it gives rise to and the point of view, has been reversed.

Once again we see an essayist playing with the possibilities of multiple voices and their contexts rather than simply using discursive prose to analyze, give us information, or tell us a straightforward, true story. Essayists can never leave well enough alone. In addition we have been given some critical insights into the powers of fiction, and this is the way an essayist will typically introduce the critical dimension. Criticism as academic discipline will have different methods than this, though some professional literary critics, once in a while, find this more creative "essayistic" approach. Lamb has also submerged the awareness of narrative to the point that we are no longer able to distinguish between a short story and an essay — this problematic margin of genres is what defines the form of writing now called "creative nonfiction" or what Shirley Neuman has also called "life writing."

Charles Dickens, Criticism and the Essayist as Fictional Character

In the first chapter we noted a character emerging in a literary essay by Dickens, "Night Walks" through the creative use of the "I" narrator. I will now develop this idea further through the inclusion of expertise and analysis, and show how we can find a wider structure about which to write. With the inclusion of biographical information, and a quotation from a literary critic, and some analysis, Dickens's ideas on London can be articulated, the notion that a large city has many levels and dimensions beyond the personal, and that they show a possibility of self-development that is not entirely positive.

Charles Dickens (1812–1870) is probably the most well-known of the great Victorian novelists; you might remember *A Christmas Carol, Great Expectations,* or *Oliver Twist.* As a child, he knew straightened circumstances; his father, once successful, spent a period in debtor's prison, and as an adolescent, Dickens worked briefly in a blacking factory — a factory for colouring shoes and boots black — experiences that formed his attitudes toward the abysmal working conditions in the 19th century factories of England, toward the injustice of British social hierarchies, and the cruel injustices of the law. He had a great narrative gift, which soon made itself known, first in journalism and then in the many novels and stories he wrote for an increasingly large audience, (Ackroyd, *Dickens*).

One of his narrative talents lies in the characters he created, some of them seeming to live to the present day, like Scrooge and Miss Haversham. At the height of his career, he was the best-known novelist of his day. Acutely concerned with the poor and outcast and with social arrogance and personal and official duplicity, his work generally shows a deep engagement with exposing social injustice and forwarding social reform. He wrote "Night Walks" when he was attempting to launch a magazine called *All the Year Round*, and it and was included in a group of essays called *The Uncommercial Traveller.*[4]

As we have seen, "Night Walks" has literary or narrative potential. How do we disclose it to a reader? Expertise about Dickens is certainly available. Here is a light touch. According to Christopher Hitchins, in a speech Dickens gave at the Garrick Club in 1854 in memory of Shakespeare's birthday, he said "We meet on this day to celebrate the birthday of a vast army of living men and women who will live for ever with an actuality greater than that of the men and women whose external forms we see around us," (Hitchins para 6). Dickens was referring to the characters in Shakespeare's plays, and his statement shows an intense faith in the power of literary character. This faith shows itself even in the relatively brief instance of "Night Walks."

In terms of point of view, "Night Walks" is couched in the familiar voice of the first person narrator. The "I" pronoun is used throughout, and, as with Montaigne, we are invited into the inner feelings of the narrator-essayist. But because he is a novelist, Dickens cannot help but play with the narrative possibilities of this voice. In "Night Walks," a familiar essayist quickly begins to employ narrative techniques in his evocation of setting and in characterization.

I noted previously that essays often report interesting travels — Montaigne composed a number of travelogues that have the exotic city or landscape as an intriguing feature; and "Of Vanity" ends with a visit to Rome. Dickens shows us, however, that a setting need not be far removed to be exotic. He organizes

---

4   See http://www.gutenberg.org/cache/epub/914/pg914.txt [Accessed Sept. 1, 2011]

"Night Walks" around a night ramble through a London neighbourhood that was well known, habitual, perhaps even uninteresting to him in daylight. But by making night the *temporal setting*, this well-known place is given mystery and deeper meaning, and the locale becomes open to interpretation and can benefit from close study.

The treatment of a travelogue borders on a narrative technique Dickens often uses in the novel or short story. As a comparison, here is an example from his *Great Expectations*. The protagonist, Pip has just appeared in London on his way up the social ladder, from a small village, and is being shown about by one Mr. Wemmick:

> ... we were at Barnard's Inn. My depression was not alleviated by the announcement, for, I had supposed that establishment to be an hotel kept by Mr Barnard, to which the Blue Boar in our town was a mere public-house. Whereas I now found Barnard to be a disembodied spirit, or a fiction, and his inn the dingiest collection of shabby buildings ever squeezed together in a rank corner as a club for Tom-cats.
>
> We entered this haven through a wicket-gate, and were disgorged by an introductory passage into a melancholy little square that looked to me like a flat burying-ground. I thought it had the most dismal trees in it, and the most dismal sparrows, and the most dismal cats, and the most dismal houses (in number half a dozen or so,) that I had ever seen. I thought the windows of the sets of chambers into which those houses were divided, were in every stage of dilapidated blind and curtain, crippled flower-pot, cracked glass, dusty decay, and miserable makeshift; while To Let To Let To Let, glared at me from empty rooms, as if no new wretches ever came there, and the vengeance of the soul of Barnard were being slowly appeased by the gradual suicide of the present occupants and their unholy internment under the gravel. (ch. 21)

Note the personifications and that the detailed observation of this setting is used not so much to set the scene of action as to give an account of Pip's state of mind and to make his "great expectations" of London more than a little ironic through deflation. The point of view is first person with Pip telling us what he is seeing, and the reader is able to look over his shoulder and position Pip's deflated expectations and the light comic irony of the presentation.

A similar characterization and travelogue approach occurs in "Night Walks." Dickens loved to walk. On the first leg into the sleeping city, we have, as in the above narrative, a well described immediate setting, the interior of a London theatre, empty at night:

Between the bridge and the two great theatres, there was but the
distance of a few hundred paces, so the theatres came next. Grim
and black within, at night, those great dry wells, and lonesome to
imagine, with the rows of faces faded out, the lights extinguished,
and the seats all empty.... I groped my well-known way to the stage
and looked over the orchestra — which was like a great grave dug for
a time of pestilence — into the void beyond. (2–3)

Dickens was a good actor and often gave public readings of parts of his novels
to appreciative audiences, so he knew these theatres from an insider position.
They certainly evoke a different atmosphere than such successes in this excerpt.
And as we move through the night streets of London, each feature opens a
possibility for commentary — from the theatres, to Newgate, London's dreaded
prison, to Bedlam the "insane asylum," to the market, to the train station. As
we progress, we uncover drunkenness, crime, poverty, alienation, and an arduous labouring or criminal life hidden beneath the daylight surface. The setting
helps us see the side of London of which most readers were perhaps only dimly
conscious, and we are also introduced to the narrator's feelings.

The narrative, literary element is clearly present. And it is most strong in
his creation of character. In *Dickens and Creativity*, (2008) Dickens's critic
Barbara Hardy finds this remarkable talent for creation of character comes
to Dickens indirectly, through a skill in allowing dialogue to form on its own,
almost as if he is listening to some other level of himself, the unconscious allowance of another voice to form with little "shaping"; he opens his feelings
to the surroundings and lets them guide his "other fashioning." According to
Hardy, Dickens thus uses the narrative structure of a night walk to widen his
personal experience and mood of loneliness to encompass the greater structure
of "houselessness" and social need that was appearing all around him.

The Traveller, the frame-narrator closest to the author in experience,
voice and affect, is not referring directly to creative work but he makes
an explicit link between personal need and empathy, demonstrat-
ing it with great energy. The identification of his restlessness and his
"amateur" houselessness with the unrest and real homelessness of city
outcasts is dramatized: the personal "I" becomes the collective "We";
the first lowercase "houselessness" is poetically transformed by sympathetic irony to the companionable "Houselessness"; the adjective
"houseless" is elaborated in moving metonymies. The key words are
ritualistically repeated in the compassionate scenes that unfold: the "fits
and starts" of late drunks, police and cabs in the Haymarket and East
End give way to a stillness in which "the yearning of the houseless mind

would be for any sign of company" and "the houseless eye looked out for lights in windows," there is "a furtive head" in a doorway, a "houseless shadow" on the road to Waterloo bridge, a cheerful tollkeeper, and the suicide-haunted river, on which "the very shadow of the immensity of London seemed to lie oppressively." (42–43)

With Hardy's expert help we can see that in this essay the reader can follow the act of creation of a character in a way that you cannot in a novel. The language leads us to probe the change itself for more meaning. We feel less of a distance between the narrator and "Mr. Houselessness." Dickens is deeply identifying with the homeless people around him. And you are invited into the creation. The use of figurative language reminds me of allegory, a code of the typical and of the representative person or animal. In an allegorical personification, "Mr. Goodness," for instance, is made into a well-dressed, healthy person, say, with an engaging personality, and "Mr. Deceit" becomes a poorly dressed weaselly kind of person. Hardy has shown us that this character, "Houselessness" is a figure for Dickens's deep empathy for the lonely and distressed homeless folk of his city.

> At length these flickering sparks would die away, worn out — the last veritable sparks of waking life trailed from some late pieman or hot-potato man — and London would sink to rest. And then the yearning of the houseless mind would be for any sign of company, any lighted place, any movement, anything suggestive of any one being up — nay, even so much as awake, for the houseless eye looked out for lights in windows.
>
> ****
>
> Walking the streets under the pattering rain, Houselessness would walk and walk and walk, seeing nothing but the interminable tangle of streets, save at a corner, here and there, two policemen in conversation, or the sergeant or inspector looking after his men. [xiii paras 1, 5, 6]

In this essayistic use of characterization we detect the steps toward the creation of a new Pip or a Wemmick or the Orlick of *Great Expectations*. We can see with Hardy's aid how this character is created. The double consciousness we have been following is again at work, character comes, for Dickens, out of a projection of emotion into a context, a shadow self is created through taking the place of others he meets underway under the pressure of his own restlessness. But we also note the awareness of the essayist, the general idea of what we now call "the homeless" taking shape and remaining as idea, London is full of them, and we can see the way it is done, both at the same time.

Virginia Woolf, The Hidden Narrator in "The Death of the Moth"

Virginia Woolf's poignant "The Death of the Moth" also has a subtle awareness of point of view and character. The narrator is looking out from a room, probably a library (where she has been reading), into a vigorous outside world of labour, natural events, and seasonal change. Her attention falls on the struggles of a moth as it flits about the window. Then she realizes that its life span is almost over, and she watches the gradual diminution of its energy and life force until its inevitable end. As I read this beautiful miniature, I felt strongly that the moth could be one of the more subtle metaphors for a self trapped behind roles or masks or of an inner being left behind in a world that does not give it much credibility, or time, or does not recognize it at all. My evidence for this reading is drawn from the text itself. Some background from other works by Woolf that I had read some time ago (*Waves* and *To the Lighthouse*) also helped.

The moth is quite like a character in a story, and its delicate, vulnerable quality in relation to the concrete presence of the sturdy life outside the window represents a clear contrast and an imbalance of power. The farmer ploughing the fields and the rooks in their intense and noisy social life are so clear, forceful, and present that the moth did not seem to have a chance against them. The imbalance struck me as so highlighted, so noticeable, that it appeared related to Woolf's own subjectivity — like the moth's life, could it also be at risk in an oblivious world? And even though the moth is called a "he," it is hard not to feel some identification between it and the narrator (and "he" is the marker for third-person narration). I think that Woolf could be showing us an allegory of a restricting force preventing self-expression and self-realization and, in the moth's rather heroic end, one of the inevitable results of this imbalance. The moth functions as something like a character and could be representing another of Woolf's selves. One important reason for a fictional "I" in an essay is then the search for a self that is deeper than our restrictive social masks or expectations allow. I think both Didion and Woolf are showing us this possibility.

However, it is one thing to come to an insight about an image like this one and quite another to write an effective paper that argues for it. I think you can now see that proof for this reading could come from biographical research into Woolf's life, from other works she might have written on similar imbalances of power and related themes, or from critics who might have written on this or related subjects. Another of her essays "In Search of a Room of One's Own" deals with similar themes. If you wished to make a case for a specific reading of the moth figure (which appears in her other works), this would be a very useful secondary source. Are there reasons to think that her well-known bouts of depression were at work somewhere in the background of the essay? What imbalances of power in her own life could you find and where would you go to find them?

Further Elements of the Narrative Voice

In previous chapters, we have uncovered additional dimensions of the narrative voice from literary reviews and a number of literary essays. The narrative approach to the organization of an essay may be the most fundamental of all of the three voices, as it allows free use of most of the standard literary points of view, and most elements of content, setting, event, outcome, theme or character development that are handled in a reduced way by the other voices. In the majority of cases however the use of narrative in the essay is limited, especially in the formal voice, because it is framed by the wider agenda of the essay. In the formal essay, higher priority is given to forwarding an idea, an experience, an "assay" of a new or old book, or a critique or insight, or evaluation of some kind. The narrative voice then becomes reduced to an anecdote, a mini-biography, or the recounting of an episode that will support the main critical idea. In these cases it is couched in the third person objective, or occasionally the "I" narrator; and after it, the essay moves from it as illustration or example back to the general idea or wider purpose which the narrative supports.

There are however, other, much more inventive uses of narrative voice in the essay. In these, the essayist experiments with narrative as the organizational envelope of the essay. The difference is that in this wider use of essayistic narrative, the angle of vision, the point of view itself, can be part of a fiction. In this "unframed" narrative voice, the author, like a novelist, can, for instance, be something of a ventriloquist and use point of view to create a character. The voice that is narrating may appear to be the "author," but is not. The events can appear to be true, but are not; the settings appear to be real but may not be. As we will see in the next chapter, Swift is expert at this technique in "A Modest Proposal" and Lamb, as we have seen, is also very good at creating a pseudonym "Elia" through which to speak and to completely make up a setting and characters. With Swift, a formal, objective tone can be fabricated through a false third-person objective point of view, and the same can be done with the "I" narrator. Deictic markers or references to the reader or the immediate context of the writer and reader can also be present, as in a short story, but they are also somewhat fictional or screens for a deeper message. The author's real personality and situation is held in the background. In this use, as reported dialogue can be present, all of the idiomatic expressions of everyday speech can be used: contractions, figures of speech, the twists and turns of conversation and discussion, as the author makes the character appear to be moderating a "real" discussion or a conversation with others, or the reader.

The focus of most of the paragraphs in this second type, is on addressing and persuading an audience, but here the whole of the essay is pointed to this task. Again, the point of view is flexible, it can move the reader away or toward the narrator, away or toward an issue, analysis or topic. There is also a range in this use of narrative: at one pole it can be impersonal and almost scientifically objective; whereas, in narrative essays which enact characters who pretend some kind of social analysis, the essayist can mix voices, or include formality and familiarity. The focus can be on almost any topic. In this second type of narrative voice, the line between fiction and truth is blurred, or fiction itself can become the focus of deeper analysis.

Your Response to The Literary Essay

How do you write a good paper about the kinds of complexity we have just studied and discussed? You now have some tools which you can use to find and evaluate this kind of significance, and analyze the textures of the literary essay. You now know that *coverage* is an important dimension of any essay, including your own. You will need then to keep this standard front and centre when you write, for instance a comparison and contrast type of essay. You need to make sure you have covered the whole of an essay and are not leaving out important elements, facts, issues or points made by the essayist that are significant and could work as confounds of your reading. Coverage is also at work in the amount of quotation you include in your own writing. Beginnings, middles and endings of the work you are analyzing are good places to find the whole of a work. Use them in your own writing.

A good paper will include enough quotation to convince that the whole has indeed been considered. Your focus is usually too narrow if you are dealing with only one episode or statement and not placing it in terms of the whole essay and this can affect the quality of good critical writing about literary works. In addition, you will likely be including *expertise* in your essays. Some of the writers you may be asked to write about will have a "critical apparatus" attached to them, especially if they from a different period or culture than your own. And you may include this expertise. As you now know there are clear rules to this inclusion; the MLA style marks them out for academic papers on literature in some detail. *Structural analysis* is a large part of most literary analysis. We find many types of larger structure in literary works, from plot lines to the working through of changes in a character over the course of a work. And, lastly, uses of *specialized terminology* is one of the strong features of literary criticism and theory and we have been following these means throughout this book.

Art, Life, and the Essay

All of our essayists in this chapter have sensitive, empathic skills in portraying the psychology of the self, and at the same time, a critical dimension; they use narrative techniques to explore both dimensions. Brand discovers a way of getting free of national myths; Bronowski uncovers a somewhat heroic image of the workings of the creative scientific mind of Galileo and corrects our narrative of him. Didion clarifies her life position in relation the expectations of others and begins to explore the difficulty of defining herself in life and narrative. Lamb allows us to see and experience the psychological sources of narrative in tragedy and loss, in the yearning for a better life. Dickens also shows us how he creates character from his own troubles. And, if my reading is on the right track, Woolf allows us to feel the trapped, ephemeral quality of some lives — perhaps on a more general level, that our subjectivity is always at risk in relation to the massive claims of the outside world and social power — a critical viewpoint is clearly present in most of these essays along with the "I" narrator. Much critical ink has been spilled on the reasons for this fictional "I" in novels and short stories — and in essays. The problem is complex, and we have had only a brief time to open the question so that you can see some of its dimensions.

One way to gain a perspective on this possibility of "self-creation" in the essay is to admit that the boundaries between our fictional and real selves are not as tight as we might think. Our tellings about ourselves and our pasts are usually very much like narratives even when we are engaged in casual conversation. Begin any conversation with "When I was four years old," and you will see what I mean. In "real life," we are often caught up in masks or personae that we, or others, relate through narration, as characters in our own story. We often show ourselves to others as such characters, or, sometimes, as Didion shows us, we become characters in narratives made up by others. There are also the many ways that we must live up to our own self-images. Think of the ways you try to convince your teachers or employers that you are diligent and intelligent or your friends that you are fashionable, hot, or cool, or think of what you might wish to project about yourself in the chilly public arena of a courtroom cross-examination. These tellings are usually somewhat idealized versions of what we are, and they also rely on narration and the "I" point of view. Narrative, as Barthes tells us in the quotation which began this chapter, is there "like life itself."

Study Questions

1. What character would you create as most like yourself in an essay? How is this related to the "I" you occasionally use in your own essay writing?
2. What friends (or non friends) do you know who are most clearly acting a role? How would you portray them in an essay about them? Satirically? Sympathetically?

3. Is there an authentic "I" in any of the essays we analyzed?
4. For you what is the value of these literary essays? What can we get out of them that we cannot get out of a more objective, formal type of writing?
5. Where would you place "narrative" as a term. Is it significant? Is it less important that say a scientific report?
6. What do you prefer: the literary essay, a short story, or a formal essay?

Key Terms

Disaspora and diasporic subject
A diaspora refers to the migration of peoples from one culture to others, usually worldwide, and caused by colonization, or warfare, natural disaster, wide starvation or other disruptions. The diasporic subject would be the psychology that arises as a result of such migrations. This subject may, for instance, have a very different view of "nationalism" than someone who was born, raised and matured in one culture in which they stayed.

Dénouement
The relaxation of tension coming after the climax in a work of fiction, the resolution of all problems.

Persona and *nom de plume*
The taking up of an alias through which to write. For Lamb it was "Elia" and there have been many others, James Bond could be thought of as a mask for author Ian Fleming. Well-known writer, Gore Vidal is the *nom de plume* of Edgar Box.

Peripeteia
The reversal of fortune in a drama or work of fiction, usually occurring just before the end and resolution.

Works Cited

Ackroyd, Peter. *Dickens*. London: Mandarin, 1994.

Barnett, George L. *Charles Lamb*, Boston: Twane, 1976.

Barthes, Roland and Lionel Duisit. *Introduction to the Structural Analysis of Narratives, New Literary History*, Vol. 6, No. 2, On *Narrative and Narratives* (Winter, 1975) The Johns Hopkins University Press, pp. 237–272. Web. November 3, 2013. * Originally published in *Communications*, 8 (1966), as "*Introduction à l'analyse structurale des récits.*"

Bronowski, Jacob. "The Reach of Imagination." *Proceedings of the American Academy of Arts and Letters.* 2nd ser. 17, 1967. In *The Norton Reader.* 8th ed. New York: Norton, 1992. 125–32.

Dickens, Charles. "Night Walks." *The Uncommercial Traveller.* N.p., 1860. 125–32. Web. 13 Aug. 2007.

— . *Great Expectations.* London: Penguin, 1985.

Halkett, Anne. Excerpt from *The Autobiography of Anne Lady Halkett.* Ed. John Gough Nichols. Westminster, England: Camden Society, 1875, 19–23. Web. 14 Aug. 2007. See online version, by Ellen Moody, (Aug 16, 2006) Web. June 1, 2011.

Hardy, Barbara. *Dickens and Creativity.* London, GBR: Continuum International Publishing, 2008.

Hazel, Paul. "Narrative: An Introduction." *Paul Hazel.com* Posted April 5, 2007. Accessed Nov. 3, 2013.

Hitchins, Christopher. "The Dark Side of Dickens: Why Charles Dickens was among the best of writers and the worst of men" *The Atlantic* (May 2010 para 6). Web, November 14, 2011.

James, Henry. "The Art of Fiction." 1884. *Partial Portraits.* Ann Arbor: U Michigan P, 1970. 375–408.

Joseph, Mia. "Wondering into Country: Dionne Brand's A Map to the Door of No Return." *Canadian Literature 193,* (Summer 2007): 75–92, 182.

Lamb, Charles *Charles Lamb & Elia,* ed. J. E. Morpurgo. Manchester: Carcanet, 1993.

Lamb, Charles. "Dream-Children: A Reverie." *English Romantic Writers.* Ed. David Perkins. Fort Worth, Harcourt Brace, 1994, pp. 691–93.

Munro, Alice. "The Peace of Utrecht." In *Oxford Book of Canadian Short Stories.* Selected by Margaret Atwood and Robert Weaver. Toronto: Oxford University Press, 1986. 191–206.

Neuman, Shirley. "Autobiography: From Different Poetics to a Poetics of Differences." *Essays on Life Writing.* Ed. Marlene Kadar. Toronto: University of Toronto Press, 1992.

Neuman, Shirley. "Life Writing." *Literary History of Canada: Canadian Literature in English.* Ed. W. H. New. 2nd ed. Vol. 4. Toronto: University of Toronto Press, 1990. 333–70.

7 The Research Essay

With him [Orwell] the essay acquires an edge or anger, a quicker temper, needed to fight for its existence and its values in an era of homogenized discourse, high-impact slogans, and images. (Graham Good, *The Observing Self*, 175)

Sources

Barbara Bengels, "Swift's A Modest Proposal" (2006)
Irwin Ehrenpreis, *Swift: The Man, His Works, and the Age* (1962)
John Richardson, "Swift, A Modest Proposal and Slavery" (2001)
Jonathan Swift, "A Modest Proposal" (1729)
David Wilson, *A History of England* (1967)

Objectives

In this chapter we will look at some ways of researching a problem in reading an essay; we then apply them to help us read and support a paper on a classic essay, Swift's satire, "A Modest Proposal" of 1729. All of the reading on voice, and the critical lore we have so far accumulated can now come into play in our analysis of this text. The result will be an exploration of how to put together a research question and begin the work required to answer it such that it can used in a term paper. In this chapter, we will:

- Return to the academic essay and explore how to evolve a research question in order to support a claim about a literary essay;
- Use the expertise found in history texts, biographies and journal articles to verify some facts about an author and a period and use them to develop your claim;
- Apply this research to an analysis of Swift's "A Modest Proposal"; and
- Propose a method for researching essays and supporting claims based on work with journal articles.

Introduction

In the following discussion I model a formal explication of a literary essay and the research that goes into an advanced reading, showing how to support a claim about the direction of the irony in Jonathan Swift's "A Modest Proposal." In my reading of the essay, I came across an acute problem. Finding a solution needed library research, much reworking of a theme in the attempt to come to some "finished thought" about Swift. Note especially the distinctions I make between the *primary text*, (Swift's essay) and *secondary texts*, (Ehrenpreis, Bengels, and Wilson) — these are the additional sources I used to help understand this essay. In addition note how these sources have been included through framing of both run-on and block quotations.

Researching the Essay: The Mask in Swift's "A Modest Proposal"

Jonathan Swift (1667–1745) has a well-deserved reputation as a deadly ironist. *Gulliver's Travels* is probably the best-known example of his skill. Born in Ireland, he left home to seek a more promising career in England. He soon became deeply involved in English and Irish politics and became friends with both Addison (his essays often appeared in *The Spectator*) and the other premier satirist of his day, Alexander Pope. When he wrote "A Modest Proposal" (1729), he was in the later phase of his career and at the height of his talent. His acid pen is now at the service of his own downtrodden Irish countrymen.

"A Modest Proposal" gives us an added problem in our reading of essayistic voice: simply put, in this case, it is the *formal voice* that is not what it seems. Swift's use of the then new science and "projector" type of approach, with its authority, general claim or "proposal," and experimental "researcher" tone is a surface or mask behind which we glimpse the change he is really calling for. I hope that you have already read the essay and discovered that the "modest proposal" is bizarre and cruelly ludicrous. Swift's style alerts us to the possibility that this formal voice with its claims to authority is sometimes *not* reliable. The clear satiric note in this essay, and its subject matter, makes it more difficult to read than our earlier essays — it is harder to find its overall intent or implication and it presents a real challenge to prove and support a reading.

We begin with an example of Swift's irony taken from the opening of the essay. In introducing us to his scheme for saving the urchins of "the great city," the narrator tells us:

> The number of souls in this kingdom being usually reckoned one million and a half, of these I calculate there may be about two hundred thousand couple whose wives are breeders; from which number I subtract thirty thousand couples who are able to maintain their own children, although I apprehend there cannot be so many under the present distresses of the kingdom; but this being granted, there will remain an hundred and seventy thousand breeders. (479)

You probably regarded the language with suspicion. Calling wives "breeders" seems insulting and ugly, yet the general tone is positive even progressive, and it is done so matter-of-factly that we almost do not hear the dissonance. But, while there might be a satiric edge, its point is hard to get. Who do you think is the target of this phrase "I calculate there may be about two hundred thousand couple whose wives are breeders"?

Effective irony works by implication. I say to a friend who asks me how I am feeling when really ill, "I'm feeling just great!" and imply that he's a bit stupid for not seeing my real state. You can see that for this kind of irony to work, context is critical. You need to hear the tone of my voice, or see the expression on my face, or be able to refer to a shared situation. What would be the effect if I said this in a hospital emergency room? Within a familiar context, you have a better chance to detect whether "I'm feeling just great!" was meant straight or not. But in "A Modest Proposal," we are confronted with a deep problem. What is the context in which this irony works? Without knowledge of the situation in which it was written it is hard to get Swift's message. The subtitle is not much help; it tells us that the essay was written "For Preventing the Children of Poor People in Ireland from Being a Burden to their Parents or Country, and for Making Them Beneficial to the Public" (478). Does Swift intend a vicious joke made at the expense of these children of the poor, or is his target Irishness? Surely not. But if this is not the case, who is the target of the irony of "A Modest Proposal"?

I think you can see that in order to answer this question satisfactorily, you would need to do some research. The historical context of the conquered Ireland in which Swift wrote "A Modest Proposal" has for all practical purposes disappeared (though its reverberations continue today), and in order to have a chance at getting the precise target of the irony we need to reconstruct some of it. We will be making this reconstruction something of a library research project. We will need to explore the context so that you can understand the literary qualities of the voice that is being used and see a possible solution to the problem of finding Swift's target, and thus the way in which his essay can be placed. Is it a formal essay, or is it something else?

I have used a history text, David Wilson's *History of England,* to help me fill in some of this missing context. My research in this secondary source tells me that the attempts to colonize Ireland were long standing. In 1155, the Catholic Pope Adrian IV authorized the English king Henry II to invade Ireland though he did not send any troops until the King of Leinster asked his assistance in 1166, and despite this nominal authority, only the area around Dublin and other parts of southern Ireland were much affected. Systematic English domination of Ireland began under Elizabeth I — when the English General Charles Blount defeated the Irish under the Earl of Tyrone and claimed all of Catholic Ireland as an English possession (1603). From this time, according to Wilson's *History of England,* England began to look upon Ireland as a colony, a place with expanded possibilities for landholding for her aristocracy and where trade would be controlled — a situation bitterly resented by most of the Irish (333). After England's own Civil War and Cromwell's period of harsh, vindictive rule of Ireland, the British often saw Ireland as a potential location of Catholic subversion and insurrection.

"The Pretender" to whom Swift refers is the son of James II (Halkett's "the duke"), James Edward Stuart, who lived in exile in France and Italy (443). The name "The Pretender" and its history have further relevance to the problem of locating the issues and the irony in Swift's essay. According to Wilson, James II had been deposed in 1688 because of his Catholicism. He sympathized with the Irish Catholics, and in 1689 he used Ireland as a base of operations in an attempt to win back his throne. However, in 1690, he was defeated in a decisive battle in Ireland (The Battle of the Boyne) by the newly chosen Protestant king, William of Orange, whose wife and co-ruler was James's daughter Mary. And as a result of this "uprising," the Irish were severely punished. One part of this punishment was the placing of legal restrictions on the Catholic middle class. But there were also equally harsh economic measures that affected shopkeepers and tradesmen more directly, and these vindictive measures essentially wrecked the Irish economy, (451).

To bring us up to the approximate date of the essay (1729), I read further in Wilson and found that in 1714, Queen Anne, (successor to William and Mary) had died and that a new king, George I, had come to the throne, (471). A new

Whig and Protestant regime would be unlikely to wish to ameliorate the desperate Catholic Irish situation. The material from Wilson's book shows us the disastrous long-term effects of the new laws on Ireland and that its poverty had reached a crisis level. This secondary material has allowed me to understand something of what was at stake in Swift's essay: the English, Protestant control of Ireland, its economic consequences, and the strong need for immediate aid to the suffering Irish.

Returning to our primary text, "A Modest Proposal," things are now a little clearer. I now know who "The Pretender" is and that "popish" refers to a belief in the authority of the Catholic Pope; the "great town" is Dublin. I can now begin to develop my understanding of some of the issues at work. The narrator's use of a rather insulting term for Catholics, "popish" and his use of "the Commonwealth" in a positive way and "the Pretender" in a negative way almost certainly mean that he is on the English and Protestant side — though he appears at first to be offering a benign solution because he begins by showing us the situation quite sympathetically. According to this "projector" (the term for the new amateur scientists and entrepreneurs of the day), Irish mothers are forced to beg for food for their children, and many poor people must leave Ireland to fight in foreign wars as mercenaries or go to the Barbados to work on plantations.

> It is a melancholy object to those who walk through this great town or travel in the country, when they see the streets, the roads, and cabin doors, crowded with beggars of the female-sex, followed by three, four, or six children, all in rags and importuning every passenger for an alms. These mothers, instead of being able to work for their honest livelihood, are forced to employ all their time in strolling to beg sustenance for their helpless infants, who, as they grow up, either turn thieves for want of work, or leave their dear native country to fight for the Pretender in Spain, or sell themselves to the Barbados. (478)

We begin "A Modest Proposal," then, with a fairly credible, sympathetic description of then current Dublin poverty. Given the background we have just explored, the narrator is probably English or pro-English and Protestant, and he is describing the scene in a way that calls for our helpful response. The tone at this stage shows the narrator is using the authoritative voice of the new scientist or amateur investigator who was learning to apply systematic kinds of reasoning to social problems. First, then, according to this new method, we must have an adequate description of the problem. The "I" narrator here is portraying himself positively, and we wonder if it may not be Swift himself talking—he will propose a solution that will make "these children sound, useful members of the commonwealth."

But very soon this reading breaks down. The narrator's language becomes so unusual that we have difficulty believing it to be Swift at all or anyone of sound mind. As we have seen, the first clue is an inappropriate use of a kind of scientific terminology. Statements like "A child just dropped from its dam" (478) and "I calculate that there may be about two hundred thousand couples whose wives are breeders" (479) warn us that something is seriously wrong with this presentation—these are terms used to describe cattle, not human beings. The statistics and calculations are driven home "objectively" in the best New Philosophy style, but this style becomes increasingly provocative. The narrator then drops a bombshell with his proposal that these suffering children should be raised for food.

> I have been assured by a very knowing American of my acquaintance in London, that a young healthy child well nursed is at a year old a most delicious, nourishing, and wholesome food, whether stewed, roasted, baked, or boiled; and I make no doubt that it will equally serve in a fricassee or a ragout. (479)

By now, you can probably detect that the objective tone and its image of authority is a false one—we are being drawn into an upside down world as the narrator, who is using a systematic and quite credible kind of reasoning supported by many facts and figures, proposes more and more horrifying "modest solutions." But what is the point of this startling inversion? Why propose such irrational and bizarre proposals? Is there a caricature here—perhaps of the scientific-economic approach of the narrator? We now have some grasp of the politics of the Irish situation and some idea of the issues at stake, but their specific alignment in this essay yet seems indirect, even obscure. Who is speaking? Would Swift himself propose these things? Is it someone else? To answer these questions and see the full import of the essay and the precise target, we need some more information about Swift himself.

As my experience in the specifics of eighteenth-century literature and history is limited, I thought that a good article or work by experts in this field might help. So I next turned to Irvin Ehrenpreis's *Swift: The Man, His Works, and the Age* (1962), a well-known biography.

From this scholarly work, I gained some further insights into Swift's text. Ehrenpreis shows that Swift often wrote satires for Church of England and Tory causes. From 1690 or so, he was deeply involved in English life and affairs—at one stage he was secretary to Sir William Temple, a court favourite, and writing for *The Spectator*, he was soon well known for his acid pen. The subject of his satire was often the New Learning of science, which he seems to have found pompous and egotistical. But more to our point, Ehrenpreis tells us that in 1714 Swift moved back to Ireland and was given the deanship of St. Patrick's Cathedral in Dublin as a reward for his support of Tory causes. He takes some time to show Swift's state of mind and the conditions he found in Ireland when he was granted this important post.

According to Ehrenpreis, Swift was intensely religious and quite well known in Ireland at this time, and he gradually became deeply immersed in the politics of the Established Church — The Anglican Church of England in Ireland. But when George I came to the throne, the Tories had fallen, and the Whigs had now gained power. Thus, Swift too had fallen from grace in England and was now far away from his favourite centres of social life and the protections of power. As his knowledge of Ireland's plight increased, he began to write against the newly ascendant Whigs — quite a different thing than writing from the vantage point of power. Ehrenpreis shows that after a period of silence, during which he gradually won over his distrustful Irish colleagues in the Church, he turned to new problems and new oppressions — particularly the economic plight of the Irish Catholics. And by 1729, he was becoming very frustrated in his quest to help the Irish poor.

For ten years or so prior to "A Modest Proposal," Swift had been writing tracts desperately urging economic change in Ireland — "The Drapier's Letters" were, for instance, a brilliant series dedicated to improving the plight of the Irish middle class. The year he wrote "A Modest Proposal" was also a year of critical shortage of food, and the crops had failed for a third time in a row, "unemployed weavers were feeding off grains and blood from the slaughterhouses. Shopkeepers who had been supporting their families respectably were now beggars." A pamphlet by another author written in August 1729 told of the city streets being "'crowded with living spectres' who wandered about, searching for food. 'If they happen to hear of the death of a horse, they run to it as to a feast'" (Ehrenpreis 627).

Let us return now to our narrator and his use of irony. You may have realized that this narrator's attitudes cannot be Swift's. The political alignment of the narrator and the biographical material summarized above show clearly that he could not hold such attitudes. Swift's impulse surely is to help his starving people. But you might still ask, "Who else's attitude could it be?" With this research behind us, all that is left now, is to put the last part of my claim in place and show you that this voice is a cleverly constructed *mask*, a *fictional* character, behind which we can just detect Swift's real message.

The Language of Extended Irony

If the history of the period tells us of a desperate situation in which Swift was sympathetically immersed, and if our research has shown that the narrator cannot be Swift, then we can conclude more certainly that this narrator is part of a fiction — or perhaps it is a "creative nonfiction." The ironic overtone comes from Swift's brilliant ability to mimic. He is adept at mimicking some of the features of the formal scientific voice of his day and the official language of English colonial power. I want to list a few of Swift's uses of this terminology and social register to show you the range of his skill.

There is for instance, the collegiality and elegance of speech of one "expert" recognizing another,

> A very worthy person, a true lover of his country, and whose virtues
> I highly esteem, was lately pleased in discoursing on the matter to
> offer a refinement upon my scheme. (481)

"Esteem," "virtue," "lately pleased in discoursing," and "worthy" show a highly refined sensibility, but the cruelty of the "scheme" makes the credibility of these claimed virtues highly doubtful. The target of the irony is this pretentious style itself. What would be the point of attacking such an elegant use of specialist language? Why would Swift use this cutting technique of satirical mimicry?

In another example, there is Swift's easy (and highly ironic) rendering of the formal language of accounting or economics:

> I have already computed the charge of nursing a beggar's child (in
> which list I reckon all cottagers, labourers, and four fifths of the
> farmers) to be about two shillings per annum, rags included. (480)

Two shillings per year was a small amount of money even in those times, and "rags included" is telling; the effect relies on the contrast of "rags" with the language of formal accounting ("computed," "reckon," "four fifths," and "two shillings per annum"). Only an inhuman and morally blind mind would compute the cost of a beggar's rags and talk about clothing beggars this way. Who is this speaker? How uncaring! Isn't this about as cynical about poverty as you can get?

We can now see that this irony is self-reflexive. It is showing up the speaker himself and doing so in a devastating way. What do you make of the following example? Again, keep in mind that the narrator is evaluating his own scheme for raising children for food:

... it is not improbable that some scrupulous people might be apt to censure such a practice (although indeed very unjustly) as a little bordering upon cruelty; which, I confess, hath always been with me the strongest objection against any project, how well soever intended. (481)

First, there is the elegant double negative, "not improbable," and then the oversensitive qualification, "a little bordering upon cruelty," and, lastly, his showy parading of his own truthfulness and compassion in the phrase starting with "I confess." The "projector" is using scientific terms correctly and has an impeccably polite and formal style, but are they appropriate in this context of Irish poverty and despair? Is this proposal only "a little bordering on" cruelty? Is it not the ultimate form of cruelty?

Answering the preceding questions about this narrator might help you determine his identity. What kind of character would make such a proposal? From what vantage point of authority or power is this person speaking? From what cultural viewpoint do you think he is seeing the Irish poor? Would you guess he was Irish? Or is he likely to be English?

Another level of support for such a reading can come from expertise in the specific work. This can usually be found in critical journals, or monographs. They pose a slightly different challenge for research than does a biography or a general history. Finding an article or excerpt on your specific research question is difficult. Here is Barbara Bengel's view of the viciousness of the image of the projector from her article on "Swift's A Modest Proposal."

Right from the first paragraph, he begins alluding to the sartorial state of the Irish as he writes of "Beggars of the Female Sex, followed by three, four, or six children, all in rags" (Swift 502; emphasis added). By the fourth paragraph he incorporates a double meaning when he writes of children "exactly at one Year old [...] who instead of wanting Food and Raiment for the rest of their Lives; they shall, on the contrary, contribute to the Feeding, and partly to the Cloathing, of many Thousands" (Swift 503). It is impossible for us on a first reading to see cloathing in this context as a noun rather than as a verb; on a second reading, however, his real meaning is clear — and horrifying. Throughout the rest of the essay there are at least seven references to clothing as clothing, per se: in paragraph 7 he speaks of "the charge of Nutriments and Rags (Swift 504); in paragraph 18 he refers to the "foreign Fineries" of the "several plump young girls in [...] Town (Swift 506); in paragraph 32, he worries about how other projectors will "find Food and Raiment, for a Hundred Thousand useless Mouths and Backs" (Swift 509).

One must question why Swift felt it appropriate to use clothing as a vehicle for his satire.... It is obvious from this quote that Swift had used clothing symbolically before writing "A Modest Proposal," (in fact he had written the "Drapier" letters five years earlier) but it is in this essay that he can exploit its usage most appropriately for his subject, a subject that deals with the ultimate exploitation of children — and of man's ultimate misuse of man.

Bengel's reading is somewhat to the side of the specific claim that the target is the abstract, scientific rationalist discourse of "the Projector." Parts of it, however might yet be used to support my claim that this is a satire of the scientific view and the horrors it can produce, both in real life and in language. She shows that Swift has clearly written satires about the differences in class and clothing before "A Modest Proposal" and the value put on clothing as a distinction of class by the English. The use of this clothing metaphor to show the "ultimate exploitation of children" could have relevance to my claim that this inhumanity is the core of the satire and that any language that describes it in a rational, reasoning way is likely part at least of the way in which the colonial system maintained it. But the connection offered by Bengel's text is a little thin.

Returning to the library, other sources promised more relevance; the precise reference that would offer support of my claim was proving difficult to find. You can often find clues to the solution of a research problem in articles that are not quite on target. Here is another example of an article in the journal *Essays in Criticism*, for October 2001. Although the author, John Richardson, writes about an undercurrent of guilt about slavery in this work, not the specific claim about the "scientific projector," he does summarize recent scholarly work on just the claim I am making:

Scholars have followed up many of the references in the proposal, but this has usually taken the form either of noting and querying specific allusions, or of identifying the ironic proposer as a parody of one or another type of contemporary speculative economist. Thus, Hermann J. Real and Heinz J. Vienken list a number of suggested sources for the cannibalism, and offer a new possible source in a traveller's account of the treatment of offspring as commodities. As for the proposer himself, George Wittkowsky's early identification in him of the kind of thinking by which "the labourer had come to be regarded as a commodity" has been generally accepted, and modern commentaries frequently contain confident asides concerning the proposal's "savage parody of contemporary economic writing."(405)

Checking the footnote attached to this paragraph, I was able to find the reference, to Wittkowsky and Kelly:

> George Wittkowsky, "Swift's Modest Proposal: The Biography of a Georgian Pamphlet," *Journal of the History of Ideas*, 4 (1943), 80; Patrick Kelly, "Conclusions by no Means Calculated for the Circumstances and Condition of Ireland": Swift, Berkeley and the Solution to Ireland's Economic Problems, in Aileen Douglas, Patrick Kelly and Ian Campbell Ross (eds.), *Locating Swift: Essays from Dublin on the 250th Anniversary of the Death of Jonathan Swift, 1667–1745* (Dublin, 1998, 49).

Investigation of some of the available journal articles on Swift, has, then, already made my idea that this was a satire of the scientist of the day, a little more precise. With the above reference, I would now be able to support my view of him as "a savage parody of economic writing," and thus that the particular type of science (18th century versions of economics) was the likely target. There is also a promise that I could go a little further and find the particular economist.

Conclusion

Swift's extended use of irony shows again one of the narrative possibilities of the literary essay. While the situation and the language is likely part of the milieu, this particular "projector" character looks fictional in "A Modest Proposal," and we detect the construction of a formal voice, though one that is absurd. The *persona* or character of the "projector" is so well crafted that you might at first have had a hard time believing that he was not Swift. His formal, authoritative (probably English) voice is a mask, and the "I" speaking it is like the voice of a character much as in a short story or novel. Swift is using the first person point of view, not to espouse his own position but to create a fictional, and entirely convincing, villain.

We seem to have broken the "non fiction" rule of the essay, and are now entirely in the mind of a character. Swift's essay could then be "troubling" the genre of the critical essay. The essay is more than an ironic portrait — technically, an example of extended irony. Swift is mimicking the formal voice of an officious English or Anglo-Irish Whig "projector." But he may also be mimicking the critical essay as such. Through this device he can show up the moral faults of both the English position and the new genre of scientific writing about society, especially economics texts. Swift is telling us that no amount of Locke's "New Science" can help if you cannot feel the depth of human suffering involved. In fact, any effort made from the point of view of formal reasoning and economics alone is going to make the Irish situation much worse. The "distance" of the new scientific language, and its form in a "report" or a "research proposal," that is supposedly "objective," is thus satirized — it now seems less helpful and more like a way of masking a deep antagonism to the Irish. It is a thin disguise for cruelty, profit-mongering, and cultural hatred. Through caricature and overstatement, Swift shows us that this proposal via rational science is unhinged because it is not attached to any human feeling and covers frightening cultural biases.

Oddly, this self-damning image of the projector was so convincing that when I did see a possible solution, I momentarily felt the intensity of Swift's feelings. Creating such a mask must have required a strong check on his own outrage. A familiar level appears to be there, then, but Swift is holding it back from direct expression. We must decipher a voice that is being "thrown" into a character just as a ventriloquist throws his voice into a dummy. And in order to arrive at Swift's moral disgust and the reasons for it, we have to undo the ventriloquism.

In the preceding explication, the problems of the formal voice in the essay, and whether it is believable were central. This irony had to be undone and interpreted before the essay could be understood. A good student essay could be written on it. Note the way in which I tracked down information about Swift and his period from outside sources like a biography, a history text and two journal articles. Not a great deal of work, but it did turn up some useful material to support my claim. What do you think of the solution — the notion of irony described above?

But I think you can now see that the narrative techniques of irony, fiction and characterization can be powerful additions to an essay's meaning, and could make interesting themes in your own writing. Those of the past almost require commentary. For now, simply note the pattern of (1) finding a problem, (2) posing a solution, and (3) supporting a solution through effective quotation from both the *primary* and *secondary* texts.

Use of Secondary Sources: and Research in Historical Context

If you recall, uncovering Swift's extended ironic portrait was made doubly difficult because Swift assumes that his readers will understand the context in which he was working. "A Modest Proposal" includes references to current Anglo-Irish politics, social tensions caused by the recent dynastic wars, the crisis state of the middle class in Ireland, the Irish emigration to the plantations in the Barbados, an acrimonious theological and legal conflict between Irish and English Protestants and Catholics, the new language of economic science, Swift's changing position on the Irish question, and his past reading and writing. Solving the problems of understanding past contexts like these is an arduous task and is one of the goals that literary scholars set themselves. Such skills are the ground for many areas of literary and humanities research and for literary criticism.

Read through the following quotation from Wilson's *History of England.* Think about how it might be used in a paper so that it would support a reading of Swift's irony. It has relevance to understanding the first paragraph of "A Modest Proposal." How could it be used to throw light on the general ironic meaning of Swift's essay? In addition think about what parts could be paraphrased, summarized, or quoted directly in pressing forward your argument.

Here is what Wilson says about the results of James II's failure at the Battle of the Boyne. James II had tried to wrest back the crown that he lost in the Bloodless Revolution of 1688. In that battle, William of Orange, husband of James's Protestant daughter Mary, had defeated James and the English were merciless in their retribution:

> The Irish received condign [suitable] punishment. They were hated and feared, both as Catholics and rebels, and England began a policy of ruthless repression and of impregnable Protestant ascendancy. Henceforth, no Catholic could hold office, sit in the Irish Parliament, or vote for its members. He could enter no learned profession save medicine. He was subject to unjust and discriminatory taxation, he suffered legal disabilities which made it difficult for him to go to law against a Protestant, and he was excluded from almost every means of acquiring wealth, knowledge, or influence....
>
> There was also a repressive economic code. The Irish were excluded from trade with the colonies, nor could colonial products come to Ireland except by way of England. Thus Ireland's shipping was all but destroyed; her many fine harbours brought her little profit. A prosperous trade in exporting cattle and sheep to England was ended....
>
> The mass of the population was thus compelled to wring a precarious subsistence from the soil. (451)

Just to refresh your memory, here are some relevant paragraphs from "A Modest Proposal." What can Wilson's material help you conclude about the narrator who is expressing them?

> It is a melancholy object to those who walk through the great town or travel in the country, when they see the streets, the roads, and cabin

doors, crowded with beggars of the female-sex, followed by three, four, or six children, all in rags and importuning every passenger for an alms. These mothers, instead of being able to work for their honest livelihood, are forced to employ all their time in strolling to beg sustenance for their helpless infants, who, as they grow up, either turn thieves for want of work, or leave their dear native country to fight for the Pretender in Spain, or sell themselves to the Barbados.... therefore, reckoning a year after Lent, the markets will be more glutted than usual, because the number of popish infants is at least three to one in this kingdom; and therefore it will have on other collateral advantage, by lessening the number of Papists among us. (518–520)

One way would be to introduce the source and the general idea of the source of the above material from Wilson in such a way that it leads, through a mixture of paraphrase and summary, to a relevant block quotation taken from his material. This is called a "frame" of the secondary source. Commenting on the quotation afterward is a good way of maintaining the frame, clearly showing the line of difference between your own voice and that of your secondary sources. In general you should take about four sentences to lead up to the points you want your reader to see in a long, block quotation. Remember the Catholic-Protestant conflict is a key that would allow you to eventually establish the narrator's English and anti-Catholic attitude, so this material is quite important. Use of the material above uncovers the narrator's real position. There are many ways in which secondary material like Wilson's can be integrated into your writing, but each of the ways, (summary, paraphrase, run-in quotation, or block quotation) has a different degree of emphasis. Too much quotation can obscure your own ideas or indicate that you do not have any on the topic; too little quotation can indicate weak or too little research. Direct block quotation of relevant material that is well integrated with your explication effectively emphasizes the importance of the ideas it contains and does so with a minimum of interruption of the flow of your argument.

You might now be interested enough in Swift's life and ideas that you want to check up on these attempts to find his position. I have shown you the process through which difficult implications and problems in reading period essays can be clarified and how you can get a start at finding issues and support an interpretation through research. Identify points you are puzzled by (difficult words or allusions), and use them to guide your research into the essay's contexts and voices. There are texts available that can help solve the interpretive problems you are likely to encounter. Most of the questions will mean that you will need more information than can be gleaned from an encyclopedia or dictionary — or

Wikipedia. Use works by experts in the field as sources for a reconstruction of obscure issues and ideas in essays and for helping you construct a possible interpretation or explication of them in a useful, well-supported paper.

Study Questions

1. What do you think of the realism of Swift's character? Is he only a work of fiction? Or is it a realistic portrait? Perhaps you find it so bizarre that you could not really hold his proposal as ever being true. If this is the case is it an ineffectual piece of fiction?
2. Could you write a piece of satire similar to Swift's? If so who would you direct it to and for what end and for what reasons?
3. What friends (or non-friends) do you know who are most clearly acting a role? How would you portray them in an essay about them? Satirically? Ironically? Sympathetically?
4. Comment on the limits of the phrase "a true story, well told." Is it an adequate definition of Swift's essay?
5. How could you make this essay into an episode in a gothic novel?

Key Terms

Irony
Variously defined and of many types. J. A. Cuddon's definition in *Dictionary of Literary Terms and Literary Theory* is five pages long. Briefly, the word stems from the Greek word for *dissimulation*, saying one thing but meaning another. As Cuddon has it, irony is more refined than mockery and satire. Most forms of irony involve, "the perception or awareness of a discrepancy or incongruity between words and their meaning, or between actions and their results, or between appearance and reality. In all cases there may be an element of the absurd and the paradoxical," (430). Swift is an expert ironist, he says one thing but means something entirely different. "A Modest Proposal" is a good example of *extended irony.*

Satire
Like irony, satire is defined by a mocking attitude but a more intensely critical tone toward some targeted subject or person. Satire is generally considered the more vulgar of the two "mockeries." It can descend to lower registers, and can be baldly humorous, reshaping its subject into a wildly idiotic or stumbling caricature. Some reputations do not survive good satire.

Caricature

Dickens's Gradgrind, or Pecksniff, are caricatures of the company boss or a money grubbing hypocrite respectively. The caricature is the favourite form of the newspaper cartoonist, and the form seems to delight in bringing out faults by making them larger, more grotesque and more visible than in real life.

The middle voice

A phrase often used to describe the 18th Century essayist, Joseph Addison. Addison is an intermediary. In *The Spectator*, he generally summarizes the current news about events in philosophy, science, literature, and art to an audience that does not know much about them. His position is closer to your own since he is quite like a (good) student who is making a report on a matter he is learning about. Unlike Bacon, Bronowski or Carson though he does not take the position of an expert; rather, he is an informed reader who is telling us what he has read and thought about this reading. When he adds his own response to the subject at hand, he puts himself more squarely between his reader and his sources. He comments on a formal treatise he has found interesting, a newly minted poem, a scientific discovery, or a new piece of music — and he is a good commentator because he keeps us interested. Addison's voice is thus in a middle register between formality and familiarity.

Works Cited

Bengels, Barbara. "Swift's A Modest Proposal," *The Explicator*, 65:1, 13–15, 2006. Web. Nov. 27, 2013.

Cuddon, J. A. *Dictionary of Literary Terms and Literary Theory*. London: Penguin Reference, 1998.

Ehrenpreis, Irwin. *Swift: The Man, His Works, and the Age*. Harvard: Harvard University Press, 1962. Web. Nov. 27, 2013.

Richardson, John. "Swift, *A Modest Proposal* and Slavery." *Essays in Criticism*, October 2001, Vol. 51 Issue 4, pp. 404–423. Web, Nov. 28, 2013.

Swift, Jonathan. "A Modest Proposal" in *The Norton Reader*. Peterson, Linda H., [*et alia*] Eds. Shorter 13th Edition. New York: Norton, 2012. 478–84.

Wilson, David. *A History of England*. New York: Holt, Rinehart and Winston, 1967.

8 Advanced Study: Essayism and Creative Nonfiction

Instead of imposing a discursive order on experience, the essay lets its discourse take the shape of experience. (Graham Good, *The Observing Self*, 7)

Sources
Philip Gerard, *Creative Nonfiction* (1996, 2004)
Graham Good, *The Observing Self: Rediscovering the Essay* (1988)
Lee Gutkind, "What is Creative NonFiction?" (2013)
Thomas Harrison, *Essayism: Conrad, Musil and Pirandello* (1992)
Margaret Singer and Nicole Walker, *Bending Genre* (2013)
Paul Woolridge, "Activist Essayism" (2012)

Objectives
In this chapter we look at a variety of critical perspectives on the essay. The essay has, as we have seen, a long and brilliant past, and if we can say with Graham Good that Montaigne began its modern form, then writers have been experimenting with it at least since its inception in the 16th century. One thing

we have learned over the last seven chapters is that the essay is a shape shifter. Essayists use elements like register, figurative language, reverse endings, characterization, general and specific terms, and point of view creatively. We have found rich interactions between familiar, formal and narrative voices in many of the essays we have studied. In this last chapter we look at some critical positions on this hybridity. Our question will be whether we can place the essay in a new category, "creative nonfiction" or whether it resists this placement. This will help us go the next step toward finding at least a working definition. In this chapter, we will:

- Evaluate the idea with which we began: that the essay is "anti-genre";
- Study the place of narrative art in the essay through the work of theorists and writers like Good, Harrison, Gerard, Singer, and Woolridge;
- Place the voices in the essay in relation to a newer form, "Creative Nonfiction"; and
- Propose a model of the essay based on the essays we have now closely read, analyzed and written.

Introduction

Creative nonfiction, essayism, the literary periods, postmodernism, literary criticism, literary theory, these are terms we have been touching on throughout this book. This chapter will introduce you to a segment of current theory about the essay. In an introductory text like this, we will not be going into this theory in great depth, but will use it to help you develop themes and build up your stock of literary terms and critical ideas for use in your own essays, and to help you come to your own decisions about essay form and style.

The critical concept of voice we have been discussing has a number of implications. One is that the three voices can be found in many different kinds of writing other than the roster of "essays" included in collections like *The Broadview Reader* or *The Norton Reader*. The titles are telling. Essays *in sich*, essays as such, or as a writing procedure distinguished from say reports, memoirs, op-ed pieces, novels, journalism, or journal articles, form only a small part of these readers. Many of the prose selections in them are excerpted from larger forms like monographs or books. However, as many theorists of the essay have recognized, essayistic forms exist within other forms. We find an essayistic, polyphonic type of writing in many guises in almost all prose. Theorists call this juxtaposition of voices by a number of terms; "essayism" (Harrison), "literary nonfiction," (Lounsberry) "creative non-fiction," (Gutkind, Gerard) "activist essayism" (Woolridge) are all attempts to find a critical lexicon and concepts for the innovative aesthetic that can occur when a writer places the familiar, formal and narrative voices in juxtaposition.

Essayism

For critic Thomas Harrison, in *Essayism: Conrad, Musil and Pirandello*, (1992) the essay is an extraordinary form, and one that has not been well understood. He has developed the term "essayism" to describe the essayist's activism; their ability to change its form and procedure, sometimes radically. As we stated at the beginning of the book, for Harrison the essay is "anti generic" — when followed through its history it does not settle into a definitive "genre" once and for all time; for Harrison, each "master practitioner" takes it up anew.

> The essay allows for these flexible perspectives, freely pursuing whatever diction, rhetoric, or supporting evidence its argument appears to require (whether factual or fictitious, exemplifying or analogical, ironic or earnest). In fact, to judge by its master practitioners from Montaigne through Roland Barthes, we might say that the essay possesses no definitive mode of procedure. What, if anything, the essayistic styles of the last four hundred years have shared is precisely a rejection of fixed, established, and authoritative literary method. (Thomas Harrison, *Essayism*, 2)

Harrison pictures the essay as a "free form" with few if any rules. But his range of works appears quite selective. The essayists he uses above are "master practitioners," but how did he arrive at this high evaluation? Roland Barthes (1915–1980), for instance, was one of the great French poststructuralist critics with works like *Mythologies* (1957) and *S/Z*, (1970). *Mythologies* is a collection of brilliant essays that showed the complex narrative structures that underlie popular cinema like the James Bond movies, popular magazines like "Paris Match," and local wrestling matches. Montaigne, as we know, is a famous originator of the familiar essay. The "master practitioners" on whom Harrison's text is based, Conrad, Musil and Pirandello, show that his choice of essays is selective as all three are canonical writers. Is Harrison's "essayism" then a statement that can be applied only to the established literary essay, those that have passed through the rigours of extensive critical analysis to become part of the accepted literary canon?

In many texts defined as "essays" in the collections we are drawing from, we find something quite different from the rejection of a stable form Harrison puts forward. Often, we have found an opposite tendency. Carson, Bronowski, Greenblatt, and Visser strive to meet the requirements and expectations of just such a "standard, definitive, authoritative" form and method. In "The Skewed Path: Essaying as Un-Methodical Method" (1988), another theorist of the essay, Lane Kauffmann, even while articulating the essay's variability, recognizes that it is "now the predominant form of writing in the human sciences," and that "it cannot avoid the challenge to define itself according to the prevailing standards of scientific knowledge and method" (66). If Harrison is writing about *literary* essays, and the shape of the *academic* essay has settled into an accepted and different procedure — it, at least, could not be included as literature. Working academics write using forms that include: consistent rules for gathering, laying out, and sequencing data or research, standards of proof, complete inclusion of evidence, rules of citation, uses of a specific terminology, and logical development. And most academic journals have a format to which prospective writers must adhere. Would the essay as it is now written in university and by countless students qualify as the type of essay pointed to by Harrison? Perhaps the academic essay is not, by Harrison's definition, an essay at all — perhaps it is closer to a report or, for students at least, merely an onerous exercise. On the other hand, if a form does not allow for the experimentation and innovation that Harrison sees as its essence, we can ask whether the disciplined academic essay has become a somewhat forced, repetitive, and uninspiring form. I would guess that you have had the urge to break out and write in a way that was more organic, more anti-genre, more personal, more inclusive than allowed in a required paper on a required theme in a required manner in a required course — you may wish at times to reject the "fixed, established, and authoritative literary methods" set down by manuals telling you how to write essays.

Taking a cue from Harrison, Paul Woolridge's concept of "activist essayism" develops this "break out" quality of the essay, but places the experimentation within a rhetorical, persuasive dimension. Woolridge notes that many critics have grappled with the problem of how to define the "activist essay." He cites the titles of works by well-known critics: Good's *The Observing Self*; Hardison's "Binding Proteus," Kauffmann's "The Skewed Path: Essaying as Unmethodical Method"; *Situations* by Sartre, *Prisms* by Adorno, *Illuminations* by Benjamin, and *Spurs* by Derrida. These titles alone, (plus their contents), are added evidence of the variability of the essay. For Woolridge, the reason for this variation is that essayists are personally engaged with the form and are using techniques of rhetoric to grapple with an audience in order to convince them that a pressing problem exists (or does not), or that their solution is the right one. They also are not interested in meeting formal expectations. For Woolridge, essay writers are more pragmatic about genre, and any stylistic experimentation is a way of convincing readers that their stand is the right one. For Woolridge, essays are more speech acts than researched facts, more about convincing others than a report, more actively deictic than formal and impersonal — the good essayist puts herself on the line and writes to change the minds of an audience. The procedure is, as he notes, to actively maintain freedom of thought, insight, or perception and their expression:

Apparent in all these titular formulations is both the overarching sense of the essay's freedom — the autonomy to observe, shape, pursue, affirm, think, reflect, critique, locate, look through, take up, reveal — and the implicit conception of the essay as an active form. That is, the essay is not simply a literary object, not merely the end product of the act of writing things called essays, but an intellectual act premised on individual action, and thus reflective of a discursively active mode of "engaging" with the world, an activity of evaluative assaying rightly named "essayism," or what I submit we refer to (non-politically) as "activist essayism." (1)

For Woolridge, as for Harrison, the essayist is not constrained by the rules of writing or the supposed form of the essay; he or she is constrained only by the need to convince an audience that a theme, affirmation, revelation, solution, interpretation, insight or thought is in fact worth paying attention to and that we should give assent to it. If their "active essay" procedure works, then the essay is successful. In our terms the essayist can use whatever voice or blend of voices that will convince an audience.

For Graham Good, the essay can be best positioned as an individual view of the world After a well-known classification of the form into four types, *the travel essay, the moral essay, the critical essay, and the autobiographical essay.* Good points out, for instance, that the travel essay is essentially a "peripatetic or ambulatory" form. It is a mini-journey taken with chance discovery in mind, (xii). This, as we know, is a hallmark of the essay, but for Good, its approach is fundamentally idiosyncratic, and individual.

Ultimately, the essayist's authority is not his learning, but his experience. The essay's claim to truth is not through its consistency in method and result with an established body of writing. Its method is not collaborative and its findings do not need corroboration. Its claim is to yield flexibly to individual experience. Instead of imposing a discursive order on experience, the essay lets its discourse take the shape of experience. (7)

This openness is also hybrid in nature and includes attention to artistic and aesthetic values. Further, the essay,

... offers aesthetic knowledge, that is to say knowledge which is organized artistically rather than scientifically or logically. The essay's open-ended approach to experience is balanced by aesthetic pattern and closure. It is not a work of art in the full sense, but a kind of hybrid of art and science, an aesthetic treatment of material that could otherwise be studied scientifically or systematically. The subject matter of the essay is constantly being taken up by disciplines like psychology, sociology and the recent attempts at systematic poetics. (14–15)

Good's more aesthetic account sees the essay as grounded in an individual experience of the world, an "observing self" and it is thus, a radically free form poised uncertainly between collectivist conventions and individual breakthroughs. An essay, following another well known definition by, Georg Lukács, is "an intellectual poem" (16) but for Good the essayist is forwarding the subjective experience, so has the power to undermine systematic positions.

Most of these ideas on the essay were worked out in the '70s to the '90s and in this period, theorists discovered something very appealing in the essay. It was a radical form that had been seriously overlooked. Earlier critics like Lukács and Woolf, and later ones like Good, and Harrison rescued this kind of prose from the *"belle-lettrist"* category, where it was seen as a lighter and refining entertainment, and reinstated it as a serious literary form that could be collected, studied, learned from and which presented many crucial problems of definition.

Essays, Creative Fiction, and Creative Nonfiction

One image that emerges from these earlier theories is that the essayist is a disruptive *collagist* or *bricoleur*. It is an appealing image. The essayist would then share ground with the breakthrough poets, artists, sculptors, film makers, and critics of the 1910s and 1920s like Gaugin, Schwitters, Picasso, or Brecht. And current trends in essay criticism connect with this sense that the essay is an experimental form, and much like a work of art. The approach has been taken up anew recently in the position, (almost now a "movement") called "creative nonfiction." The "essayism" idea and the "creative nonfiction" idea share some agreements about the true shape of the essay as shape shifter and collage. But, how would such positions place what Good calls the "critical essay"?

Here is how one of the practitioners of *creative nonfiction*, Lee Gutkind, defines and raises the banner of, a new anti-genre.

> What is Creative Nonfiction?
> The banner of the magazine I'm proud to have founded and I continue to edit, *Creative Nonfiction*, defines the genre simply, succinctly, and accurately as "true stories well told." And that, in essence, is what creative nonfiction is all about.

In some ways, creative nonfiction is like jazz — it's a rich mix of flavors, ideas, and techniques, some of which are newly invented and others as old as writing itself. Creative nonfiction can be an essay, a journal article, a research paper, a memoir, or a poem; it can be personal or not, or it can be all of these.

The words "creative" and "nonfiction" describe the form. The word "creative" refers to the use of literary craft, the techniques fiction writers, playwrights, and poets employ to present nonfiction — factually accurate prose about real people and events — in a compelling, vivid, dramatic manner. The goal is to make nonfiction stories read like fiction so that your readers are as enthralled by fact as they are by fantasy.

Perhaps though, this amalgam of "true story" and creative use of narrative, (literary craft) is what really sets this approach apart from essayism. There yet seems room in Gutkind's description for essays as a separate form — he says "it can be an essay" and we gather that other essays are not creative nonfiction. Does the essay as we have read it fit into this new literary category? Or does it share some of its elements, but not others? Philip Gerard, in *Creative Nonfiction: Researching and Crafting Stories from Real Life,* defines creative nonfiction as a deeper form of journalism, as journalism with an added resonance. We have looked at a number of essays that analyze a subject through finding a wider or deeper structure, and for Gerard, this is one of the principles of good creative nonfiction. But there is more to it. He finds five "hallmarks" that define this new hybrid genre:

First, it has an apparent subject and a deeper subject.... Second, and partly because of the duality of the subject, such nonfiction is released from the usual journalistic requirement of *timeliness*. Long after the apparent subject ceases to be topical, the deeper subject and the art that expresses it remain vital.... Third, creative nonfiction is narrative, it always tells a good story.... Fourth, creative nonfiction contains a sense of *reflection* on the part of the author. The underlying subject has been percolating through the writer's imagination for some time, waiting for the right outlet. It is *finished* thought.... Fifth, such nonfiction shows serious attention to the craft of writing. It goes far beyond the journalistic "inverted pyramid" style — with interesting turns of phrase, fresh metaphors, lively and often scenic presentation, a shunning of clichés, and obvious endings, a sense of control over nuance, accurate use of words, and a governing aesthetic sensibility. (7–11)

Gerard's text is something of a textbook, he is a writer, and teaches both the writing of fiction, and creative non-fiction in a creative writing class. But his ideas are also a refreshing commentary on most essay writing and they align in some ways with the ideas forwarded by Good and Harrison. His definitions of creative nonfiction have a number of essayistic features. In the terms we have been developing, according to Gerard, creative nonfiction should use the "I" narrator, and develop its story using the familiar voice. We have seen much of this in essays like Didion's "On Going Home" and Rhenisch's "A World of Water." Gerard's guidelines also include uncovering "the deeper idea"; that is, nonfiction stories should break out of the limit of "timeliness" (the journalistic ethic of topicality or "news"); and especially that the subject should be *reflected* upon, or present "finished thought." As we have seen these are characteristics of the formal, critical voice couched in a slightly different way; essays like Bronowski's or texts like Carson's certainly present critical, "finished thought." And, last, he forwards the strong rule that creative nonfiction is a species of narrative art — thus what we have called the narrative voice is also included. Chapter 6 uncovered this art in Lamb's "Dream Children," where we found a persuasive example of narrative technique, the surprise ending.

This summary of the elements of "creative nonfiction" may then adequately describe both the "literary essay" and at least some instances of the "formal essay." But Gerard's inclusion of *narrative* in such a careful, appreciative, but limited way might also define a limit of "creative nonfiction" and help our attempt to define its relation to the essay. Bacon, Astell, Gould, and Bronowski fit in some ways in the category of creative nonfiction — while they use a formal, methodical, factual and logical kind of approach, (they are trying for truth not fiction) they sometimes do juxtapose it to either familiarity or narrative and can include a "true story well told." But the creative nonfiction of a practitioner like Anderson's "Man on the Tracks" shows a compelling difference — none of the four authors above would experiment with narrative art in this way. In the following excerpt, note that the layout has the freedom of poetry:

When you watch a man on the tracks before an oncoming train, that's exactly what you do: watch.

You can shout at him.

You can yell, "Train!"

You can grip your *New Yorker* and suck in your breath.

You can exhale when the Brooklyn-bound A stops twenty feet short.

You can widen your eyes when the man stumbles in your direction, toward the platform where you await the Manhattan-bound A.

You can gasp when the man steps over the electrified third rail.

You can listen to the Manhattan-bound A train barrel down.

Anderson's visual design, the layout of her text on the page, with its artfully placed line breaks, would not be found in Bacon's, Carson's or Bronowski's style of essay, nor would the experiment with a second person "you" point of view which shifts about midway in "Man on the Tracks" to a first person narrator,

> The two men on the platform grip the man's arms. I stand five feet from the men on the platform. I lunge toward the men on the platform. I pause.

On the other hand, Lamb's essay "Dream Children" does incorporate something like this narrative technique in which the point of view abruptly changes. But is it a "true story," or a "fiction"? "Dream Children" can be seen as a narrative that uncovers (and enacts) how fiction itself can be made up out of desires for overcoming the tragic negations of life — for the narrator, Elia, the missed opportunity with Alice. It certainly includes fictional children, fictional houses, fictional grandparents, but with no stated idea or theme included. The reader has to interpret for the theme at the end.

> "We are not of Alice, nor of thee; nor are we children at all. The children of Alice called Bartrum father. We are nothing; less than nothing, and dreams. We are only what might have been, and must wait upon the tedious shores of Lethe millions of ages before we have existence, and a name." (693)

A theme of how dreams might work is poetically invoked with the shores of Lethe reference, but we are yet attached to the *persona* Elia, and not necessarily to Lamb's "true story." There is no clear uncovering of any other fiction at the end. Can creative nonfiction deal with pseudonyms like Elia? And as we saw in Swift's "A Modest Proposal," once the reader has deciphered it, the complete essay seems to shift from its moorings in one form, the formal-critical "proposal," and come to reside wholly within the fiction category. This projector's voice is not the copying down of an interview. No one said these terrible things in this way; it is made up. Are we then forced to place such essays in a different category than "creative nonfiction"? Some essays are critical-formal, some are personal, and some indeed are literary and play, as does creative nonfiction with the relation between fiction and truth, but in these instances essay writers play almost wholly on the side of fiction. The reader gets to uncover the truth.

Perhaps we can reach a decision if we include more specific elements of narration. Another significant difference between creative nonfiction and the essay is implied by Gerard's perspective on point of view. Gerard sifts through some of the possible points of view allowed in creative nonfiction, noting that the third-person omniscient form, (the prevailing form of the novel or short story) where the narrator knows and reports on the inner life of characters, clearly and emphatically *cannot* be the prevailing angle from which a nonfiction story is told,

> The best the nonfiction writer can do is to present the *illusion* of interior lives, giving the reader insight and private information about real people, but stopping short of claiming to *know* what cannot be known — without making it up.
>
> ****
>
> All nonfiction must be told in either dramatic or first person point of view, or it becomes, by definition, fiction.
>
> ****
>
> In practice.... it almost always is told technically from the first-person point of view (the writer being the "I" witness, whether or not he alludes to himself). (116)

Gerard thus points to one solution to our problem of categorization. One easy difference has now at least become clear: the formal, critical essay practiced in universities today cannot diverge from its scholarly parameters and include an "I" narrator as must a writer of creative nonfiction. Once chosen the critical approach settles into a standard form, the academic essay, and much good work has been done in this form. The essay that includes a trustworthy "I" narrator, (Didion, Angelou, Woolf) might be included in the category creative nonfiction. But the essay that experiments with untrustworthy "I" narrators (Swift and Lamb) are yet outside the margins of creative nonfiction. As in life, so in the essay, a plurality of types and forms results in hybridity. In essays, the "I" narrator is not a guarantee, fiction and nonfiction can yet merge into each other, and can separate from each other. The tendency to meet formal requirements and the tendency to experiment share a creative relationship in the essay. Almost from Montaigne on, amalgamation of the intellectual, critical side of writing, with the creative poetic, personal, lyrical side of writing has been the essay's domain.

For Gutkind, "the primary goal of the creative nonfiction writer is to communicate information, just like a reporter, but to shape it in a way that reads like fiction" (xi *The Best Creative Nonfiction* Vol. 1). Singer finds this a limited view.

> Creative nonfiction certainly shares with fiction the elements of detail, image, description, dialogue, and scene.... Yet Gutkind's defin-

ition seems too limited. Surely the goal of creative nonfiction is not just to "communicate information" but also to bring the reader on a journey of discovery as we explore our selves and our experience of the world. And what about the wide range of essays whose emphasis is on idea rather than story, on meditation rather than reportage? What about creative nonfiction that feels more like poetry than fiction, relying on lyric compression rather than narrative to achieve its aims? (3)

Note that Singer includes essays in this critique of Gutkind, she implies that essays which have "poetry," "idea," and "meditation" as their method can also be classified as creative nonfiction. Remember, Lukács found genre hybridity in the essay in his idea that it was an "intellectual poem." But although Singer is trying for inclusivity in her definitions, she does not leave us with a clear line of division between nonfiction and the essay. As we have seen with Dickens, Lamb and Didion, the literary essay problematizes this boundary. If it becomes a complete fiction then it also runs the risk of losing its essay status to become a short story, say, or a novelette. Perhaps we can end with a compromise. Is creative nonfiction the underlying procedure of a type of essay in which experiment with narrative, especially with point of view, is predominant? The canonical essayists we have studied played in this boundary, actively blurring it to include both sides. Jonathan Swift blurred the division, and produced cutting satire, Lamb also blurred it and produced lyricism and an insight into how fiction is produced. I suggest though, that the essay may be the larger, wider form, at least up to this point in its development. It can play in areas that would likely not work for good creative nonfiction. The highly formal, the highly fictional, and experiments with hybrid points of view outside the "centre of consciousness" or "I narrator" are not included in the definitions of creative nonfiction we have so far studied. I doubt there is a place in "creative nonfiction" for a standard, academic, critical essay; I am not so sure about the play between narrative and formal voices in "The Death of A Moth," "Dream Children" or "A Modest Proposal."

Critics such as Gerard, Good, Woolridge, Singer, Gutkind, and Harrison, all have further things to say on the abstract and narrative aspects of the essay and they show us that when combining the three voices, the literary essayist, can be engaged in exciting, experimental work that shares ground with creative nonfiction. Montaigne, Swift, Woolf, and Lamb certainly seem at times to be disruptive collagists of voice who experiment with fictions in order to point to the truth.

The Essay

The description and definition that follows is a summary and tentative integration of the various forms and ideas about the essay we have been gradually accumulating and sifting through in this book.

First and most important, the essay is an old form. As the *"essai,"* it has been around since the 16th Century in France and its practitioners have continued to experiment with its voices, length, duties, literariness, definitions, and inclusivity unabated since that time. It shows no signs of slowing its development of possible shapes and the nature of its activism. A critical renaissance of sorts occurred in the 20th century in which many erudite analyses of the essay were put forward (from Lukács and Woolf, to Harrison, and Graham Good), and this assessment continues to the present day. The latest development appears to be its sometimes inclusion in the category of "creative nonfiction," though the essay may be the more inclusive of the two genres. It has now migrated to the Internet and is continuing to experiment there, most long-term blogs, wikis, web encyclopedias, data bases, e-zines, websites have some or all of the creative essayistic features we have analyzed.

We have noted three major voices predominant in the essay. And these could lead us to proposing three major types of essays based on these voices. Graham Good uses a four part typology of *the travel essay, the moral essay, the critical essay, and the autobiographical essay* (xii). In our terms these could be reducible to three types, the "familiar essay" can clearly include the autobiographical; moral and critical essays could fit under the "formal essay"; and what Good terms the travel essay seems to me to be a blend of familiar and narrative voices — the story of a real journey. Typologies of the essay, however, likely deserve a book of their own. We have also noted, as does Good, that the essay freely combines these types and voices. In fact this free hybridity, this mixing and blending of voices is one of its defining features.

In terms of the familiar essay, we have defined it by its use of the "I" pronoun and its allowance of multiple references to context, and to audience and speaker. The exploration of the problem of the self or the essayist's relation to the authority, controls, priorities, and rewards of social often family life is another marker of this voice. The familiar essay has features of "creative nonfiction" but also, as we have seen in Lamb, Dickens, and Swift, in contrast, it can deliberately make up fictional characters, a fictional "I" when it suits the essayist to do so. This flexibility may make the essay the more inclusive form. It can both create characters and get inside their minds, and it can yet, we think, be accurate to truth, something two theorists of "creative nonfiction," Gutkind and Gerard say is not possible within creative nonfiction. Though Singer, is yet sure that essayistic "genre bending" may be available to nonfiction as well.

The second major form is the formal essay. It has been well covered in this book and is very much alive and used in the academic and professional worlds. It is composed of a voice that is "field oriented" and has a more objective tone; it uses the *third-person objective point of view,* and is thin on the use of the "I" pronoun. General language is clearly present but so are specific details, and this relation organizes the whole of the formal essay. These essays are, in a word, *thematic:* As we have noted their focus is on addressing and persuading an audience about issues other than the relation of the writer's self to expectations and roles.

The final form we have studied is the narrative voice especially in Lamb, Woolf, Rhenisch, and Swift. These essays are recognizably literary and use features of narration, like figuration, plot, characterization, point of view, theme, and setting. They are sometimes challenging enough we have had a difficult time placing them as essays, rather than as a form of fiction, though creative nonfiction also comes close to describing them.

We can now attempt to define the essay as the form of writing that is free enough to incorporate and juxtapose the familiar, formal and narrative voices in an almost infinite variety. It does so with freedom of scope and point of view, moving into its subject as it needs to, bending genre when it needs to, staying within strict genres boundaries when required. The essay can include fictional characters, made up scenes, caricatures, plot lines, dreamscapes, but also at the same time, a critical view, a view that revises the narrative and makes us see it "as such." The essay can incorporate most of the features of creative nonfiction, but is likely the more inclusive form in that it can break the adherence to "nonfiction" and step into imagined worlds and points of view that break the rules of journalism and challenge most of the expectations of genre.

I will end with a number of notes and a collection of interesting perspectives on the essay and on fiction in the hope that we retain variety to the end:

Here is Montaigne from one of his earlier essays, "Of the Vanity of Words" (Book I of the *Collected Essays*) and one of his later ones "On the Art of Discussion" (Book III):

> Aristotle wisely defines rhetoric as the science of persuading the people; Socrates and Plato, as the art of deceiving and flattering. And those who deny this in the general definition verify it everywhere in their precepts. The Mohammedans forbid its being taught to their children, because of its uselessness. And the Athenians, perceiving its perniciousness, for all its complete prestige in their city, ordained that the principal part of it, which is to stir the emotions, should be eliminated, together with the exordiums and perorations.

I love and honour learning as much as those who have it; and in its true use it is man's most noble and powerful acquisition. But in those (and their number is infinite) who have their fundamental capacity and worth on it, who appeal from their understanding to their memory, *hiding under the shadow of others* [Seneca], and can do nothing except by the book, I hate it, if I dare say so, a little more than stupidity.

Here is the American poet Robert Frost on relation of the voice to prose:

A dramatic necessity goes deep into the nature of the sentence. Sentences are not different enough to hold the attention unless they are dramatic. No ingenuity of varying structure will do. All that can save them is the speaking tone of voice somehow entangled in the words and fastened to the page for the ear of the imagination. That is all that can save poetry from sing-song, all that can save prose from itself. (Introduction, *A Way Out*)

Here are two well-known European critics of the essay:

The essay form has not yet, today, travelled the road to independence which its sister, poetry, covered long ago; the road of development from a primitive, undifferentiated unity with science, ethics, and art. (Lukács, 13)

Luck and play are essential to the essay. It does not begin with Adam and Eve but with what it wants to discuss; it says what is at issue and stops where it feels itself complete — not where nothing is left to say. (Adorno, 152)

Here is a piece of creative nonfiction that squarely faces the problem of genre confronted by the essay. It is taken from Michael Mortone's "Hermes Goes to College."

I am worried that we don't worry enough about the subliminal influences of the institutions in which we find ourselves housed, colleges and universities, which for me seem to be diabolic engines for sorting, categorizing, defining.... The institution is a critical institution and insists we act critically. We want to think of such influence as benign, but it is not. We have adapted our writing, this writing, to the academic model, to the critical turn of mind. It must be seen as serious, empirical, enlightened. Even now in this essay, in this collection of essays that is interested in blurring the lines of genre, we still must use words like genre. We are interested in the confusion of genre, the borrowing of technique between the genres, the tension that exists as one genre rubs up against the other. But still we are quite conscious and quite ready to admit to the easy use of "genre" altogether. We worry the categories of fact and fiction. Nonfiction and fiction. Prose and poetry. What we don't worry well enough is the category of category, the genre of *genre*. (54)

Vladimir Nabokov would have likely have not liked the "true story well told" idea because he was in love with the fictional, probably more than the true.

Literature was born not the day when a boy crying wolf, wolf came running out of the Neanderthal valley with a big gray wolf at this heels: literature was born on the day when a boy came crying wolf, wolf and there was no wolf behind him.

****

There are three points of view from which a writer can be considered: he may be considered as a storyteller, as a teacher, and as an enchanter. A major writer combines all three — storyteller, teacher, enchanter — but it is the enchanter in him that predominates and makes him a major writer. (574)

And some last words from creative nonfiction.

Hoagland: "the artful 'I' of an essay can be as chameleon as any narrator in fiction." (26)

Singer: We all know that something crucial happens to how we read a story when we understand that its events really occurred, that the people and places described really exist. There's no question that there's a special intimacy that comes from recognizing the voice of an essay or memoir as the author's, from listening to that author think and wonder, reminisce, confess, reflect. But what distinguishes creative nonfiction as a genre, we propose is not only the truth-value of the writing. It's the ways in which the raw material of "reality" is transformed into literary art. (2)

Study Questions

1. Is there an authentic "I" in any of the essays we have analyzed?
2. For you what is the value of a literary essay like Swift's? What can we get out of them that we cannot get out of a more objective, formal type of writing?
3. Where would you place "narrative" as a term? Is it significant? Is it less important that say the organizing principle of a scientific report?
4. What do you prefer: reading a literary essay, a short story, a familiar essay, creative nonfiction, a narrative essay, or a formal essay?
5. Comment on the limits of the phrase "a true story, well told." Is it an adequate definition of the essay? Is it adequate to creative nonfiction?
6. In what ways does the essay "splice together elements of other genres to create a hybrid"? (Singer, 2)
7. Is the blog another form of the essay?
8. What is a genre?

Key Terms

Genre

The more or less stable pattern or form of a literary or other text. The term is related to "general" or "type" "generic," perhaps even "gene," and as we have found, the essay usually does not try to produce a complete system of explanation or thought, though there are exceptions. Locke's *Essay on Human Understanding*, was book length. For some critics the literary genres include, drama, poetry, the novel, the short story; others prefer the classical types of epic, tragedy, lyric, comedy and satire. Cuddon would also add the novel and short story. The term has a literary sense as above, but also a wider sense which includes film genres like the *crime noir* film, or the gothic novel. The essay is considered by Harrison and others to be an "anti-genre."

The middle voice

A phrase often used to describe the 18th Century essayist, Joseph Addison. Addison is an intermediary. In one of the first magazines, *The Spectator,* he generally summarizes the current news about events in philosophy, science, literature, and art to an audience that does not know much about them. His position is closer to your own since he is quite like a (good) student who is making a report on a matter he is learning about. Unlike Bacon, Bronowski or Carson though he does not take the position of an expert; rather, he is an informed reader who is telling us what he has read and thought about this reading. When he adds his own response to the subject at hand, he puts himself more squarely between his reader and his sources. He comments on a formal treatise he has found interesting, a newly minted poem, a scientific discovery, or a new piece of music — and he is a good commentator because he keeps us interested. Addison's voice is thus in a middle register between formality and familiarity.

Creative nonfiction
We have defined it in the previous discussion as, "A true story well told," but for many current practitioners it can involve hybridity of genre, a questioning of conventions about narration, meditations and ideas, poetic technique and lyricism, and it may be at the growing margin of the essay. In relation to the essay it may however be restrained by its dedication to "nonfiction."

Works Cited

Adorno, T. W. "The Essay as Form." *New German Critique* 32 (Spring-Summer, 1984): 151–71.

Cuddon, J. A. *Dictionary of Literary Terms and Literary Theory*. London: Penguin Reference, 1998.

Gutkind, Lee. *Creative Nonfiction True Stories, Well Told*. "What is Creative Nonfiction?" Issue #0, Web. Nov. 15, 2013.

Harrison, Thomas. *Essayism: Conrad, Musil & Pirandello*, Baltimore: The Johns Hopkins University Press, 1992.

Good, Graham. *The Observing Self: Rediscovering the Essay*, London: Routledge, 1988.

Gerard, Philip. *Creative Nonfiction: Researching and Crafting Stories of Real Life*. Longrove, Illinois: Waveland Press Inc, 2004.

Hoagland, Edward. *The Tugman's Passage*. NY, New York: Random House Publishing Group, 1982.

Lukács, George. "On the Nature and Form of the Essay." *Soul and Form*. Trans. Anna Bostock. Cambridge, MA: MIT Press, n.d.

Michael Martone. "Hermes Goes to College" in *Bending Genre: Essays on Creative Nonfiction*. New York: Bloomsbury Academic, 2013, 53–57.

Nabokov, Vladimir. "Good Readers and Good Writers" in *The Norton Reader*. Peterson, Linda H., [*et alia*] Eds. Shorter 13th Edition. New York: Norton, 2012, pp. 571–575.

Singer, Margot and Nicole Walker eds. *Bending Genre: Essays on Creative Nonfiction*. New York: Bloomsbury Academic, 2013.

Woolridge, Paul. "Activist Essayism." Opticon1826 (3), 2012 DOI: http://dx.doi.org/10.5334/opt.030702 Web. Nov. 30, 2013.

Bibliography

On the Essay

Adorno, T. W. "The Essay as Form." *New German Critique* 32 (Spring–Summer, 1984): 151–171.

Adorno, T. W. *Prisms* Tanslators Samuel and Shierry Weber. Cambridge, MA: MIT Press, 1981.

Anderson, Chris, ed. *Literary Nonfiction: Theory, Criticism, Pedagogy.* Carbondale: Southern Illinois University Press, 1988.

Anderson, Chris. "Teaching Students What Not to Say: Iser, Didion, and the Rhetoric of Gaps" *JAC: A Journal of Rhetoric, Writing, Culture, and Politics*, Vol. 7, Issue #½ Double Issue, 1987, 2006.

Atkins, Douglas G. *Estranging the Familiar: Towards a Revitalized Critical Writing.* Athens, Georgia: The University of Georgia Press, 1992.

Atwan, Robert. "Essayism" *The Iowa Review*, Vol. 25, No. 2 (Spring-Summer, 1995), 6–14.

Belsey, Catherine. *Critical Practice.* London: Methuen, 1987.

Benjamin, Walter. *Illuminations.* Ed. Hannah Arendt, Trans., Harry Zohn. New York: Schocken Books, 1988.

Brodski, Bella, and Celeste Shenk, eds. *Life/Lines: Theorizing Women's Autobiography.* Ithaca: Cornell University Press, 1988.

Butryn, Alexander J. *Essays on the Essay: Redefining the Genre.* Athens, Georgia: University of Georgia Press, 1989.

Derrida, Jacques. *Spurs: Nietzsche's Styles.* Introduction by Stefano Agosti; Trans., Barabara Harlow. Chicago: University of Chicago Press, 1979.

Eaken, Paul John. *Fictions in Autobiography.* Princeton: Princeton University Press, 1985.

Gerard, Philip, *Creative Nonfiction: Researching and Crafting Stories of Real Life.* Longrove, Illinois: Waveland Press Inc., 2004.

Good, Graham. *The Observing Self: Rediscovering the Essay*. London: Routledge, 1988.

Gutkind, Lee. *Creative Nonfiction True Stories, Well Told*. "What is Creative Nonfiction?" Issue #0, Web. Nov. 15, 2013.

Halper, Daniel, ed. *The Autobiographical Eye*. Hopewell, NJ: Ecco Press, 1982.

Hardison Jr., O. B. "Binding Proteus: An Essay on the Essay." *The Sewanee Review*, Vol. 96, No. 4 (Fall, 1988), 610–632.

Harrison, Thomas. *Essayism: Conrad, Musil & Pirandello*. Baltimore: Johns Hopkins University Press, 1992.

Joeres, Ruth-Ellen Boetcher, and Elizabeth Mittman. *The Politics of the Essay: Feminist Perspectives*. Bloomington: Indiana University Press, 1993.

Kauffmann, R. Lane. "The Skewed Path: Essaying as Unmethodical Method" *Diogenes* September 1988 36: 66–92.

Koen, Anne. "Democracy and Women's Autobiographies." *American Studies* 35.5 (1990): 321–326.

Lukács, George. "On the Nature and Form of the Essay." *Soul and Form*. Trans. Anna Bostock. Cambridge, MA: MIT Press, n.d.

Neuman, Shirley. "Life Writing." *Literary History of Canada: Canadian Literature in English*. Ed. W. H. New. 2nd ed. Vol. 4. Toronto: University of Toronto Press, 1990. 333–370.

Neuman, Shirley. "Autobiography: From Different Poetics to a Poetics of Differences." *Essays on Life Writing*. Ed. Marlene Kadar. Toronto: University of Toronto Press, 1992.

Singer, Margot and Nicole Walker eds. *Bending Genre: Essays on Creative Nonfiction*. New York: Bloomsbury Academic, 2013.

Walker, Hugh. *The English Essay and Essayists*. 1915. London: Dent, 1928.

Woolridge, Paul. "Activist Essayism." *Opticon 1826* (3), 2012 DOI: http://dx.doi.org/10.5334/opt.030702. Web. Dec. 2, 2013.

Anthologies

Aaron, Jane E., ed. *The Compact Reader: Short Essays by Theme and Form*. 4th ed. Boston: Bedford, 1993.

Boyd, Alex, Al-Solaylee, Kamal. *The Best Canadian Essays 2010*. Toronto, ON: Tightrope Books, 2010. Web. Nov. 23, 2013.

Corbett, Edward P., and Sheryl L. Einkel, eds. *The Essay: Old and New*. Englewood Cliffs, NJ: Prentice-Hall, 1993.

Delany, Paul, ed. *Vancouver: Representing the Postmodern City*. Vancouver: Arsenal Pulp Press, 1994.

Fakundiny, Lydia. *The Art of the Essay*. Boston: Houghton Mifflin Company, 1991.

Flick, Jane, Rosengarten, Herbert. *The Broadview Reader*. Peterborough, Ontario: Broadview Press, 1998. Web. Nov. 23, 2013.

Lynch, Gerald, and David Rampton, eds. *The Canadian Essay*. Toronto: Copp Clark Pitman, 1991.

Marx, Paul. *Modern and Classical Essayists: Twelve Masters*. Mountain View, California: Mayfield Publishing Company, 1995.

Muller, Gilbert H., ed. *Major Modern Essayists*. Englewood Cliffs, NJ: Prentice-Hall, 1991.

Muller, Gilbert H., ed. *Major Modern Essayists*. 2nd ed. Englewood Cliffs, NJ: Prentice-Hall, 1994.

Peterson, Linda H., [*et alia*] eds. *The Norton Reader*. Shorter 13th Edition. New York: Norton, 2012.

Smart, William ed. *Eight Modern Essayists*. 2nd ed. New York: St. Martin's Press, 1973.

Authors

Achebe, Chinua. "An Image of Africa: Racism in Conrad's *Heart of Darkness*." *Heart of Darkness*. Ed. Robert Kimbrough. 3rd ed. New York: W. W. Norton, 1988.

Achebe, Chinua. *Hopes and Impediments: Selected Essays, 1965–1987*. London: Heinemann, 1988.

Achebe, Chinua. *Things Fall Apart*. London, Heinemann, 1958.

Ackroyd, Peter. *Dickens*. London: Mandarin, 1994.

Addison, Joseph. "The Spectator No. 519. Oct. 25th, 1712." *The Works of Joseph Addison*. Ed. Richard Hurd. London: George Bell, 1898.

Addison, Joseph. *Critical Essays from the Spectator with Four Essays by Richard Steele*. Ed. Donald E. Bond. New York: Oxford University Press, 1970.

Anderson, Erika. *Creative Nonfiction*, Issue #49, Summer 2013. Online. https://www.creativenonfiction.org/online-reading/man-tracks. Web. Oct. 8, 2013.

Angelou, Maya. *I Know Why the Caged Bird Sings*. New York: Bantam, 1971

Angelou, Maya "Graduation" in *The Norton Reader*, Eds. Linda Peterson *et al*. Shorter 13th ed. New York W.W. Norton, 2012. 10–19.

Asimov, Isaac. "The Eureka Phenomenon." *The Norton Reader: An Anthology of Nonfiction*. Shorter 11th ed. Eds. Linda Peterson and J. Brereton. New York: Norton, 2004. 130–39.

Archibald, Sasha. *Rumpus*. blog review of *Unruly Voices: Essays on Democracy, Civility and the Human Imagination* (2012) a collection of essays written by Mark Kingwell. Web. Jan. 6, 2013.

Arendt, Hannah. *Eichmann in Jerusalem: A Report on the Banality of Evil*. New York: Viking Press; 1963.

Arendt, Hannah. *On Revolution*. London: Penguin, 1990.

Arendt, Hannah. *The Origins of Totalitarianism*. 1951. Rev. ed. New York: Schocken, 2004.

Arendt, Hannah. "Power and Violence." *The Essay: Old and New*. Ed. Edward P. J. Corbett and Sheryl L. Finkle. Englewood Cliffs, NJ: Prentice Hall, 1993. 315–23.

Arnold, Matthew. "Preface." In *The Poems of Wordsworth*. London, 1879. v–xxvi. Also Published in *Macmillan's Magazine* 40 (July 1879): 193–204 and in *Essays in Criticism*, Second Series, 1888.

Astell, Mary. "A Serious Proposal to the Ladies." *The Norton Anthology of Literature by Women*. 2nd ed. Eds. Sandra Gilbert and Susan Gubar. New York: Norton, 1996.

Astell, Mary. Excerpt from *A Serious Proposal to the Ladies for the Advancement of Their True and Greatest Interest.* London, 1694. Web. Aug. 8, 2011. See the *Luminarium* website: http://www.luminarium.org/eightlit/astell/

Atwood, Margaret. "Footnote to the Amnesty Report on Torture," in *Two-Headed Poems*, Toronto: Oxford University Press, 1978, 14–15.

Bacon, Francis. *The Advancement of Learning. Collected Works of Francis Bacon.* Vol. 4. Eds. Robert Leslie Ellis, Douglas Denon Heath, and Graham Rees. London: Routledge/Thoemmes Press, 1996.

Bacon, Francis. *Selected Writings of Francis Bacon.* New York: Modern Library, 1955.

Bacon, Francis. "Of Revenge." *Essays* (various editions, 1597–1625). Web. Aug. 13, 2007.

Bacon, Francis. *The Advancement of Learning.* Web. Oct. 11, 2013.

Barker, Pat. *Regeneration.* London: Viking, 1991.

Barnett, George L. *Charles Lamb.* Boston: Twayne, 1976.

Barthes, Roland. *Mythologies.* Trans. Anette Lavers. London: Paladin Grafton Books, 1989.

Barthes, Roland. *New Critical Essays.* Trans. Richard Howard. New York: Hill and Wang, 1980, 1972.

Barthes, Roland. "From Work to Text." *Textual Strategies: Perspectives in Post-Structuralist Criticism.* Ed. Josue V. Harari. Ithaca: Cornell University Press, 1979.

Barthes, Roland and Lionel Duisit. *Introduction to the Structural Analysis of Narratives, New Literary History*, Vol. 6, No. 2, On *Narrative and Narratives* (Winter, 1975) The Johns Hopkins University Press, pp. 237–72. Web. Nov. 3, 2013. Originally published in *Communications*, 8 (1966), as "*Introduction à l'analyse structurale des récits.*"

Baugh, Hume. "Fred Wah's Diamond Grill," in *Quill & Quire*, (Sept. 1996). Web. Dec. 8, 2013.

Beauvoir, Simone de. *Adieux: A Farewell to Sartre.* Trans. Patrick O'Brian. New York: Pantheon Books, 1984.

Beauvoir, Simone de. *The Second Sex.* (1949). Trans. H. M. Parshley. New York: Knopf, 1952.

Berger, Peter L., and Thomas Luckmann. *The Social Construction of Reality: A Treatise in the Sociology of Knowledge.* Garden City, NY: Anchor Books, 1966.

Berlin, Isaiah. "The Magus of the North." *New York Review of Books* 40.17 (1993): 64.

Berlin, Isaiah. *Concepts and Categories: Philosophical Essays.* Oxford: Oxford University Press, 1980.

Bettelheim, Bruno. *The Informed Heart: Autonomy in a Mass Age.* Glencoe, IL: The Free Press, 1960.

Bettelheim, Bruno. "A Victim." *The Norton Reader: An Anthology of Expository Prose.* Ed. Linda H. Peterson, John C. Brereton, and Joan E. Hartman. 9th ed. New York: W. W. Norton, 1996. 11–13.

Booth, Wayne C. *The Rhetoric of Fiction.* 2nd ed. Chicago: University of Chicago Press, 1983.

Booth, Wayne C. *The Vocation of a Teacher: Rhetorical Occasions. 1967–1988.* Chicago: University of Chicago Press, 1988.

Bressler, Charles. *Literary Criticism: An Introduction to Theory and Practice*. Upper Saddle River, NJ: Prentice-Hall, 1998.

Bronowski, Jacob. *The Ascent of Man*. Boston: Little, Brown, 1973.

Bronowski, Jacob. "The Nature of Scientific Reasoning." *The Norton Reader: An Anthology of Nonfiction*. Shorter 12th ed. Eds. Linda Peterson and J. Brereton. New York: Norton, 2008. 562–66.

Bronowski, Jacob. "The Reach of Imagination." *Proceedings of the American Academy of Arts and Letters*. 2nd ser. 17, 1967. In *The Norton Reader*. 8th ed. New York: Norton, 1992. 125–32.

Bronowski, Jacob. *William Blake, 1757–1827: A Man without a Mask*. New York: Haskell House, 1967.

Brown (Jr.), George E. "Can Scientists 'Make Change their Friend'?" *Scientific American* 268.6 (1993): 158.

Burgess, Anthony. *A Clockwork Orange*. New York: Norton, 1962.

Burgess, Anthony. *Earthly Powers*. London: Hutchinson, 1980.

Burke, James. "Connections: From Bottled Veggies to a Pointillist Picnic." *Scientific American* Sept. 1996. 176–77.

Carroll, Lewis. *The Annotated Alice: Alice's Adventures in Wonderland, Through the Looking Glass*. Introduction and Notes by Martin Gardner. New York: Meridian, New American Library, 1960.

Carr, Nicholas. "Is Google Making Us Stupid?" *The Norton Reader*. Eds Linda H. Peterson et alia. Shorter 13th ed. New York: Norton, 2013. 150–159

Carson, Rachel. "The Obligation to Endure." *Silent Spring*. Greenwich Conn.: Fawcett, 1962.

Chadburn, Melissa, *Saturday Rumpus*, "Interview of Dana Johnson." Web. Jan 5 2013.

Chatwin, Bruce. *On the Black Hill*. New York: Viking Press, 1982.

Chatwin, Bruce. *The Songlines*. Markham, Ontario: Viking, 1987.

Chen, Ing-Ho MD; Chien, Jui-Teng MD; Yu, Tzai-Chiu MD. "Transpedicular Wedge Osteotomy for Correction of Thoracolumbar Kyphosis in Ankylosing Spondylitis: Experience With 78 Patients." *Spine* 26.16 (2001): E354-E360.

Choy, Wayson. "The Ten Thousand Things." *The Norton Reader*. Eds. Linda H. Peterson and John C. Brereton. Shorter 11th ed. New York: Norton. 2004, 12–17.

Coulter, Gerry. "Jean Baudrillard and the Definitive Ambivalence of Gaming" *Insomnia Essays*. Web. Nov. 27, 2013.

Dickens, Charles. *Great Expectations*. London: Penguin, 1985.

Dickens, Charles. "Night Walks" from *The Uncommercial Traveller*. The Project Gutenberg EBook of *The Uncommercial Traveller*, by Charles Dickens (#23 in series by Charles Dickens) Web. Oct. 11, 2013.

Didion, Joan. "On Going Home" in *The Norton Reader*, Eds. Linda Peterson *et al.* Shorter 13th ed. New York W.W. Norton, 2012. 1–3.

Didion, Joan. *The White Album*. New York: Simon and Schuster, 1979.

Didion, Joan. *Play It As It Lays*. Harmondsworth: Penguin, 1973.

Didion, Joan. "Why I Write" *New York Times*, Dec. 5, 1976.

Didion, Joan. *Blue Nights.* New York: Vintage International, 2012.

Didion, Joan and Darryl Pinckney. "On Elizabeth Hardwick (1916–2007)." *The New York Review of Books* (online). Web. Dec. 21, 2012.

Dillard, Anne. "Terwilliger Bunts Out." *The Norton Reader: An Anthology of Nonfiction.* Shorter 11th ed. Eds. Linda Peterson and J. Brereton. New York: Norton, 2004. 69–74.

Eco, Umberto. *The Open Work.* Trans. Anna Cancogni. Introduction by David Robey. Cambridge, MA: Harvard University Press, 1989.

Ehrenpres, Irvin. *Swift: The Man, His Works and the Age.* 3 vols. Cambridge MA: Harvard University Press, 1986.

Elliott, J. H. *Europe Divided 1559–1598.* Glasgow: Fontana, 1975.

Ellul, Jacques. *The Technological Society.* Trans. John Wilkinson. New York: Knopf, 1967.

Ellul, Jacques. *Propaganda: The Formation of Men's Attitudes.* New York: Vintage, 1973.

Emerson, Ralph Waldo. *Emerson's Essays: First and Second Series.* New York: Gramercy Books, 1993.

Esterhammer, Angela. Review of *The Cambridge History of Literary Criticism. Vol. 5: Romanticism in English Studies in Canada* 29. 3&4, 2003. 258–61.

Fowler, Roger. *Literature as Social Discourse: The Practice of Linguistic Criticism.* London: Batsford Academic and Educational, 1981.

Fowler, Roger. *Linguistic Criticism.* Oxford: Oxford University Press, 1986.

Frame, Donald M. *Montaigne: A Biography.* London: H. Hamilton, 1965.

Frye, Northrop. *The Bush Garden: Essays on the Canadian Imagination.* Toronto: Anansi, 1971.

Gager, Valerie L. *Shakespeare and Dickens: The Dynamics of Influence.* Cambridge: Cambridge University Press, 1996.

Garvey, John. "Thinking in Packages." *Short Essays.* 7th ed. Ed. G. Levin. Boston: Heinle and Heinle, 1994. 201–207.

Gilbert, Sandra, and Susan Gubar, eds. *Norton Anthology of Literature by Women.* 2nd ed. New York: Norton, 1996.

Gingerich, Owen. "Neptune, Velikovsky and the Name of the Game. *Scientific American* Sept. 1996: 181–83.

Gould, Stephen Jay. (1979). "Darwin's Middle Road." *The Norton Reader: An Anthology of Nonfiction.* Shorter 11th ed. Eds. Linda Peterson and J. Brereton. New York: Norton, 2004. 600–06.

Gould, Stephen Jay. "Evolution as Fact and Theory." *Major Modern Essayists.* Ed. Gilbert H. Muller. Englewood Cliffs, NJ: Prentice-Hall, 1991, 379–85.

Goodheart, Adam. "9.11.01: The Skyscraper and the Airplane." *The Norton Reader.* Eds. Linda H. Peterson and John C. Brereton. Shorter 11th ed. New York: Norton, 2004. 187–93.

Grant, George. *The George Grant Reader.* Ed. William Christian and Sheila Grant. Toronto: University of Toronto Press, 1998.

Grant, George. *Lament for a Nation: The Defeat of Canadian Nationalism.* Ottawa: Carleton University Press, 1965.

Grant, George. *George Grant in Process: Essays and Conversations.* Ed. Larry Schmidt. Toronto: Anansi, 1978.

Greeley Andrew. *Why Can't They Be Like Us? Facts and Fallacies about Ethnic Differences and Group Conflicts in America.* Pamphlet Series, Number 12. New York: Institute of Human Relations Press, The American Jewish Committee, 1969.

Greenblatt, Stephen. J. "Shakespeare and the Exorcists" *Shakespearean Negotiations: The Circulation of Social Energy in Renaissance England.* Oxford/Berkeley and Los Angeles: OUP/U California Press, 1988.

Grekul, Lisa. "Inspiring and Uninspired," *Canadian Literature,* 8 Dec. 2011. Web. Feb. 3, 2013.

(This review originally appeared in *Canadian Literature* #194 (Autumn 2007), *Visual/Textual Intersections.* 145–147.

Halkett, Anne. Excerpt from *The Autobiography of Anne Lady Halkett.* Ed. John Gough Nichols. Westminster, England: Camden Society, 1875, 19–23. Web. Aug. 14, 2007. See online version, by Ellen Moody, (Aug. 16, 2006) Web. Jun. 1, 2011.

Hardwick, Elizabeth. "In the Wasteland." *New York Review of Books* Vol. 43, Number 17 31 Oct. 1996. Web. Dec. 21, 2012.

Havel, Vaclav. "The Post-Communist Nightmare." *The New York Review of Books* 41.10 (1993): 8–10.

Hitchins, Christopher. "The Dark Side of Dickens: Why Charles Dickens was among the best of writers and the worst of men" *The Atlantic* (May 2010). Web. Nov. 14, 2011. http://www.theatlantic.com/magazine/archive/2010/05/the-dark-side-of-dickens/8031/. Web. Sept. 20, 2011.

Hixson, M. D. "Ape Language Research: A Review and Behavioral Perspective." *The Analysis of Verbal Behavior* 15 (1998): 17–39.

Hoagland, Edward. *The Tugman's Passage.* NY, New York: Random House Publishing Group, 1982.

Hughes, *William Critical Thinking: An Introduction to the Basic Skills.* Peterborough: Broadview Press, 1996.

Hutcheon, Linda. *The Canadian Postmodern, A Study of Contemporary English-Canadian Fiction.* Toronto: Oxford University Press, 1988.

Iser, Wolfgang. *Prospecting: From Reader-response to Literary Anthropology.* Baltimore and London: Johns Hopkins University Press, 1989.

James, Henry. "The Art of Fiction." 1884. *Partial Portraits.* Ann Arbor: University of Michigan Press, 1970. 375–408.

Johnson, Harry M. *Sociology: A Systematic Introduction,* ed. Robert K. Merton. New York: Harcourt, Brace and World, 1960.

Joseph, Mia. "Wondering into Country: Dionne Brand's A Map to the Door of No Return." *Canadian Literature* 193, (Summer 2007): 75–92, 182.

King, Martin Luther. *Stride Toward Freedom: The Montgomery Story.* New York: Harper, 1958.

Knight. G. Wilson. "The Embassy of Death." The Wheel of Fire. Rev. ed. London: Methuen & Co., 1954. 38–39.

Kuhn, Thomas. *The Structure of Scientific Revolutions.* Chicago: University of Chicago Press, 1962.

Lamb, Charles. "Dream-Children: A Reverie." *English Romantic Writers.* Ed. David Perkins. New York: Harcourt, 1967.

Lamb, Charles. *Miscellaneous Essays and Sketches.* London: Dent, 1929.

Lamb, Charles. *Charles Lamb & Elia*, ed. J. E. Morpurgo. Manchester: Carcanet, 1993.

Laurence, Margaret. *Heart of a Stranger.* Toronto: McClelland and Stewart, 1976.

Link, Perry "Does This Writer Deserve the Prize?" *The New York Review of Books,* Dec. 6, 2012, Vol. 59, No 19.

Lowman, John. "The Hypocrisy of Prostitution Law: A Challenge to the Politicians of Canada." *Summary of the 1997 Sterling Prize in Support of Controversy Lecture,* September 24, 1997.

Mackelm, Michael, trans. *Champlain: Voyages 1599–1603.* Ottawa: Oberon, 1971.

Martone, Michael. "Hermes Goes to College" in *Bending Genre: Essays on Creative Nonfiction.* New York: Bloomsbury Academic, 2013, 53–57.

Matthews, G. A. *Pesticide Application Methods.* 2nd ed. Oxford: Blackwell, 1992.

McLuhan, Marshall. "The Role of New Media in Social Change." *Marshall McLuhan: The Man and His Message.* Eds. G. Sanderson & F. Macdonald. Golden, Colorado: Fulcrum, 1989. 34–40.

McMillan, J. H., & Schumacher, S. *Research in Education: A Conceptual Introduction.* 5th ed. New York: Longman, 2001.

Mills, C. Wright. *The Sociological Imagination.* New York: Oxford University Press, 1959.

Momaday, Natachee Scott. *The Way to Rainy Mountain.* Albuquerque: University of New Mexico Press, 1969.

Montagu, Basil. *The Works of Francis Bacon, Lord Chancellor of England: With a Life of the Author.* Vol. 3. Philadelphia: Carey and Hart, 1848.

Montaigne, Michel de. *The Essays of Michel de Montaigne.* Trans. M. A. Screech. London: Penguin, 1987.

Montaigne, Michel. de "Of the Vanity of Words." *Essays of Michel de Montaigne.* Vol. 8. Trans. Charles Cotton. Ed. William Carew Hazlitt. 1877. http://www.gutenberg.org/dirs/3/5/8/3588/3588.

Montaigne, Michel de. "Of the Art of [Discussion]Conference." *Essays of Michel de Montaigne.* Vol. 16. Trans. Charles Cotton. Ed. William Carew Hazlitt. 1877. http://www.gutenberg.org/dirs/3/5/9/ 3596/ 3596.

Munro, Alice. "The Peace of Utrecht." In *Oxford Book of Canadian Short Stories.* Selected by Margaret Atwood and Robert Weaver. Toronto: Oxford University Press, 1986. 191–206.

Nabokov, Vladimir. "Good Readers and Good Writers" in *The Norton Reader.* Peterson, Linda H., [*et alia*] Eds. Shorter 13th Edition. New York: Norton, 2012. 571–75.

Nadelmann, Ethan Avram. *Cops across Borders: The Internationalization of U.S. Criminal Law Enforcement.* University Park: Pennsylvania State University Press, 1993.

Nadelmann, Ethan A. "Legalize Drugs." *The Compact Reader: Short Essays by Theme and Form.* Ed. Jane E. Carson. 4th ed. Boston: Bedford Books, 1993. 301–05.

Ngugi wa Thiong'o. *Detained: A Writer's Prison Diary.* London: Heinemann, 1981.

Ngugi wa Thiong'o. *Decolonizing the Mind: The Politics of Language.* London: Heineman, 1986.

Ngugi wa Thiong'o. *Moving the Centre: The Struggle for Cultural Freedoms.* London: Heineman, 1993.

Njeri, Itabari. "Who is Black?" in *Essence* Sept. 1991: 64–66.

Ondaatje, Michael. *Running in the Family.* Toronto: McClelland and Stewart Inc., 1982.

Ondaatje, Michael. *The English Patient.* Toronto: Vintage, 1993.

Ondaatje, Michael. *Coming through Slaughter.* Toronto: Anansi, 1976.

Ondaatje, Michael. *In the Skin of a Lion.* London: Picador, 1988.

Orwell, George. Afterword. *1984: A Novel.* By Erich Fromm. New York: New American Library, 1961.

Orwell, George. "Anti-Semitism in Britain." *1945. England, Your England and Other Essays.* London: Secker and Warburg, 1953. Web. Aug. 13, 2007.

Orwell, George. *Burmese Days.* Harmondsworth: Penguin, 1967.

Orwell, George. *Collected Essays, Journalism, and Letters.* Ed. Sonia Orwell and Ian Angus. New York: Harcourt, Brace & World, 1968.

Orwell, George. *Homage to Catalonia and Looking Back on the Spanish War.* Harmondsworth: Penguin, 1966.

Orwell, George. *Down and Out in Paris and London.* London: Secker & Warburg, 1986.

Perkins, David, ed. *English Romantic Writers.* New York: Harcourt, Brace, Jovanovich, 1967.

Rhenisch, Harold. *Out of the Interior.* Vancouver: Ronsdale Press, 1993.

Rollin, Betty. *Last Wish.* New York: Linden Press/Simon and Schuster, 1985.

Rollin, Betty. "Motherhood: Who Needs It?" (*Look* Sept. 22, 1970). The Norton Reader. Ed. Linda H. Peterson and John C. Brereton. New York: Norton, 2008. 369–77.

Roszak, Theodore. *Person/Planet.* New York: Anchor Press/Doubleday, 1979.

Roszak, Theodore. *The Making of a Counter Culture: Reflections on the Technocratic Society and Its Youthful Opposition.* 1970. London: Faber, 1979.

Sagan, Carl. *The Dragons of Eden: Speculations on the Evolution of Human Intelligence.* New York: Random House, 1977.

Sanders, Scott R. *Aurora Means Dawn.* New York: Bradbury Press, 1989.

Sanders, Scott Russell. "The Singular First Person." *Essays on the Essay: Redefining the Genre.* Ed. Alexander J. Butrym. Athens: University of Georgia Press, 1989. 31–42.

Shumpeter. "The 'Breaking Bad' school: The best show on television is also a first-rate primer on business" *The Economist*, Sept. 28, 2013, 64. Web. Nov. 8, 2013.

Shawn Syms, "Brian Fawcett, *Human Happiness*," *Quill & Quire*, Feb. 2012. Web. Jan 1, 2013.

Sloan, J. H., *et al.* "Handgun Regulations, Crime, Assaults, and Homicide: A Tale of Two Cities." *New England Journal of Medicine* 319 (1988): 1256–62.

Sontag, Susan. *"Against Interpretation" and Other Essays.* New York: Farrar, Straus & Giroux, 1966.

Sprat, Thomas. *A History of the Royal Society.* (1667). Eds. J. I. Cope and H. W. Jones. London: Routledge and Kegan Paul, 1959.

Swift, Jonathan. *Gulliver's Travels and Other Writings.* Ed. Ricardo Quintana. New York: The Modern Library, 1958.

Tarle, George, and Simon P. Swordy, "Cosmic Antimatter." *Scientific American* Apr. 1998. 36–41

Tarnopolsky, Damian, "Theory for Beginners" Review of *In Search of Authority: An Introductory Guide to Literary Theory. Books in Canada* 26.3 (1997): 26

Tarnopolsky Damian, *Books in Canada* Review: *In Search of Authority: An Introductory Guide to Literary Theory* by Stephen Bonnycastle (1997).

Thoreau, Henry, David. "Civil Disobedience." *The Broadview Reader.* 3rd ed. Peterborough, Ontario: Broadview Press, 1998. 348–368.

Visser Margaret. *The Rituals of Dinner: The Origins, Evolution, Eccentricities, and Meaning of Table Manner.* Toronto: HarperCollins, 1991.

Visser, Margaret. "Feeding, Feasts, and Females." *The Broadview Reader.* Ed. Herbert Rosengaren and Jane Flick. Peterborough, Ontario: Broadview Press, 1992, 347–56.

Wilson, David. *A History of England.* New York: Holt, Rinehart and Winston, 1967.

Winchell, Mark Royden. *Joan Didion Revisited.* Rev. ed. Boston: Twayne Publishers, 1989.

Wollstonecraft, Mary. *Political Writings.* Ed. Janet Todd. London: W. Pickering, 1993.

Woolf, Virginia. *Collected Essays.* New York: Harcourt, Brace & World, 1966.

Woolf, Virginia. "Leslie Stephen." *The Captain's Death Bed and Other Essays.* Ed. Leonard Woolf. London: The Hogarth Press, 1950. 67–73.

Woolf, Virginia. *The Death of the Moth and Other Essays.* New York: Harcourt Brace Jovanovich, 1942.

Wooster College. "Writing in the Historical/ Literary Presents" Web. May 27, 2006.

Wordsworth, Mary. *Dorothy Wordsworth's Journal, Written at Alfoxden from 20th January to 22nd May 1798.* Web. Oct., 2013.

Critical Works

Abrams, M. H. *A Glossary of Literary Terms.* New York: Holt Rinehart and Winston, 1981.

Adorno, Theodor W. *The Culture Industry: Selected Essays on Mass Culture.* Ed. J. M. Bernstein. London: Routledge, 1991.

Baker, Sidney J. *The Australian Language.* Sydney: Currawong Publishing, 1966.

Bengels, Barbara. "Swift's A Modest Proposal," *The Explicator,* 65:1, 13–15, 2006. Web. Nov. 27, 2013.

Blake, N. F. *An Introduction to the Language of Literature.* Houndmills: Macmillan Education Ltd., 1990.

Coe, Richard M. *Process, Form and Substance: A Rhetoric for Advanced Writers.* 2nd ed. Englewood Cliffs, NJ: Prentice-Hall, 1990.

Corbett, Edward. P. *Classical Rhetoric for the Modern Student.* 2nd ed. New York: Oxford University Press, 1971.

Cuddon, J.A. *Dictionary of Literary Terms and Literary Theory.* London: Penguin Reference, 1998.

Dornan, Edward A., and Charles W. Dawe. *The Brief English Handbook.* 3rd ed. New York: HarperCollins, 1990.

Dubrow, Heather. *Genre.* no 42 in *The Critical Idiom* Ed. John. D. Jump. London: Methuen, 1982.

Elbow, Peter. *Writing With Power: Techniques for Mastering the Writing Process.* New York: Oxford University Press, 1981.

Ehrenpreis, Irwin *Swift: The Man, His Works, and the Age.* Harvard: Harvard University Press, 1962. Web. Nov. 27, 2013.

Fowler, Roger. *Linguistic Criticism.* Oxford: Oxford University Press, 1986.

Giltrow, Janet. *Academic Writing: How to Read and Write Scholarly Prose.* Peterborough, Ontario: Broadview Press, 1990.

Hardy, Barbara. *Dickens and Creativity.* London, GBR: Continuum International Publishing, 2008.

Hazel, Paul. "Narrative: An Introduction." *Paul Hazel.com* Posted April 5, 2007. Accessed Nov. 3, 2013.

Hitchins, Christopher. "The Dark Side of Dickens: Why Charles Dickens was among the best of writers and the worst of men" *The Atlantic* (May 2010 para 6). Web. Nov. 14, 2011.

Hughes, William. *Critical Thinking: An Introduction to the Basic Skills.* Peterborough, Ontario: Broadview Press, 1992.

Leech, Geoffrey, and Jan Svartik. *A Communicative Grammar of English.* London: Longman, 1975.

Messenger, William E., and Jan de Bruyn. *The Canadian Writer's Handbook.* 2nd ed. Scarborough: Prentice-Hall, 1986.

Neuman, Shirley. "Autobiography: From Different Poetics to a Poetics of Differences." *Essays on Life Writing.* Ed. Marlene Kadar. Toronto: University of Toronto Press, 1992.

Neuman, Shirley. "Life Writing." *Literary History of Canada: Canadian Literature in English.* Ed. W. H. New. 2nd ed. Vol. 4. Toronto: University of Toronto Press, 1990. 333–70.

Richardson, John. "Swift, *A Modest Proposal* and Slavery." *Essays in Criticism*, Oct. 2001, Vol. 51 Issue 4, pp. 404–23. Web. Nov. 28, 2013.

Roberts, Edgar V. *Writing Themes about Literature.* 5th ed. Englewood Cliffs, NJ: Prentice-Hall, 1983.

Shields, David. *Reality Hunger: A Manifesto.* New York: Knopf, 201, 5.

Taylor, Charles. *The Malaise of Modernity*. Concord, Ontario: Anansi, 1991.

Winchell, Mark Royden. *Joan Didion*. Boston: Twayne Publishers, 1980.

The Sciences and Disciplines

Berger, Peter. *Invitation to Sociology: A Humanistic Perspective*. New York: Anchor, 1963.

Birney C. Robert, and Richard C. Teevan, eds. *Instinct: An Enduring Problem in Psychology*. Princeton: Van Nostrand, n.d.

Brookman, Christopher. *American Culture and Society Since the 1930s*. The Contemporary United States Series. London: Macmillan, 1984.

Brown, Gillian, and George Yule. *Discourse Analysis*. Cambridge England: Cambridge University Press, 1983.

Gutting, Gary, ed. *Paradigms and Revolutions: Appraisals and Applications of Thomas Kuhn's Philosophy of Science*. Notre Dame: University of Notre Dame Press, 1980.

Hoyningen-Huene, Paul. *Reconstructing Scientific Revolutions: Thomas S. Kuhn's Philosophy of Science*. Trans. Alexander T. Levine. Chicago: University of Chicago Press, 1993.

Johnson, M. Harry. *Sociology: A Systematic Introduction*. Ed. Robert K. Merton. New York: Harcourt, Brace and World, 1960.

Kuhn, Thomas S. *The Structure of Scientific Revolutions. International Enclycopedia of Unified Science* 2.2. Chicago: University of Chicago Press, 1970.

Lévi-Strauss, Claude. *Tristes Tropiques*. Trans. John & Doreen Weightman. New York: Atheneum, 1975.

Lévi-Strauss, Claude. *The Way of the Masks*. Trans. Sylvia Modelski. Vancouver: Douglas & McIntyre, 1979.

McGoldrick, Monica, John K. Pearce, and Joseph Giordano, eds. *Ethnicity and Family Therapy*. New York: The Guilford Press, 1982.

Mills, C. Wright. *The Sociological Imagination*. New York: Grove Press, 1959.

Moscovici, Serge. "The Myth of the Lonely Paradigm: A Rejoinder." *Social Research* 51.4 (Winter 1984): 939–67.

Nussbaum, Fredrick L. *The Triumph of Science and Reason: 1660–1685*. New York: Harper & Row, 1953.

Stebbing, L. Susan. *A Modern Introduction to Logic*. New York: Harper & Brothers, 1961.

Index of Authors, Essays, and Dates

This book's text is set in Warnock, a
contemporary typeface grounded in the
classic proportions of oldstyle Roman
type. The headings are set in Cronos,
which derives its appearance from the
calligraphically inspired type of the Italian
Renaissance. Both typefaces were designed
by Robert Slimbach.

This book was printed by Hignell Book
Printing on Ph neutral paper that
is processed chlorine free.